GW01080838

Ibsen and Chekhov on the Irish Stage

In memory of Ros Dixon

'[Theatre] is live, immediate, and dangerous.
It is beautifully tragic and ephemeral.'
R. Dixon, September 2010

My work with Ros Dixon began in 2008. Together we organized the conference on Ibsen and Chekhov on the Irish Stage which took place in November 2009 and where the essays presented in this book were first tried out. In spite of her illness Ros continued working on the book, organizing a review panel, commenting on the essays, and providing indispensable advice. It is a rare privilege to have worked with Ros and an honour to have been her friend. Her interest in people, her indomitable humour, and her keen and calm intellect can be glimpsed in the fine article included in this volume. I hope that this project is a fitting tribute to the memory of a wonderful scholar and a person of courage and grace.

Irina Ruppo Malone

Ibsen and Chekhov on the Irish Stage

edited by

Ros Dixon and Irina Ruppo Malone

Carysfort Press

A Carysfort Press Book
Ibsen and Chekhov on the Irish Stage
edited by Ros Dixon and Irina Ruppo Malone

First published in Ireland in 2012 as a paperback original by
Carysfort Press, 58 Woodfield, Scholarstown Road
Dublin 16, Ireland

ISBN 978-1-904505-57-0
©2012 Copyright remains with the authors

Typeset by Carysfort Press
Cover design by eprint limited
Printed and bound by eprint limited
Unit 35
Coolmine Industrial Estate
Dublin 15
Ireland

This book is published with the financial assistance of
The Arts Council (An Chomhairle Ealaíon) Dublin, Ireland

Caution: All rights reserved. No part of this book may be printed or reproduced
or utilized in any form or by any electronic, mechanical, or other means, now
known or hereafter invented including photocopying and recording, or in any
information storage or retrieval system without permission in writing from the
publishers.

This book is sold subject to the conditions that it shall not, by way of trade or
otherwise, be lent, resold, hired out, or otherwise circulated in any form of
binding, or cover other than that in which it is published and without a similar
condition, including this condition, being imposed on the subsequent
purchaser.

TABLE OF CONTENTS

CHEKHOV IN IRELAND

ACKNOWLEDGEMENTS

This book, dedicated to the memory of Ros Dixon, is also her legacy – the result of her meticulous work as well as her knowledge of the Irish academic and theatrical worlds.

Several of the opinions represented in this volume belong to Ros's close friends and colleagues. In thanking them for their support of the conference and contribution to this book, I acknowledge their friendship with Ros and their dedication to her memory.

The book began with a conference on 'Ibsen and Chekhov on the Irish Stage' that was held at the Moore Institute, National University of Ireland Galway in November 2009. I would like to warmly thank Adrian Frazier. The idea of a joint publication on Ibsen and Chekhov belongs to him, and he remained a wonderful source of advice and support throughout the project.

I am grateful to Lionel Pilkington and Sean Ryder, Riana O Dwyer, and Patrick Lonergan. Special thanks also go to Dearbhla Mooney and Irene O'Malley. I thank Miglena Ivanova, Kathleen Heininge, and all of those who contributed to the conference, the authors of the essays, and participants of the roundtable discussions. Special thanks are due to the Norwegian Ambassador to Ireland, His Excellency Öyvind Nordsletten.

I would like to mention with gratitude the writers and theatre practitioners – Thomas Kilroy, Michael West, Máiréad ní Chróinín, Lynne Parker and Arthur Riordan – as well as the moderators of the round-table discussions, Kurt Taroff, and Adrian Frazier. I thank Linzi Simpson. Excavation Director (Margaret Gowen & Co), whose lecture on 'Dublin's Smock Alley theatre, 1662-1788: Lost and Found' was a particularly anticipated and exciting event on the conference programme. I thank Shelley Troupe whose professional handling of key administrative matters ensured the smooth running of the conference.

The conference and the ensuing publication were enabled by the generosity of the following institutions: the Embassy of Norway, Dublin, the Moore Institute, National University of Ireland, Galway, the Discipline of English National University of Ireland, Galway, the MA in Drama and Theatre, National University of Ireland, Galway, and the NUI Galway Aid in Publications Grant.

I would like to thank Maura Campbell and Máiréad Delaney for making available the photographs of Abbey Theatre productions; I thank Kathleen Barrington for her advice during my search for some of the images. For the Royal Court images of *The Seagull,* I thank John Hayes and Eleanor McKeown of the Lebrecht Music and Arts Library. I am grateful to the staff of the James Hardiman Library, NUI Galway and would like to specially thank Kieran Hoare and Margaret Hughes for their kind assistance and for making it possible to use images from the archive of Taibhdhearc na Gaillimhe.

I would like acknowledge with gratitude the help of the anonymous peer-reviewers. I am very grateful to Carysfort Press for their steadfast support of the project. Special thanks are due to Eamonn Jordan, Dan Farrelly, Lilian Chambers, and Margaret Hamilton.

I am grateful to all my friends and family, especially Marina Ruppo, Paul Malone, and Alice Malone.

This book would not have been the same were it not for the support of Ros Dixon's partner, Elizabeth Fitzpatrick, and the work of Victor Dixon, whose careful copy-editing of the manuscript was a labour of love for his beloved daughter.

My greatest debt of gratitude is to my friend Ros Dixon whose memory I will always cherish.

A Note on Transliteration

There are several deviations from the Library of Congress transliteration system used throughout the book. Original transliteration is retained in all quoted material. Articles dealing with Tom Murphy's translation of *The Cherry Orchard* adopt, in the main text, Murphy's transliteration of the characters' names. In addition, standard anglicized version of Stanislavsky's name is used. Similarly, the soft sign at the end of Maria Knebel's name is omitted.

LIST OF ILLUSTRATIONS

Introduction

Irina Ruppo Malone

The names of Henrik Ibsen (1828-1906) and Anton Chekhov (1860-1904) often appear together in English language theatre journalism, textbooks, and critical literature. In the public eye, they have been turned into near contemporaries by the proximity of the dates of their deaths and the processes involved in the cross-cultural transmission of their works. This perception exists in spite of the radical differences between the life stories and work of the two authors. These differences are frequently subsumed in a type of comparative analysis which ascribes, for instance, better insight into the 'nature of the actor's art' to Chekhov and keener awareness of 'the nature of the dramatist's art' to Ibsen – as if the two writers were in a kind of eternal competition.[1] Whether as progenitors of modern drama, modern classics, or even 'honorary British playwrights',[2] these authors appear to have a joint power, a power that depends, perhaps, on the friction between the two.

Rejecting the superficial (yet persistent) notion of Ibsen and Chekhov as barely distinguishable realist playwrights, *Ibsen and Chekhov on the Irish Stage* presents a collective study of the reception of their plays in Ireland and their influence on the development of Irish drama. The book is divided into two parts: Irish Ibsenites, and Chekhov in Ireland. These parts have a similar structure: an article on wider issues of cross-cultural reception is followed by articles which taken together provide an episodic history of the reception of each playwright; these are followed by articles dealing with recent adaptations. The round-table discussion on Ibsen features insights from Irish directors; the concluding discussion by Thomas Kilroy and Michael West is centred on *The Seagull* but ranges widely, referring back to the issues explored in the entire volume.

In 2008, when Ros Dixon and I planned the conference which led to this collection, it was already possible to speak of a tradition of Irish literary adaptations of Ibsen and Chekhov. Thomas Kilroy's *The Seagull* (1981), Brian Friel's *Hedda Gabler* (2008), or Frank McGuinness's *Peer Gynt* (1988; publ. 1990) or *John Gabriel Borkman* (2010), to use but a few key examples, are not merely actable versions of the plays suitable for Irish actors. Possessing different degrees of reverence (and irreverence) toward the original, these works portend to claim Ibsen and Chekhov for Ireland and for its unique brand of English language. These adaptations exist in conversation with each other. Friel's *Hedda Gabler* might be an answer to McGuinness's version of that play (1994), while Kilroy's *The Seagull* could have partially influenced Tom Murphy's *The Cherry Orchard* (2004)). Moreover, they relate to other works of these Irish contemporary playwrights. Thus, as is pointed out in three articles in this volume, Chekhov's influence on Tom Murphy is not measured by his *The Cherry Orchard* alone, but by the earlier *The House* (2000). Further, the cultural roots of these adaptations go back to the Irish Revival, when plays by Ibsen and Chekhov were premièred in Ireland inspiring a generation of Irish playwrights, and to the early years of the Irish Free State, when their plays were staged by the Abbey, and by the Gate, as well as by the Irish-language theatre, An Taibhdhearc na Gaillimhe.

Central to *Ibsen and Chekhov on the Irish Stage* is the need to destabilize the prevalent twentieth-century belief in the separateness of national literary and dramatic canons. The notion that a country's dramatic tradition develops in cultural isolation is challenged by the significance of Ibsen and Chekhov (and by implication other world playwrights) for the history of Irish drama. It was at the peak of Irish national romanticism that these playwrights were introduced to Irish readers and audiences, becoming entrenched in the Irish dramatic writing and affecting the development of Irish modernism.

Yet it is often a custom, in the wider world as well as in literary studies, to see the notions of 'tradition' and 'foreignness' as binary opposites – as if migration of literary works (or indeed migration of people) were possible only in the present. In dispelling this view, the present volume offers a model of looking at the history of Irish drama as a history of cultural immigration and trans-cultural dialogue.

Nor should the works of Ibsen and Chekhov be seen as static entities; they are continuously changed and developed by absorbing the interpretations of their international audiences. In different ways, the materials presented here demonstrate that established interpretations of classic works of the theatre exist in order to be subverted by critics and stage interpreters; static interpretations usually tell us more about the bias of a particular culture than about the plays in question.

These issues are apparent in the opening article by Tore Rem. Having charted the history of the reception of Ibsen in his home country and the recent impact of international interpretations of the canonized national author, Rem notes that 'the way ... to liberate Norwegian theatre and Norwegian Ibsen traditions is to let go, not to insist on ownership, and acknowledge that Ibsen belongs to the world, that he will always be characterized by the fact that he is received in translation, in new versions, even before the play begins'. In addition to providing a background to the articles dealing with the Irish reception of Ibsen, Rem's article may interest the reader as a model for approach to the cultural ownership of Irish playwrights mentioned in this book.

The idea of international theatre as a liberating force is counterbalanced by Cynthia Marsh's analysis of certain aspects of the contemporary theory and practice of staging Russian theatre in English. Identifying three different approaches to translation: collision, hybridization, and acculturation, Marsh proceeds to examine the ensuing fate of a translated text, as mediated by the director, the design team, marketing, and finally, reviewers. Marsh carefully documents the pull of the stereotype as a cultural short-hand and a marketing strategy and reveals the accrued losses suffered by the translated texts. The cross-cultural transferral of a play is shown to betray the local latent attitudes to other cultures, reminding the reader of 'the danger of colonialism and cannibalism, which the Irish, American and other examples seek to attack, but in so doing they in fact adopt precisely the methods they decry'.

The contradictory and unpredictable workings of dramatic influence are explored by Christopher Murray. Ibsenist realism seemed, in the early days of the Irish Revival, to be opposed to Yeatsean poetic drama and peasant play, but, in 1938, the actor-playwright Micheál MacLiammóir declared that 'every Irish play that I know is what I would call a problem play', a claim that resounded for several decades. A central role in this process was occupied by 'Ibsen's middle-man', G.B. Shaw. Murray examines the interrelated influences of both playwrights on the Irish dramatic writing of the early twentieth century, noting the ideological difficulties involved in the reception of both anti-idealist writers in both pre-and-post-independence Ireland.

Murray's article is paralleled by Robert Tracy's account of the staging of Chekhov's plays at the Irish Theatre from 1915 to 1917. In the hands of poets and revolutionaries, the performances became sensitive responses to Chekhov's dramatic methods and moments of cross-cultural recognition – affecting future Irish responses to Chekhov. Reading these performances in the context of pre-1916 and pre-World War I Irish drama, Tracy outlines their significance for the participants of the Easter Rising and their surviving friends.

Christopher Morash's article takes its title from Lennox Robinson's comedy which imagines the disastrously comic impact of the performances of plays by Chekhov and Ibsen on the residents of a small Irish town in 1930s. A leading playwright of his day, Robinson claimed to be 'Ibsen-foolish', writing articles on Ibsen and consciously imitative plays as well as directing his plays at the Abbey Theatre. Through an analysis of the role of Ibsen's writings in 'shaping Robinson's engagement with post-Independence Ireland and its possibilities', Morash addresses the effect of the policies and ideologies of the post-independence Ireland on the nationalist artists.

Focusing on the works of Denis Johnston, my own article likewise engages with the cultural disillusionment at the start of the De Valera decade. However, the main objective of my article is to address a gap in the study of Ibsen's reception in Ireland. I suggest that in consciously imitating Ibsen such playwrights as Robinson, T.C. Murray, Seamus O'Kelly, and R.J. Ray ignored the non-realistic, modernist aspects of Ibsen's drama. I therefore examine the beginnings of Irish engagement with the modernist Ibsen through a discussion of the Ibsenite echoes in Denis Johnston's *The Old Lady Says 'No!'* (1929) and *A Bride for the Unicorn* (1933).

The subsequent articles deal with more contemporary events in the stories of Ibsen and Chekhov in Ireland. Patrick Burke draws on his experience of directing plays by Ibsen and Friel to provide a comparative analysis of *John Gabriel Borkman, Faith Healer, When We Dead Awaken,* and *Performances.* His article underscores common preoccupations of these works and their concern with theatrical space. The title of Helen Lojek's article evokes McGuinness's well-known jocular lament: 'I've lost my Henrik ... I've lost him surely, I've lost my only Ibsen, my only Ibsen of the Western World ...'. Lojek offers an overview of Ibsen's significance for McGuinness, the common features of his adaptations, including their ability to 'mediate between Norway and Ireland', and the similarities of his original plays to Ibsen's.

Nicholas Grene charts a history of Irish engagements with Chekhov from Hubert Butler's translation to Murphy's *The Cherry Orchard* and his creative response to Chekhov, *The House*. Querying the origins of the well-established association of Chekhov's country estates with the Irish Big House, Grene shows 'how Irish playwrights have been able to take off from Chekhov in their own dramatic visions'.

Ros Dixon's article on Maria Knebel's production of *The Cherry Orchard* at the Abbey provides a bridge between the analysis of problems of cross-cultural transferral in Marsh's article and the points made by Grene. The article discusses Knebel's experience of working at the Abbey in 1968, the differences in working practices between Soviet and Irish theatres, and the legacy of this production. It indicates how in 1968 the perception of Chekhov's central characters as returned exiles was key to an understanding of the play for its Irish cast, and concludes by suggesting how later in 2000 this idea was re-imagined by Tom Murphy in *The House*.

Zsuzsa Csikai also focuses on Murphy's *The Cherry Orchard*, but approaches the play from a more theoretical perspective. Unlike Grene, who believes that Murphy's *The Cherry Orchard* is little more than 'a good actable version', Csikai sees it as a bold move away from the approach to re-translation established by Kilroy and Friel. In a close textual analysis of the translation, Csikai argues that Murphy's refusal to domesticate the play and the emphasis he places on the foreign elements of the play 'demonstrates an opening up to a larger scale of other voices in Irish theatre, which instead of defining itself in opposition to the English influence, now conceives of itself as part of a global, multicultural world'.

Ibsen and Chekhov on the Irish Stage is above all an episodic history of Irish drama seen from a new angle. Hopefully the variety of the approaches presented here will stimulate further interest in the Irish engagement with international drama. The thematic continuity across the essays is due partly to the contributors' willingness to approach the conference as a collaborative study and undertake specific areas of research and partly to the nature of the subject. The links between the present-day translations of Ibsen and Chekhov and the encounters with these playwrights during the Revival become particularly notable during the round-table discussions. These sections, far-ranging and conversational, include several invitations for further scholarly investigations; among them is the discussion of the Irish language reception of Ibsen and world drama. For future scholars, the two round-table discussions transcribed in this volume offer particularly valuable material, not only in terms of the scholarly insight they offer, but also as a record: a freeze image of an ongoing process and an attempt to capture theatre as it is being created and reinterpreted.

---

[1] Peter Ustinov, Introduction, *Plays about People* (London: Jonathan Cape, 1950). Cited after 'Sundry Stages', *Irish Times* 19 August 1950: 6.

[2] Gunilla M. Andermann, *Europe on Stage: Translation and Theatre* (London: Oberon Books, 2005): 8.

IRISH IBSENITES

1 | Is There a Norwegian Ibsen? Ibsen at Home and Abroad

Tore Rem

I

When the National Theatre in Oslo opened on 1 September 1899, it was with massive statues of two living writers, Bjørnstjerne Bjørnson and Henrik Ibsen, in front of the theatre's main facade.[1] The one, outwardly directed, confidently looking into the future; the other, represented as his colleague's very opposite, an introvert, seemingly concerned with his own, inner life. The foundation of the Nationaltheatret, as well as the choice of location, were the results of a long debate, with resistance not least from the university, which was worried about getting a theatre opposite its own dignified, neoclassical buildings.[2] The plans won through, however, albeit after the authorities had agreed to some of the demands from the university, among other things pertaining to the height of the building. The centre of Christiania, present-day Oslo, thus became dominated by four national institutions: The Parliament (Stortinget), the Royal Palace, the University and the Theatre.

Norway by this time had its reasons to affirm the status of the theatre in such a conspicuous way. In traditional histories of the Norwegian theatre, the two figures in front of Nationaltheatret laid the foundations of a national drama.[3] In these narratives, however, the dynamic between national and international, a key point in what I am going to discuss in this article, has hardly been taken into account at all. One of the most intriguing aspects of Ibsen is that he was a writer who moved, in a relatively short time, from the periphery to the centre, from habitually being labelled as provincial to becoming securely established as belonging to world literature.

In 1885 Bjørnson wrote to Ibsen, after the latter's artistic triumphs in Germany: 'This is a victory for more than yourself, your poetry, Norwegian life and dramatic art more generally. This is our only way of being represented, and it necessarily imposes a respect for our right to be ourselves.'[4] There are three authors which the entire world knows, wrote literary critic and historian Jens Braage Halvorsen in Ibsen's *Festschrift* for his 70th birthday in 1898: Zola, Tolstoy and Ibsen.[5] The sense that Ibsen, the man represented as an introvert in front of Nationaltheatret, had helped his small nation become a mighty nation culturally, with the help of Grieg, and, to a smaller extent Bjørnson, the extrovert, should not be underestimated. The intellectual historian Narve Fulsås, editor of Ibsen's letters in the new critical Ibsen edition, *Henrik Ibsens Skrifter*, has recently pointed out the exceptional, not to say miraculous, nature of the evolution of a strong, Norwegian literature in the second half of the nineteenth century.[6] After the question of literary copyright had been debated at a meeting of Nordic booksellers in 1856, it resulted in a new law on literary property in Denmark the following year; symptomatically, in Norway the issue was thought to be irrelevant. Only a couple of decades later, however, Norwegian literature was among the leading literatures of Europe. Fulsås convincingly shows how there were particular, Scandinavian conditions, not least regarding publishing and habits of reading, which helped make this possible. Ibsen's society plays were no doubt also controversial at home, but it was at the same time difficult to dispute that his international success had gradually also become something of a national resource.

II

When the artist Erik Werenskiold painted a portrait of Ibsen in 1895, at a time when Ibsen's Europe-wide fame was well established, he began by depicting the playwright as a private persona, sitting in an armchair.[7] The result was a fine likeness, but Werenskiold is said to have realized that this great poetic genius had to be portrayed with snow-clad, Norwegian mountains in the background. Thus the armchair had to give way, and Ibsen was moved outdoors, standing. The painting now belongs to the National Gallery, and when the country's then leading professor of literary history, the famous Ibsen editor Francis Bull, concluded an article in the year of the fiftieth anniversary of Ibsen's death, in 1956, he identified Werenskiold's painting as exemplary. Bull noted that here was a visualization of Ibsen's loftiness, loneliness, and artistic ideals, as well as, at the same time, a representation of the country in which he had his 'roots'. Through Ibsen's works this country had become 'a living country for an entire world public'.[8] There may be a number of reasons for Bull's focus on the Norwegianness of Ibsen, and on Ibsen's importance to his own country – and this focus has indeed for a long time been the dominant mode in Norwegian Ibsen scholarship – but there can nevertheless be little doubt that the almost sensationally strong Europe-wide interest in Ibsen from the late 1880s also led to a new interest in other things Norwegian.

Another fifty years and it was time for a new anniversary, the centenary of Ibsen's death. Even before the year-long events of 2006 were underway, the director of the official celebrations noted that the 'Ibsen brand' had been underestimated in Norway, claiming that this year represented 'a unique chance for Norway to show itself as a nation of culture'.[9] The Minister of Culture confirmed, in a near-identical formulation, that this was a 'unique opportunity for showing off Norway'.[10] These statements were not isolated remarks made by individuals in public speeches, but part of a thinking which also manifested itself in public policy documents. By 2006 Ibsen had become a tool to be used in another phase of nation building, more specifically in terms of soft diplomacy, nation branding and the experience economy, in a new convergence between the fields of culture, economics and politics. 'Is this centenary about Norway's Ibsen or Ibsen's Norway?', one commentator asked.[11] There is little reason to doubt that the Ibsen who was being promoted throughout this year, at least as he was envisaged by the National Committee of the centenary, was still a very Norwegian Ibsen.

There is a fundamental paradox at work here. An author worth celebrating on this scale, and on behalf of the Norwegian nation, must almost necessarily be international. Without international fame, and thus with other ownerships than the Norwegian one, an anniversary of this kind, marked in eighty countries around the world, would have been impossible. The conspicuous turn back to the nation in official Norwegian rhetoric clearly goes counter to recent academic trends within both literary studies and national historiographies, and may be related to the sense of a need for affirmations of national identity in an era of globalization. In spite of this perhaps surprising return to an emphasis on the national ownership of Ibsen, something has nevertheless happened to the Norwegian sense of the Norwegianness of Ibsen, to the point of no return.

III

Ibsen and Norway

Someone approaching the scholarship on Ibsen from the outside, be it from other fields of literature or theatre studies, or from other national traditions, is likely to be surprised by one conspicuous fact of Norwegian Ibsen scholarship, impressive as it is in many respects: there has been little interest in the Dano-Norwegian reception of Ibsen's works, whether in print or in the theatre. While there are anthologies in English which provide the scholar and student with numerous and representative examples of Ibsen's reception in Britain and the US, such as James W. McFarlane's *Henrik Ibsen: A Critical Anthology* (1970) and Michael Egan's *Ibsen: The Critical Heritage* (1972), no such resource is available in respect of Ibsen's Dano-Norwegian reception. Paradoxically (and I have to admit that I have helped create this paradox myself, perhaps as a gentle provocation), there is even an anthology of Ibsen's British reception available in Norwegian, *Henry Gibson/Henrik Ibsen: Den provinsielle verdensdikter* (2006).

The practical consequence of this situation is that each conscientious new scholar or student of Ibsen's first Dano-Norwegian reception is being sent back to the archives. It is at least in part possible to explain such a serious shortcoming with reference to the main trends in Norwegian Ibsen scholarship in the twentieth century. After a long period in which the so-called 'historical-biographical' school was dominant, and in which much attention was paid to Ibsen's biography, with a particular focus on its relationship to the texts, as well as to the impressive historical and editorial work which for decades went into The Centenary Edition of Ibsen's works, New Criticism finally won the day in Norway in the 1950s. In the following decades, and up until surprisingly recently, at least when considering international trends in theatre and literary studies, Ibsen scholarship has been characterized by approaches which may generally be called formalist, whether they have been new critical, structuralist or deconstructionist.[12] The focus has, furthermore, been literary, concentrating on Ibsen's texts, with relatively little attention being paid to performance, not to say to context or historicity more generally.

The implicit theoretical assumptions of this academic tradition have led to scant interest in how Ibsen was received in his time, in his own cultural sphere and domestic market. These have to do with unformulated notions of textual stability, assumptions about unmediated access to the original, and perhaps also with a narrow-minded focus on professional readers. It is as if Ibsen were transparent to Norwegians, or at the very least to Norwegian scholars of literature.

IV

The traditional narratives about Ibsen and Norway relate the story of a genius who was too great for his country, who was misunderstood, perhaps even persecuted, at home, and who escaped abroad in order to become what he had to become. This is the story created by those who won the 'culture wars' of the late nineteenth century, the 'cultural radicals', with the Danish critic Georg Brandes as the leading figure; and it is a story which has had such force in literary historiography that it is still being uncritically repeated. As recently as in 2008, a prominent American Ibsen scholar would claim that Ibsen left Norway after 'years of merciless attacks from the Norwegian press'.[13] Ibsen was said to have exposed 'the conspiracy between church and state'[14] and to have triumphed over hypocrisy and conservatism. Such a caricature of winners and losers, and, by implication, of Ibsen's agency in changing the course of Norwegian history, makes a more nuanced and open approach to Ibsen's first receptions seem unnecessary, uninteresting or, perhaps, unimaginable.

In this often-told version of Ibsen's relationship to his native country, it was the world which saved Ibsen from his nation. Since then, Norway has taken him back, but not without a strong sense of guilt. Historical scholarship of recent years, including that of the most recent Norwegian biographer of Ibsen, Ivo de Figueiredo, shows a more complex reality, however.[15] Ibsen was made director of two theatres while still in Norway, awarded a generous travel grant from the state, and later received a substantial state stipend. He was also, by the way, for a long time, and in a number of significant ways, himself a conservative. It is of course possible to argue that Ibsen should have been met with even greater acknowledgment in younger years, but it might also be worth remembering that he had not then become Ibsen, as we know him in retrospect. In one of his introductions to the new critical edition of Ibsen's letters, Fulsås documents how Ibsen was shown considerable generosity in his native country during the early part of his career.[16] The reception of his works was mixed, and no doubt on the whole for good aesthetic reasons, but he ended on a note of resounding success with *The Pretenders* (1863), the last play to be staged before he left Norway.

Ibsen himself had first participated in creating a national-romantic drama, but was relatively soon to distance himself from this tradition. There is satire on Norwegian nationalism already in *Love's Comedy* (1862), whereas *Brand* (1866), *Peer Gynt* (1867), and *Emperor and Galilean* (1872) show a more explicit turning away from the ideology of nationalism towards a new individualism.[17] Nevertheless, and in part because of the very artistic autonomy which he managed to obtain, the internationally famous Ibsen, as pointed out at the beginning of this article, was put to the service of the young Norwegian nation at the end of the century.

V

In terms of his reception, it is possible to trace the Norwegian Ibsen, as he has been constructed in his native country, in a number of ways, but in the following I would particularly like to note his influence on the Norwegian theatre. From the late nineteenth century a particular Ibsen tradition of a psychological-realistic kind was established and came to dominate Norwegian theatre for many decades, even for the greater part of the twentieth century.[18] The theatre historian Keld Hyldig has shown how this tradition was closely associated with the establishment of the Norwegian National Theatre, and how its first director Bjørn Bjørnson (son of Bjørnstjerne Bjørnson) was instrumental in shaping parts of this tradition, namely its emphasis on 'external realism'.[19] Others, not least the critic and playwright Gunnar Heiberg, also contributed to these long-lasting conventions for staging Ibsen, albeit with greater emphasis on 'internal realism'. The actor-led tradition which developed was strongly associated, due to its institutional home, with the national, and thus with a presumably authentic and Norwegian Ibsen. In the ritual references to the 'shadow of Ibsen', or even the curse of Ibsen, in recurring Norwegian debates about the state of the theatre, it was often tradition which was the object of attack.

There are important, though isolated incidents and episodes which break with this tradition, such as the New Norwegian (i.e., the minority version of written Norwegian, 'nynorsk') and anti-romantic *Peer Gynt* at The Norwegian Theatre (Det Norske Teatret) in 1948, but on the whole it was conserved and maintained in the first three decades of the post-war period.[20] The more open rebellions occur in the 1960s, and the key figure here may be the Brecht-inspired playwright Jens Bjørneboe. Bjørneboe started out as an admirer of Ibsen on literary grounds, but when he moved into practical work in the theatre, he very much came to resist his influence as it was manifested in the Ibsen tradition. Bjørneboe would typically claim that Norway had 'the heaviest Ibsen tradition in Europe, and therefore the emptiest theatres', and he rebelled against actors attempting to be '"full of soul" and "meaningful" and "secretive" à la the Norwegian Ibsen theatre'.[21] Still, it is clear that the Ibsen tradition survived at least in terms of its methods of acting, even in Bjørneboe productions, such as in his celebrated *The Bird Lovers* at the Nationaltheatret in 1966.

VI

Breaking Out

The Ibsen tradition can be said to have dominated, and strongly felt to oppress, both the Norwegian theatre and the Norwegian academy at least until the 1980s. It has been suggested that the establishment of a number of new regional state theatres in the 1970s helped weaken the dominance of the Nationaltheatret, and that this in turn helped loosen up that theatre's age-old Ibsen hegemony.[22]

From the 1980s and 1990s, a new director's theatre, influenced by German expressionism, also signalled new beginnings and a renewal of Norwegian approaches to Ibsen. More recently and perhaps more importantly, the Ibsen festival at the Nationaltheatret, which began in 1990, and became a biannual affair from 1992, has contributed strongly to a new, more international orientation. Because the festival has brought in some of the best and/or most interesting Ibsen productions from around the world every other year, Norwegian theatre has inevitably been challenged and encouraged to engage in dialogue with these foreign importations. Most often, the best and best-received productions of the Ibsen festival have indeed been foreign. These direct encounters with other Ibsens, in which local productions have been measured against foreign ones, may (in turn) also have stimulated a more extensive use of more experimentally oriented foreign directors. Recent years have even seen a modest turn towards interculturalism, including the staging of a Bollywood-inspired *The Lady from the Sea* in Oslo in 2006.

Compared with the situation in the Norwegian theatre debates twenty years ago, it is hard to dispute that a change has taken place. The almost ritual references to the theatre's miserable existence in the shadow of Ibsen are now hard to come by; the attempts at murdering the father figure are few and far between. New theatre conventions have shown new possibilities, and the theatre is less actor-led than before. In the last decade, Norwegian playwrights have also been seen to demonstrate a greater confidence, inspired by Jon Fosse's international success. There is more freedom in the interpretation of Ibsen, and the approaches on the whole seem less insular, more outward-oriented.

In spite of its insular tendencies, 'Ibsen 2006', the world-wide marking of the Ibsen centenary which I noted at the beginning of this article, proved an interesting indicator of Ibsen's contemporary international status. In addition to a great number of other events, there were over three hundred Ibsen premières around the world.[23] The new website Ibsen.net had around fourteen million hits during that year alone. This website was established in the long build-up to 'Ibsen 2006', and has since been made permanent, one of its key tasks being the documentation and registration of all Ibsen productions. These surveys are of course not perfect or complete, but the figures may still tell us something about the relationship between the Norwegian and foreign Ibsens. While the year 2000 saw 16 Ibsen productions in Norway and 124 world-wide, last year saw 177 world-wide and twenty in Norway. The peak was of course 2006 with 308 productions, of which fifty-seven took place in Norway. One of the inescapable, if indirect, effects of Ibsen.net lies in changing Norwegian perceptions of Ibsen, simply as a result of its documentation of the numerous foreign ownerships of Ibsen.

VII

In 1983 the journal *Edda* published a strong attack on Norwegian Ibsen scholarship, written by the literary scholar Jørgen Haugan. Apart from noting that this tradition on the whole represented a form of idealist aesthetics, Haugan identified a 'nationally restricted attitude towards literature' as one of the major weaknesses of existing Ibsen scholarship.[24] This diagnosis now seems to have been right in the most important respects, but it was a long time before Haugan's perspective was recognized.

William Archer, perhaps Ibsen's most important middleman in his early English-language reception, claimed already in 1901 that '[n]ever before has a poet of world-wide fame appealed to his world-audience so exclusively in translation'.[25] Perhaps the way further to liberate Norwegian theatre and Norwegian Ibsen traditions is to let go, not to insist on ownership, and acknowledge that Ibsen belongs to the world, that he will always be characterized by the fact that he is received in translation, in new versions, even before the play begins. In the last couple of decades much work has been done on Ibsen's reception in many countries, from China to Ireland. As a contribution to this turn, I have myself claimed, somewhat polemically, that 'Ibsen is English'.[26] In doing so, I of course wanted to draw attention to the fact that there are so many foreign ownerships of Ibsen, that studies of his reception show that he lives a great number of lives which are only tentatively connected with Norway and the Dano-Norwegian language in which he wrote, and that the English language has been an extremely important vehicle for his continuing life in the world. In order to enter the world, Ibsen became dependent on what Pascale Casanova calls 'foreign exchange brokers',[27] and his success in English has helped both to establish and maintain his position within a Western and even world canon of literature and theatre. As a writer from what may be called a 'literarily impoverished space', Ibsen obtained much of his cultural capital by being received in the centre.

The biggest current research project on Ibsen, with the exception of the critical edition which has just been completed, is called 'Ibsen between Cultures' and is led by Frode Helland, the director of the Centre for Ibsen Studies at the University of Oslo. This project finds its empirical material in Ibsen productions in China, India and Bangladesh. Refusing to conceive of culture as 'national', it stresses the importance of what it calls 'localizing acts', echoing Jacques

Derrida in seeing 'the local performance as the original itself'.[28] Ibsen, this project claims, and not without taking a critical stand against a certain Ibsen tradition and certain political uses of Ibsen, is not '"imported" out of an interest in Norway, but [...] in relation to a specific situation within this culture, originating within its own theatre'. A not insignificant dimension of this project is 'self-reflexive', in that it wants to analyze the role taken by Norwegian authorities in 'the dissemination of Ibsen throughout the world'. Such an analysis may also 'shed light on the blind spots and dead ends in the Norwegian appreciation or valuation of "Ibsen"'. Not only that, but the project aims to serve as a 'corrective to a Norwegian tradition of Ibsen studies that is predominantly textually and nationally oriented'. Such a project, even based at the Centre for Ibsen Studies, would have been inconceivable, or at the very least thought of as highly provocative, even a few years ago.

VIII

'Our Northern Henry'

Our 'literary unconscious' is still to a large degree national.[29] Ibsen is a writer who begins in Dano-Norwegian, but he clearly does not stop there. Already in the first substantial article written on Ibsen in English, the attempt was made, before the fact, to place the Norwegian playwright at the centre of European culture. Writing in 1873, the young Edmund Gosse, having worked his way through *Love's Comedy, Brand,* and *Peer Gynt,* wrote about the unknown Norwegian dramatist in *Fortnightly Review.* 'Where shall we look for a young great poet among continental nations?', Gosse asked.[30] He listed a few candidates, none of whom were deemed to be qualified as 'world-poets'. The answer lay, presumably to the surprise of the journal's readers, to the north: 'It is my firm belief that in the Norwegian, Henrik Ibsen, the representative of a land unknown in the literary annals of Europe, such a poet is found.'

The international Ibsen starts here, if not before. Twenty years later his fame was becoming secure, and he published his works almost simultaneously in the big European languages. In spite of (and perhaps because of this) 'Ibsen 2006' most conspicuously, and perhaps even notoriously, ended up affirming a particular version of a Norwegian Ibsen. When the organizers wanted to mark the centenary of the playwright's death, they chose a spectacular final event in Egypt. Director Bentein Baardson claimed that this was the self-evident and only way to do it, by bringing Peer Gynt back to the pyramids.[31] The result was 'Gynt in Giza' and a rather unfortunate attempt at branding the Norwegian nation. The very choice of play is in fact telling. On first reading it, Bjørnson had called it 'a satire on Norwegian self-love, insularity and selfishness'.[32] Both the play's first reception and the later scholarly readings of the text confirm the clear satirical dimensions of this play, and its attacks on Norway and certain notions of Norwegianness, yet this has not been the dominant Norwegian version of *Peer Gynt*. Ibsen may himself in fact be seen to have contributed to the inception of a 'national-romantic' *Peer Gynt* tradition by inviting Edvard Grieg to compose music for the stage première of the play at Christiania Theater in 1876, and through his own cuts in the text.[33] From the 1890s onwards, Bjørn Bjørnson was to develop the same tradition, with Peer presented as a charming Norwegian rogue. Then, in Egypt in 2006, *Peer Gynt* was played in Norwegian, with the Cairo Symphony Orchestra providing the music. Thousands of Norwegian tourists and VIPs flew in, but it was very difficult to see how this production, apart from perhaps its music and light effects, would communicate with a local audience, even if much was made of the meeting between cultures. The main message from the 'Ibsen 2006' committee, manifested in its habitual and de-contextualized references to a letter Ibsen wrote to the Swedish king, was that Ibsen wanted to teach his fellow countrymen to 'think big!'[34]

With hindsight, it seems clear that 'Ibsen 2006', i.e., the committee in charge of the anniversary, made its worst mistakes as a result of not taking the time to reflect more critically on the relationship between Ibsen and the nation. The insular and very Norwegian version of Ibsen which was communicated, inevitably, and involuntarily, thus got out of control.

IX

By way of conclusion, there is a particular point to be made regarding the tensions between the national and the international Ibsen. In *The Norton Anthology of World Masterpieces*, first published in 1956, René Wellek notes that 'Ibsen more than anyone else widened the scope of world literature beyond the confines of the great modern nations ... Since the time of Ibsen, the other small nations have begun to play their part in the concert of European literature'.[35] During Ibsen's relatively early British reception, in 1897, Henry James memorably labelled him 'the provincial of provincials'.[36] Both to James and many of his contemporaries, Ibsen's origin in Norway, so clearly removed from Europe's cultural centres, was a problem which simply had to be confronted. Those most hostile to Ibsen during his first British reception used such labels simply to dismiss him, but even the 'Ibsenites', the playwright's most vocal defenders, felt that they somehow had to negotiate these puzzling complexities of the Ibsen phenomenon. At the same time, James also called Ibsen 'our Northern Henry', clearly wishing to be associated with his namesake.

Since then, perhaps the provincial has in many ways become the central in world literature, and perhaps Ibsen therefore can be seen as exemplary, and something of a pioneer, in this respect. He was a writer who came from the periphery, or at least from what, not least because of him, may be considered a literary semi-periphery. But he achieved recognition in the centre, and thus no longer, or no longer exclusively, belongs to the periphery, or certainly not to one particular periphery.

Judging by his status today, Henrik Ibsen belongs to the world. He is nearly fully out of Norwegian control. That said, there is of course a particular responsibility involved for Norwegian Ibsen scholars in negotiating between the language in which Ibsen was first received and his numerous new appearances. Interventions from those with the knowledge of Ibsen's Dano-Norwegian texts, their language and historicity, can still be important and valuable. But at the same time, both academics and people in the Norwegian theatre have been forced to recognize that there is another 'real Ibsen' who exists more or less independently of the Norwegian ones.

Writing rather self-consciously as a Norwegian Ibsen scholar in this context, I would hope and think that the new focus on the many different Ibsens abroad may also lead to a renewed interest in our own Ibsens, how these have differed historically, and how they may differ today. Is there a Norwegian Ibsen? No, would be my tentative and theoretical answer, there are many. And some of these Ibsens are still in the process of being constructed, and that to an ever-greater extent as part of dialogues with other Ibsens, from other parts of the world, Ireland included.

---

[1] Many thanks to Irina Ruppo Malone and the late Ros Dixon for their input, as well as to an anonymous reader. Thanks also to Lene Vibeke

Hansen for help in collecting some of the empirical material for this article.

2 Narve Fulsås, 'Litteraturen, universitetet og det moderne gjennombrotet', *Kunnskapens betingelser: Festskrift til Edgeir Benum*, eds John Peter Collett, Jan Eivind Myhre and Jon Skeie (Oslo: Vidarforlaget, 2009): 168-92.

3 Keld Hyldig, *Realisme, symbol og psykologi: Norsk Ibsen-tradition belyst gennem udvalgte forestillinger på Nationaltheatret 1899-1940*, Doctoral Dissertation (University of Bergen, 2000): 31 and 36.

4 Bjørnstjerne, Bjørnson and Henrik Ibsen, 'Utrykte brev mellem Bjørnson og Ibsen 1882-98. Meddelt ved Øyvind Anker', *Edda* 38 (1938): 121.

5 J.B. Halvorsen, 'Ibsens verdensry', *Henrik Ibsen: Festskrift*, ed. Gerhard Gran (Bergen: John Grieg, 1898): 284.

6 Fulsås, 'Litteraturen', 168.

7 Francis Bull, 'Henrik Ibsen og Norge', *Edda* 56 (1956): 253.

8 Ibid.

9 'Ibsen-året 2006', *Aftenposten* 11 January 2006: 3

10 Gisle Selnes, 'Peer og imperiet', *Klassekampen* 7 November 2006: 14-15.

11 Gisle L. Johannessen, 'Norges Ibsen eller Ibsens Norge?', *Bergens Tidende* 4 December2005: 3.

12 Even if there obviously were, even during this period, remnants of an 'old historicist' tradition within Norwegian Ibsen scholarship.

13 Joan Templeton, *Munch's Ibsen: A Painter's Visions of a Playwright* (Seattle: U. of Washington P.,2008): 4.

14 Ibid.

15 Ivo de Figueiredo, *Henrik Ibsen: Mennesket* (Oslo: Aschehoug, 2006): 121-350.

16 Fulsås, Innledning [Introduction], *Henrik Ibsens Skrifter: Brev 1844-1871* (Oslo: Aschehoug, 2005), vol. 12: 27-28.

17 Keld Hyldig, 'Ibsen-tradisjonen i norsk teater', *Norsk Shakespeare- og teatertidsskrift* 3-4 (2006): 6.

18 Keld Hyldig, *Realisme, symbol og psykologi*: 1.

19 Ibid., 44

20 Hyldig, 'Ibsen-tradisjonen', 10.

21 Tore Rem, *Født til frihet: En biografi om Jens Bjørneboe* (Oslo: Cappelen Damm, 2010): 50.

22 Hyldig, 'Ibsen-tradisjonen', 8.

23 Tore Rem, 'Ute av kontroll: Ibsen-året i skyggen av pyramidene', *Samtiden* 1 (2007): 128-139.

24 Jørgen Haugan, 'Krisen i norsk Ibsen-forskning', *Edda* 1 (1983): 46.

25 William Archer, 'The Real Ibsen', in *William Archer on Ibsen: The Major Essays, 1889-1919*, ed. Thomas Postlewait (London: Greenwood P., 1984): 54.

[26] Tore Rem, *Henrik Ibsen/Henry Gibson: Den provinsielle verdensdikter* (Oslo: Cappelen,2006): 17.

[27] Pascale Casanova, *The World Republic of Letters* [1999] (Boston: Harvard U.P., 2004): 21 and 17.

[28] 'Ibsen between Cultures', project description, http://www.hf.uio.no/ibsensenteret/research/research_projects/Ibsen_between_cultures.html.

[29] Casanova, *The World Republic of Letters*, xi.

[30] Edmund Gosse, 'Ibsen, the Norwegian Satirist', *Fortnightly Review* 19: 74-88.

[31] Bentein Baardson, in 'Peer Gynt inntar pyramidene', *Dagsavisen* 25 October 2006: 50-51.

[32] 'Verdenspeer', *Bergens Tidende*, 14 January 2006.

[33] Hyldig, *Realisme, symbol og psykologi*, 29.

[34] Rem, 'Ute av kontroll', 128-139.

[35] René Wellek, 'From Tolstoy to Ibsen', *The Norton Anthology of World Masterpieces*, ed. Maynard Mack, with René Wellek et al. [1956] 4th ed. (London: Norton, 1979): 728.

[36] Henry James, 'John Gabriel Borkman', *Harper's Weekly* 6 February 1897: 78.

2 | Shaw's Ibsen and the Idea of an Irish Theatre

Christopher Murray

> I am with Synge in thinking that the Irish should do their own Ibsenizing; and in fact all your [Abbey Theatre's] successes have been nothing else than that as far as they have been concerned with the works of young Irishmen.
>
> (Shaw to Lady Gregory, 3 September 1916)

There cannot have been anywhere in the world such a champion of Ibsen and Ibsenism as Shaw. The first edition of his book *The Quintessence of Ibsenism* appeared in 1891, to be established as a standard work, if not a classic, after the revised edition of 1913. But Shaw had been on platform and podium long before 1891 haranguing his audiences into recognition of the new drama, especially as translated by his friend William Archer. The gospel according to Shaw was that Ibsen was greater than Shakespeare: 'He gives us not only ourselves, but ourselves in our own situations.'[1] The core of Ibsen's dramaturgy, according to Shaw, lay in the emphasis on discussion or debate: he rejoiced in the paradigm provided by that section in Act III of *A Doll's House* where Nora insists that Torvald sit down and discuss where exactly their marriage failed. This was the 'technical novelty' in Ibsen's new social drama, and it was to provide the cornerstone of Shaw's own plays, where his characters do a lot of sitting down to thrash out thorny issues in lively dialogue. Thus it has rightly been said that the *Quintessence of Ibsenism* 'served as a manifesto for [Shaw's] theatrical aims.'[2]

In addition, as critic for the *Saturday Review* in the later half of the 1890s Shaw not only recorded but shaped the taste of his day by constantly invoking the name of Ibsen as a touchstone of dramatic excellence. Repeatedly, Shaw argued that the best contemporary English actors were frustrated in roles from so-called new English realism which were actually exposed as highly artificial in the light of 'the relentless holding up of the mirror to nature as seen under Ibsen.'[3] Ibsen, he claimed in the same forum, had taken the European drama by the scruff of the neck, as Wagner had taken the opera, and 'willy nilly, it had to come along'.[4] He saw his own dramatic career as bound up with Ibsen's achievement. It is amusing to find in one review – of *Rosmersholm* in March 1895 – Shaw's delight in spotting a volume of his own plays in Rosmer's library on stage, though he feared the actor playing Rosmer who consulted this book might 'forget all about his part'.[5] In this instance Shaw obviously trained his opera glasses on the stage with a degree of vanity. He saw it mirroring his own Ibsenism.

On meeting Ibsen in 1887 William Archer noted how much he was 'essentially a kindred spirit with Shaw – a paradoxist, a sort of Devil's Advocate, who goes about picking holes in every "well-known fact"', allowing Shaw's biographer to conclude: 'It was this similarity that helped to give Shaw such an instinctive insight into Ibsen's plays.'[6] At the same time, it may be added that while championing Ibsen, Shaw the playwright was decidedly his own man, whose vision of life was strikingly different: comic where Ibsen's was tragic, and consequently intellectually playful and optimistic where Ibsen was Darwinist, deterministic, and pessimistic.

As an extension of his missionary spirit, which was very much implicated with that English brand of liberal-socialism known as Fabianism (because of its lack of a revolutionary dimension), Shaw accepted the term 'problem play' as applicable to Ibsen's social drama, so long as it was not to be confused with the accursed 'well-made play' of Eugène Scribe and his followers, which he roundly dismissed as not an art but an 'industry'.[7] The problem play, according to a modern Norwegian scholar, implies the embodying of 'contemporary social problems through the medium of an individual's destiny'.[8] Shaw found the term limiting, since 'every social question furnishes material for drama,'[9] and went beyond Ibsen in calling for 'a frankly doctrinal theatre'.[10] In that respect, in his relations with the new Irish theatre Shaw possibly gave a hostage to fortune and particularly to W.B. Yeats, who as a symbolist poet

was quick to voice his dislike of utilitarian art. Yeats was openly
hostile to Ibsen and the modern movement in realism. Having seen
in London 'the first truly successful production of Ibsen in
England'[11] in 1889, Archer's translation of *A Doll's House*, Yeats
hated it: 'I resented being invited to admire dialogue so close to
modern educated speech that music and style were impossible.'[12]
Shaw conceded that *A Doll's House* would be 'as flat as ditchwater'
when *A Midsummer Night's Dream* would 'still be as fresh as paint'
but insisted that 'it will have done more work in the world.'[13] He
adhered to this position all his writing life. Indeed, in engaging with
the English playwright Terence Rattigan in 1950 on the theme of the
play of ideas Shaw claimed categorically that 'the quality of a play is
the quality of its ideas.'[14] His advocacy of Ibsen derived from this
conviction.

Shaw's commitment to such an aesthetic was to have its
counterpart in the cultural-nationalist project of the twentieth-
century Irish national theatre. In a strange way, the unlikely sharing
by Shaw's *Arms and the Man* and Yeats's *The Land of Heart's
Desire* of a programme offered by J.T. Grein's Independent Theatre
in London in 1894 prefigured the sharing of realism and symbolism
at what was to become the Abbey Theatre in Dublin. In summing up
the productions of Ibsen he saw in London in the 1890s Shaw
surprisingly generalized that the best productions of 'true modern
drama' had to be in a form of 'poetically realistic illusion'.[15] In
destabilizing the accepted theatrical values in London Shaw at this
time showed himself open to the kind of art theatre developing in
Paris and about to flourish in Dublin.

In the 1890s Shaw would have had a kindred spirit in George
Moore, who, like Shaw, was a supporter of and playwright for the
radical Independent Theatre in London. They shared an Ibsenist
view of modern drama. Moore, in turn, had complete domination
over Edward Martyn, who adored Ibsen, so that when Moore and
Martyn joined up with Yeats to launch the Irish Literary Theatre
(hereafter ILT) in 1899, the Irish problem play was born. The
literary historian Ernest A. Boyd, writing in 1918, actually asserted
that the ILT owed its title and for the most part its existence less to
Yeats than to Edward Martyn, 'whose interest in the drama was
avowedly stimulated by the revelation of Ibsen and the
Scandinavian and Russian dramatists to a belated London public.'[16]
Martyn's plan was to emulate the Independent Theatre, and with his
kinsman Moore establish the 'drama of ideas', as Boyd phrases their

work.[17] Indeed, Boyd goes so far as to claim that 'in Martyn we get the essence of Ibsenism, rather than that quintessence extracted by Bernard Shaw.'[18] Whatever about that, it is arguable that the problem play as first naturalized by Martyn and Moore between 1899 and 1901 was mainly the product of Shaw's Ibsenism. In spite of Yeats's suspicion of the form, it was to enjoy a long life in the Irish theatre.

When many years later the actor and playwright Micheál MacLiammóir gave a lecture on the topic he could therefore claim: 'Every Irish play that I know is what I would call a problem play [...] While Ireland remains Ireland there will be problems; and while the Abbey Theatre stands, those problems will find their way to the light in the form of plays.'[19] Appropriately, at this Abbey Festival in 1938 Ernest Blythe also featured as lecturer, albeit on drama in the Irish language. Blythe was to become general manager of the Abbey after Yeats's death, and saw its role as staging certain social and political problems so that 'matters which could be sources of misunderstanding and division may well be combed out on the stage and rendered innocuous by thorough ventilation there.'[20] Here, in a nutshell, is what the Abbey policy became. But even before the Abbey was founded in 1904, *pace* Yeats the Irish dramatic movement was already committed to the naturalization of the Ibsenist problem play. In that year Yeats uncharacteristically asked Shaw for a new play for the Abbey, due to open in December, and was thus the midwife for *John Bull's Other Island*.

To be mentioned also among the shapers of the Ibsenist aesthetic at the Abbey, as filtered through Shaw's teachings, is the influence of Frank Fay, one of two brothers, both actors of the kind who knew everything about the theatre and its history and who knew in addition how to apply the latest ideas. They ran the Ormonde Dramatic Society between them and were eventually to help create the Irish National Theatre Society, which evolved into the Abbey. Frank was also a drama critic in the late 1890s and for a short time after. His reviews in the *United Irishman* make it clear that Shaw was his ideal critic. I would argue that it was mainly through Fay that Shaw's idea of a theatre penetrated the new Irish movement. Writing in May 1901 Fay tried to push Yeats into an Ibsenist dramaturgy: 'In Ireland we are at present only too anxious to shun reality. Our drama ought to teach us to face it. Let Mr Yeats give us a play in verse or prose that will rouse this sleeping land.' [21] Yeats actually obliged by providing the rabble-rousing *Cathleen Ni*

Houlihan (1902) for the Fays to act in. Summing up the achievements of the ILT, then come to the end of its three-year programme, Fay remarked: 'there was in each of them [the plays] something to make one think – a rare occurrence in a Dublin theatre, except when a play by Ibsen or Maeterlinck, or George Bernard Shaw, or Oscar Wilde is acted.'[22] The ILT plays, Fay went on, no doubt thinking of the early problem plays of Martyn and Moore, 'kept one awake; there were ideas in them, and we had to use our brains. That is the class of play we want in Ireland'.[23] His main point once again was that 'the country needs to be roused from its lethargy. People must be taught to think, and then to act',[24] here echoing Shaw's own 'pragmatist ethic'.[25] The circulation of such ideas shaped the development of the Irish dramatic movement.

This development was in naturalism and the naturalistic style of acting and production. 'A popular error still identifies W.B. Yeats with the training of the Irish players and the establishment of the acting tradition which has kept the Abbey theatre alive through the last fifty years,' wrote one of the early trainees. 'If the poet was alive now he would be the first to disagree with such a theory. To Frank Fay must go the credit of training the actors. Without Willie Fay there might never have been an Irish theatre company; without Frank Fay there might never have been a competent one.'[26] Gabriel Fallon, who acted in O'Casey's plays in the 1920s, agreed: 'The Fays were the "onlie begetters" of what is known as the Abbey Theatre tradition in acting.'[27] It was to survive for most of the twentieth century and its success is symbiotically related to the prevalence of realism in the Abbey repertory and production style.

Yeats's rejection of *John Bull's Other Island* must have stung because in his 1906 preface to the published text Shaw allowed himself a sneer against the whole Abbey project: 'Only a quaint little offshoot of English pre-Raphaelitism called the Gaelic movement has got a footing by using Nationalism as a stalking-horse, and popularizing itself as an attack on the native [*sic*] language of the Irish people, which is most fortunately also the native language of half the world, including England.'[28] Although Shaw had certainly begun to think of *John Bull* as destined for the Court Theatre in August 1904, which he was to join with fellow-playwright Harley Granville Barker and the manager John Eugene Vedrenne in an epoch-making venture, he knew it could stir an Irish audience. In fact, so did Yeats, who wrote to Shaw: 'You have said things in this play which are entirely true about Ireland, things which nobody has ever said before, and these are the very things that are most part of the action.'[29] It was too big a play and too challenging for the Abbey actors and their tiny stage, and yet 'that queer elephant', as Yeats dubbed it,[30] Shaw's clever dramatic analysis of Ireland and the land question, should obviously have been accepted. Frank Fay said as much after *John Bull* proved a hit in England, and added: 'But Yeats is an impossible creature to head a theatre. His complete ignorance of acting is in itself sufficient to incapacitate him.'[31] The point is that Shaw's plays are 'actorly' in the extreme,[32] and *John Bull* would have enabled the Fays to develop the art of acting at the Abbey rather more than they did before Yeats got rid of them in 1908.

Happily, rejection of *John Bull's Other Island* did not keep Ibsenist modernism out of the new Abbey repertory. The enemy was already within. Ibsen was present in the plays of minor writers such as William Boyle and Padraic Colum. In the same year as Shaw published his play with its provocative preface Colum acknowledged Ibsen's recent death in Arthur Griffith's weekly newspaper: 'Henrik Ibsen should be of interest to us in Ireland if only as the great representative of a minor nationality.' But then he shifts into Shavian gear: '[Ibsen] has brought seriousness back into drama, he has restored drama as a great form. He has created dramatists in many countries by the shock of his new and living form. He has given them the dramatic point of view, and no reading of Shakespeare, Molière or the dead Greeks could have done this.'[33] In his own early plays, notably *Broken Soil* (1903) and especially in *The Land* (1905), Colum dramatized themes central to *John Bull's Other Island*, themes which Daniel Corkery was later to categorize as definitive of the Irish as opposed to the Anglo-Irish writer, namely, the land, nationalism and religious consciousness.[34] A slightly later Colum play, *Thomas Muskerry* (1910), set in a workhouse, was regarded as dangerously Ibsenist and has been described as 'certainly the most debated drama of the year'.[35]

What Colum's plays and their reception show is that the economic problem could not be separated from the political in the way Shaw as Fabian believed desirable. Further, for Shaw the issue of identity was of no real significance. Racial stereotypes were merely the invention of popular writers. As Shaw saw it, difference was based on wilful insistence on ideals, which should be exposed Ibsen-style as either ridiculous or dangerous or both. But to the Irish writer of this time and for many years after the colonial question was settled and a major post-colonial problem remained, ideals were definitive, and if Ibsen cried out for their deconstruction in drama then the Irish writers needed to redirect Ibsen's ideas anew.

I would argue that this is what happened. After the death in 1909 of Synge, who had remained strangely hostile to both Ibsen and Shaw[36] during his short, meteoric career as Abbey playwright, Lennox Robinson and T.C. Murray came forward with the sort of plays Colum had initiated. They were darker, more pessimistic, than Colum's work and in that respect more Ibsenist. Robinson, newly appointed manager at the Abbey at age twenty-four, had a brief period as Shaw's secretary in London in 1910, where as apprentice he attended Shaw's rehearsals of a new play, *Misalliance*. At the time he also attended the rehearsals of Granville-Barker's *The Madras House*. 'I spent a magical six weeks,' Robinson says in his autobiography.[37] It must have been rather like Brian Friel's stay at the Guthrie Theater in Minneapolis in 1963 and with comparable results. Robinson brought back to the Abbey a determination to make the new realism and production methods central to the repertory. As dramatist Robinson began his career as an Ibsenist playwright with *The Clancy Name* and other dark critiques of rural conventional values, even if he was to mock all of this in rather Shavian style in *Drama at Inish: An Exaggeration in Three Acts* (1933). [38] However, Robinson's little primer *Towards an Appreciation of the Theatre* (1945) shows that *A Doll's House* remained for him the best example of modern dramatic construction.

T.C. Murray likewise based his realism on Ibsen's model, re-applied to rural Irish social conditions and problems. Murray's *Birthright* (1910), *Maurice Harte* (1912), and his masterpiece *Autumn Fire* (1924) managed to wed peasant drama to Ibsenist tragedy. But while adhering to Ibsen's form Murray was unable to move beyond it.[39] By the 1920s the peasant drama was outmoded and the Shavian style of urban drama was dominating the Abbey repertory,[40] leaving Murray's style of quiet realism behind.

Through a twist of fate, Shaw's presence had begun to be felt more at the Abbey following the controversial production there in 1909 of *The Shewing Up of Blanco Posnet*. Banned by the Lord Chamberlain in England, this piece was seized on by the Abbey as a *cause celèbre* that might restore its status as a radical theatre, badly damaged by the reception of Synge's *Playboy* by the nationalists. The triumph of *Posnet* at the Abbey was ably promoted as a blow against Dublin Castle and its attempt at censorship. Ironically, as Shaw had insisted, *Posnet* on stage was a danger to nobody. Indeed, many openly claimed themselves disappointed that the thing wasn't in the least naughty. The novelist George A. Birmingham said in his review:

> In Dublin, the most religious city in the world, the provincial visitors who put in an appearance during Horse Show week are incapable of understanding Shaw [...] Such of them as ventured to attend the opening performance do not know that they have been enticed to a theatre to listen to a sermon. When they find it out they will be very angry, indeed, and quite rightly, for it is a clear case of obtaining money under false pretences to advertise a blasphemy and produce a sermon.[41]

Shaw could hardly have put the matter better himself. Here was the prophet as jester accepted in his own country. *Posnet* is a 'Mousetrap play' – Shaw's term, borrowed from Hamlet's play-within-the play 'to catch the conscience of the king' for Ibsen's style of drama – but a Mousetrap play with a difference, and the difference is truly Irish in its sustained use of irony.

It has to be underlined that none of Ibsen's plays was staged at the old Abbey. Therefore one is speaking at all times here either of Ibsen *sub rosa* or of Shaw applying Ibsenist discussion for his own mischievous purposes. From 1916 on, when *John Bull's Other Island* was first performed at the Abbey, Shaw's plays began to be staged with regularity, especially when the actor J. Augustus Keogh became manager.[42] Shaw was suddenly kosher. Lady Gregory adopted him as one of her own. The Shaw season of 1916-1917, which featured six plays – *John Bull, Widowers' Houses, Arms and the Man, Man and Superman, The Inca of Perusalem,* and *The Doctor's Dilemma* – can be recognized as 'an act of repatriation' for Shaw the playwright.[43] It is noteworthy that after 1916 *John Bull* 'was revived for at least a week's run every year until 1931'.[44] Shaw's attitude to the 1914-18 war, to Home Rule, and to the execution of the leaders of the 1916 Rising made a lasting impression in Dublin. He was now 'one of our own', as the phrase is, who took his holidays in Kerry.

It is appropriate, consequently, that Shaw's collected comments on the Irish question are dedicated by his editor to Sean O'Casey.[45] As playwright, O'Casey developed under the formative influence of Shaw, to whom he wrote in 1919 for a preface to a book of polemical essays he had in mind; though turned down he got good advice. A great admirer – alongside Jim Larkin – of *John Bull's Other Island,*

O'Casey would boast that it was Shaw's preface which made him a socialist.[46] When he saw *Androcles and the Lion* at the Abbey in 1919 he began to model his own plays satirically. One of these (rejected) texts has recently come to light, set in a public house in Dublin on the brink of the first election after the civil war.[47] It is a comic debate with a farcical outcome, pointing towards the kind of play O'Casey was mainly interested in; this *Cooing of Doves* was to re-appear in disguise as Act II of *The Plough and the Stars* (1926). In the meantime, O'Casey's two popular plays, *The Shadow of a Gunman* (1923) and *Juno and the Paycock* (1924), while highly original as reflections of recent Irish life at a time of violence and confusion, showed many signs of Shaw's influence, mainly in the lively, challenging dialogue, the gendered representation of women as superior to men in common sense and initiative, and the provocative anti-war stance taken in the plays. Yet the inevitable traces of Ibsen in modern Irish drama may be discerned in O'Casey's use of autobiographical detail and the use of space as indicative of social determinism, bringing to mind Raymond Williams's remark that one feels that 'Ibsen had to make rooms on the stage in order to show men trapped in them.'[48] O'Casey's subject was tenement life in impoverished, war-torn Dublin. It is interesting that he felt he could mock Ibsen, however, as when in *Juno and the Paycock* Captain Boyle, who carries a slight flavour of Jacob Engstrand about him, derides his daughter's efforts to improve herself by reading, 'nothin' but thrash, too,' he adds. 'There's one I was lookin' at dh'other day: three stories, The Doll's House, Ghosts, an' The Wild Duck – buks only fit for chiselurs! [children]'[49] The irony is that his daughter Mary Boyle, like any Shavian heroine, Vivie Warren or Ellie Dunn, is vigorously in league with the Life Force. O'Casey thus established a hybrid drama in Ireland, in accordance with Shaw's idea of a theatre.

Denis Johnston, a younger, more intellectual Irish playwright, assumed an even more Shavian stance, to the point of writing witty, iconoclastic prefaces to his plays while following O'Casey into satirical critiques of postcolonial Ireland. *The Old Lady Says 'No'!* (1929), *The Moon in the Yellow River* (1931), and other plays down to that rather postmodernist rewriting of O'Casey's 1916 play under the parodic title *The Scythe and the Sunset* (1958) seem to marry Shaw's anti-war sentiments with Shaw's later use of fantasy. Cleverly, however, Johnston, who knew Shaw personally, remarked that having found that Shaw had clay feet when it came to acting the sage, he decided to listen to Shaw's advice 'with becoming respect' but to go on 'to do the opposite.'[50] The Ibsenist form, by the same token, was with time being freely adapted into expressionism.

Less experimental Irish playwrights than Johnston carried on the established blend of Ibsen and Shaw at the Abbey into the 1930s and beyond. These writers included Paul Vincent Carroll, Louis D'Alton and John O'Donovan. Carroll wrote strong, anti-clerical, realistic plays for the Abbey before being turned away with the rejection of *The White Steed* (1938), subsequently staged with great acclaim on Broadway. He has said: 'fortunately for my work, Ibsen took a sure and disciplined hand in my development.'[51] His *Things That Are Caesar's* (1932, revised 1944) has been compared to *A Doll's House*. His later work, satirical and whimsical, was more in Shaw's vein and inclined to be over-didactic. D'Alton's *Lovers Meeting* (1941), while mining again rural Irish realism, daringly addressed such Ibsenist themes as the loveless marriage, infidelity, illegitimacy, incest and suicide. As Ciara O'Farrell has demonstrated, 'D'Alton's premature death undoubtedly was a major loss to the Irish stage.'[52] His posthumously produced *This Other Eden* (1953) was the longest-running success the Abbey ever had. Here D'Alton adopted Shaw's style by invoking *John Bull's Other Island* as a means of scrutinizing the shortcomings of postcolonial Ireland. Obsessed with Shaw, John O'Donovan wrote *The Shaws of Synge Street* (1960) for the Abbey, as well as the memoir *Shaw and the Charlatan Genius* (Dolmen 1965), and in life affected the abrasive style of Shaw. His most successful play for the Abbey was *The Less We Are Together* (1957), a satire on Irish partition: 'dealing with the subject as I did was equivalent to saying that the Communists weren't wholly demonic when Senator McCarthy was at the height of his power.'[53]

Ideologically, Shaw was probably less appealing to conservative Abbey audiences than was naturalized Ibsen. On the other hand, Irish taste is more for comedy than for tragedy. From O'Casey through to Beckett tragicomedy is thus the preferred modern Irish dramatic form. Ibsen as filtered through Shaw is one way of describing this development.

Finally, it has to be pointed out that once the Gate Theatre was established by two Englishmen in Dublin in 1928 Shaw, alongside Wilde and Shakespeare, became mainly associated with that theatre, easily identifiable as the Abbey's 'other'. From the 1930s Shaw disappeared from the Abbey repertory until after the new theatre opened in 1966. The original Gate was both more intellectual and more committed to modern theatrical production values than was the old Abbey. It stole Shaw as it stole Wilde and tried to make off with Johnston and many another. But even as stolen goods Shaw in production at the Gate can cast light on the Abbey by showing it up, or should that read 'shewing up'? By staging *Back to Methuselah*, by making Shotover – Shaw's alter ego – in *Heartbreak House* one of Hilton Edwards's enduring roles, and by staging act three of *Man and Superman* as a vehicle for MacLiammóir as an Irish devil, the Gate ironically served to critique the Abbey ethos after 1930. Shawless, the old Abbey had then to make do with Ibsen and bog water.

---

[1] Bernard Shaw, *The Quintessence of Ibsenism: Now Completed to the Death of Ibsen* (New York: Hill and Wang, 1957): 182.

[2] Christopher Innes, '"Nothing but talk, talk, talk, – Shaw talk": Discussion Plays and the Making of Modern Drama', *The Cambridge Companion to George Bernard Shaw*, ed. Christopher Innes (Cambridge: Cambridge University Press, 1998): 162.

[3] Bernard Shaw, *Our Theatres in the Nineties*, 3 vols (London: Constable, 1932): 2, 241. There are seventy-two references to Ibsen in these reviews collected from *The Saturday Review*.

[4] Shaw, *Our Theatres in the Nineties* 2, 258.

[5] Shaw, *Our Theatres in the Nineties* 1, 73.

[6] Michael Holroyd, *Bernard Shaw: The One-Volume Definitive Edition* (London: Vintage, 1998): 113.

[7] George Bernard Shaw, Preface, *Three Plays by Brieux* (1911), reprinted as 'Against the Well-Made Play', *Modern Theories of Drama: A Selection of Writings on Drama and Theatre 1850-1990*, ed. George W. Brandt (Oxford: Clarendon P, 1998): 102.

[8] Bjørn Hemmer, 'Ibsen and the Realistic Problem Drama', *The Cambridge Companion to Ibsen*, ed. James McFarlane (Cambridge: CUP, 1994): 71.

[9] Bernard Shaw, 'The Problem Play – A Symposium', *Shaw on Theatre*, ed. E.J. West (New York: Hill and Wang, 1959):59.

[10] Shaw, *The Quintessence*, 187.

[11] Robert F. Whitman, *Shaw and the Play of Ideas* (Ithaca and London: Cornell UP, 1977): 109.

[12] W.B. Yeats, *Autobiographies* (London: Macmillan, 1961): 279. This was to be Yeats's firm bias against 'the play of modern manners'. See Yeats, *Essays and Introductions* (London: Macmillan, 1961): 274-77.

[13] Shaw, 'The Problem Play – A Symposium', 63.

[14] Shaw, 'The Play of Ideas', *Shaw on Theatre*, 290. See also John Russell Taylor, *The Rise and Fall of the Well-Made Play* (London: Methuen, 1967): 81-91.

[15] Shaw, 'Ibsen Triumphant' (22 May 1897), *Our Theatres in the Nineties*, 3, 139.

[16] Ernest A. Boyd, *The Contemporary Drama of Ireland* (Dublin: Talbot Press; London: Fisher Unwin, 1918): 5.

[17] Ibid., 7. It was after he and Arthur Symons saw *Ghosts* at Antoine's Théâtre Libre in Paris in May 1890 that they decided to found the Independent Theatre in London, with J.T. Grein. See Adrian Frazier, *George Moore, 1852-1933* (New Haven and London: Yale UP, 2000): 213-14.

[18] Boyd, 19.

[19] Michael MacLiammóir, 'Problem Plays', *The Irish Theatre*, ed. Lennox Robinson (London: Macmillan, 1939): 202, 227.

[20] Ernest Blythe, *The Abbey Theatre* [pamphlet] (Dublin: The National Theatre Society Ltd, n.d.), no pagination.

[21] *Towards a National Theatre: The Dramatic Criticism of Frank J. Fay*, ed. Robert Hogan (Dublin: Dolmen Press, 1970): 53.

[22] Ibid., 83.

[23] Ibid., 83.

[24] Ibid., 84.

[25] Alfred Turco, Jr, *Shaw's Moral Vision: The Self and Salvation* (Ithaca: Cornell UP, 1976): 53.

[26] Máire Níc Shiubhlaighh, *The Splendid Years* (Dublin: James Duffy, 1955): 9.

[27] Gabriel Fallon, 'The Abbey Theatre Acting Tradition', *The Story of the Abbey Theatre*, ed. Sean McCann (London: New English Library, 1967): 107.

[28] Shaw, *Collected Plays*, 2:471.

[29] Yeats to Shaw, 5 October 1904, Bernard Shaw, *Collected Letters 1898-1910*, ed. Dan H. Laurence (London: Max Reinhardt, 1972): 453.

[30] Ibid.

[31] Frank Fay to Máire Garvey, cited by Robert Hogan and James Kilroy, *The Modern Irish Drama: A Documentary History* vol. 3, *The Abbey Theatre: The Years of Synge 1905-1909*, (Dublin: Dolmen Press; Highlands, NJ: Humanities Press, 1978): 308.

[32] See Jan McDonald, 'Shaw and the Court Theatre', *The Cambridge Companion to George Bernard Shaw*, 261-82.

[33] Padraic Colum, 'Ibsen and National Drama', *Sinn Fein* 2 June 1906: 3.

[34] Daniel Corkery, *Synge and Anglo-Irish Literature* [1931] (Cork: Mercier Press, 1966): 19. To Corkery, Shaw had, like Wilde, sold out to the enemy: 'is it not a strange thing that servitude to the stranger should eventuate in brilliancy?' Shaw the jester was not 'one of ourselves' (19).

[35] Robert Hogan, Richard Burnham and Daniel P. Poteet, *The Modern Irish Drama: A Documentary History IV: The Rise of the Realists*

1910-1915 (Dublin: Dolmen, 1979): 32. See also Christopher Murray, 'Padraic Colum's *The Land* and Cultural Nationalism', *Hungarian Journal of English and American Studies*, 2.2 (1996): 5-15.

36 One has but to point to Synge's preface to his *Playboy of the Western World* (1907) for evidence of Synge's hostility to Ibsen and his followers, although it is equally plain that the *Playboy* is indebted to *Peer Gynt*, and *The Well of the Saints* in some measure to *The Wild Duck*. See Jan Setterqvist, *Ibsen and the Beginnings of Anglo-Irish Drama*, 1, *John Millington Synge* (Uppsala: U. of Uppsala, 1951). Morerover, Synge's first complete play, never acted at the Abbey, *When the Moon Has Set* (1900-1902), is deeply indebted to *Ghosts*. For Synge's 'anxiety of influence' in this regard, and his hostility to Shaw, see Christopher Murray, *Twentieth-Century Irish Drama: Mirror up to Nation* (Manchester: Manchester UP, 1997): 64-87.

37 Lennox Robinson, *Curtain Up: An Autobiography* (London: Michael Joseph, 1942): 25.

38 Michael J. O'Neill, *Lennox Robinson* (Boston: Twayne, 1964): 49-53. He was not confined to Ibsenism, however. See Hartmut Vormann, *The Art of Lennox Robinson: Theoretical Premises and Theatrical Practice* (Trier: WVT, 2001): 262-68.

39 Albert J. DeGiacomo, *T.C. Murray, Dramatist: Voice of Rural Ireland* (Syracuse: SUP, 2003):35. See also Richard Allen Cave, Introduction, *The Selected Plays of T. C. Murray* (Gerrards Cross: Colin Smythe; Washington, DC: CUAP, 1998): xix-xx.

40 Mícheál Ó hAodha, 'T.C. Murray, Dramatist (1873-1959)', *Plays and Places* (Dublin: Progress House, 1961): 23-25.

41 Cited by Hogan and Kilroy, *The Abbey Theatre: The Years of Synge*: 301.

42 See *Shaw, Lady Gregory and the Abbey: A Correspondence and a Record*, eds Dan H. Laurence and Nicholas Grene (Gerrards Cross: Colin Smythe, 1993): xx-xxii.

43 Christopher Morash, *A History of Irish Theatre 1601-2000* (Cambridge: CUP, 2002): 159.

44 Dan H. Laurence and Nicholas Grene, Introduction, *Shaw, Lady Gregory and the Abbey*, xxii.

45 Bernard Shaw, *The Matter with Ireland*, eds David H. Greene and Dan H. Laurence (London: Hart-Davis, 1962).

46 Sean O'Casey, *Autobiographies*, 2 vols (London: Macmillan, 1963), 1:557-72; O'Casey, *Under a Colored Cap* (London: Macmillan, 1964): 263.

47 See 'Sean O'Casey's *The Cooing of Doves*: A One-Act Play Rediscovered', introduced and edited by Christopher Murray, *Princeton University Library Chronicle*, LXVIII No. 1 & 2 (Autumn 2006-Winter 2007): 327-56.

48 Raymond Williams, *Drama from Ibsen to Brecht*, revised edition (London: Penguin, 1968): 387.

[49] Sean O'Casey, *Collected Plays*, vol. 1 (London: Macmillan, 1949): 23.

[50] Denis Johnston, *The Dramatic Works of Denis Johnston*, vol. 2 (Gerrards Cross: Colin Smythe, 1979): 5.

[51] Paul A. Doyle, *Paul Vincent Carroll* (Lewisburg: Bucknell UP, 1971): 19.

[52] Ciara O'Farrell, *Louis D'Alton and the Abbey Theatre* (Dublin: Four Courts, 2004):198.

[53] Cited by Robert Hogan, *After the Irish Renaissance: A Critical History of the Irish Drama Since* The Plough and the Stars (London: Macmillan, 1968): 77.

3 | Ibsen in Inish: Lennox Robinson, Ibsen, and the Censorship of Publications Act

Christopher Morash

Being Ibsenish

If he is remembered at all today, Lennox Robinson is recalled as the author of a series of forgotten plays that every decade or so surprise enterprising directors (and audiences) by turning out to be much better than we remember them.[1] We might think of the Barabbas production of *The Whiteheaded Boy* in 1997, or Conall Morrison's 2007 production of *The Big House*, or the 2009 off-Broadway production of *Drama at Inish*, staged under its original American title, *Is Life Worth Living?*[2] However, Robinson was much more than a playwright. From 1909, he spent two terms as manager at the Abbey, was almost continuously producing plays, and was one of the prime movers behind the Dublin Drama League, which did so much to bring key modernist plays to Irish audiences. From the 1920s, Robinson was also a critic, a prose writer, the founder of the Irish chapter of PEN, a tireless organizer for the Carnegie Libraries, and generally an inescapable figure in that intimate, sometimes disillusioned, and always contested world of Irish culture in the years during which the Irish Free State was trying to define itself in the fading aftermath of the excited idealism of its founding.

Throughout this period, it was clear that both the figure of Ibsen and Ibsen's dramaturgy played a significant role in shaping Robinson's engagement with post-Independence Ireland and its possibilities. By the early 1930s, the extent to which Ibsen had become a sort of prism through which he saw Irish society would become so clear to Robinson that he would use it as the basis for *Drama at Inish*, a play about the comic disruption caused in a 'deadly dull'[3] Irish seaside town – Inish – by the performances of a travelling theatre company whose summer repertoire includes Ibsen's *A Doll's House*. However, the core of this idea goes back much earlier for Robinson, and he would later claim that elements of this scenario could almost be taken 'for a fragment of autobiography', fondly recalling that as a young man he had watched from the gods as Octavia Kenmore's touring company played the Gaiety Theatre in the early years of the century. The management, he reminisced, knew that there would be only a paltry audience for such plays, so they booked the company for 'the worst week of the year, the week before Holy Week'. 'And so there would be, for me, a glorious week split up between *A Doll's House*, *Hedda Gabler*, *An Enemy of the People*, with, perhaps, a *Rosmersholm*, thrown in as makeweight.'[4]

From that point until the end of his life, Robinson championed Ibsen's work in Ireland with an almost evangelical zeal. For instance, writing on the front page of the *Irish Times* in March of 1928 to mark the centenary of Ibsen's birth, Robinson proclaimed that 'the modern Irish theatre seems to be founded on the Ibsen tradition.' Twenty five years later, he would pick up this theme again in an article for the *Irish Press*. 'Joyce imitated Ibsen and wrote *Exiles*, a bad, dull play', he notes, 'but on other Irish dramatists the influence was more fruitful. A notable example is Séamus O'Kelly's *The Bribe* … I think I see a touch of Ibsen in [Padraic] Colum's *Thomas Muskerry*; in St. John Ervine's early serious plays; in my own *Patriots*.'[5] At one level, Robinson's sustained admiration for Ibsen was firmly grounded in dramatic practice. For instance, in a late piece entitled 'Making A Play' from the 1950s (but which echoes the same point from essays going back to the early 1920s), he argues that *John Gabriel Borkman* is a model of effective dramatic form, in that all of the significant action has taken place before the play begins, and the audience faces what Robinson evocatively calls 'the cinders from a volcano – hence the long and often unnatural explosions.' In other articles, however, he makes it clear that the example of Ibsen for Irish drama was more than simply structural; it was equally the revelation that theatre could be made from ordinary lives. 'We have learned the great Ibsen lesson – life does not mainly concern itself with fashionable drawing-rooms; it spreads to the suburbs, to the slums, to the countryside, and history, local and national, impinges deeply on common people's lives.'[6] Luke Gibbons has recently written of Joyce that 'one of the most traumatic aspects of the "nightmare of history" in *Ulysses* is that the past is not confined to dream but may visit its terrors again on the present.' [7] This was a lesson that Robinson had already learned from Ibsen in the 1920s.

Robinson began writing these articles at a time when he was among the most influential figures in Irish theatre, directing more than fifty productions in the decade 1920-1930 alone, including the première of O'Casey's *The Plough and the Stars*.[8] Indeed, in an unpublished letter to Lady Gregory, Robinson confessed that, in his view, O'Casey's play 'lacks a character strongly running through it and it is seriously hampered by long rambling speeches',[9] a criticism clearly shaped by his own preference for the dramaturgical values of Ibsen's late plays, which are dominated by strong central characters who speak, for the most part, with restraint. Later, Robinson unfavourably compared O'Casey's Juno – who is 'quickly presented to us in the round; she does nothing to astonish us' – to Nora in *A Doll's House*, who 'develops and surprises us from the first scene to the last, her greatest surprise, her most staggering development being reserved for the last fifteen minutes of the play.'[10]

As the Abbey's main producer of plays in the 1920s and early 1930s, Robinson was in a position to make sure that the Irish public's awareness of Ibsen was not confined to print. Beginning in 1923, he produced the first of what the *Irish Times* in 1926 was already referring to as the 'annual presentation of *A Doll's House* by the Abbey company',[11] usually mounted in the last week of September or early October. These productions generally attracted a good house, and enthusiastic notices. In 1925, for instance, Robinson was able to report to Lady Gregory, who was home in Coole Park, that 'the return of "Dolls House" will astound you. The theatre was absolutely full on Saturday night. I couldn't get a seat high or low.'[12] That year, the *Irish Times* thought the production 'was better than any seen at the Abbey Theatre for a long time'.[13] Robinson went on to produce *John Gabriel Borkman* in 1928 as part of the Ibsen centenary, to a similarly rapturous critical response. 'As one sat in the crowded theatre last night it was hard to reconcile oneself to the admitted fact that Ibsen, in these countries, is not popular in the ordinarily accepted meaning of the term',[14] enthused the *Irish Times*. Later, in 1932, Robinson staged *Rosmersholm* at the Abbey.

For audiences today who know Robinson's own plays primarily from comedies such as *The Whiteheaded Boy* or *Drama at Inish*,

Robinson's close association with Ibsen's work might come as something of a surprise (although his admiration for a late point of attack in narrative structure is evident in *The Whiteheaded Boy*). However, there are other Robinson plays, less well known today, in which Ibsen is much more clearly a model. Perhaps the best example is a play from 1925, *The White Blackbird*,[15] in which a strong-willed, visionary character, William Naynor, returns to inherit the house and copper mine that the rest of his family can only see as a means of bankrolling lives of aimless leisure. William baffles his family (apart from his artist sister, Bella) by exhausting himself in trying to save the mine, not for financial gain, but because 'it was father's dream ... that's inexplicable. – Thank God it is. I couldn't live if life could be explained.'[16] Bella (for whom he holds an incestuous torch) tells him that he is 'just like that white blackbird'. 'White blackbird?' he asks. 'I'm trying to be Ibsenish', she tells him, '– of course you don't know what that means.' 'It sounds impossibly beautiful – a white blackbird', he says; to which she replies: 'It's neither impossible nor beautiful.'[17] In short, in William Naynor, the strong-willed visionary pursuing an ideal just at the limits of definition, Robinson creates his own master builder, his 'Ibsenish' hero.

Branded as a Blasphemer

The White Blackbird premièred on 12 October 1925, immediately after that year's Abbey production of *A Doll's House*. Both productions took place just after Robinson's place in Irish public life was undergoing an abrupt shift, and he was, as he dryly observed to Lady Gregory, 'being branded as a blasphemer.'[18] The roots of the incident go back to the middle of the previous decade when, having been temporarily dismissed as the Abbey's manager, Robinson threw himself with characteristic vigour into managing the Carnegie Library Trust in Ireland, quickly rising to a position on its managing Committee (a position he maintained after he resumed his role as Abbey manager in the early 1920s). At the same time, he continued to publish, and in 1924 Robinson contributed a story he had originally written back in 1911, 'The Madonna of Slieve Dun', to the first issue of an arts journal started by Francis Stuart and Cecil Salkeld, *To-morrow*. Other contributors included Joseph Campbell and Yeats, who published 'Leda and the Swan' in the journal. Yeats also anonymously contributed the first editorial, in which he provocatively proclaimed that 'we can forgive the sinner, but abhor the atheist, and ... we count among atheists bad writers and Bishops of all denominations.'[19]

This was clearly incendiary material, and was intended as such. In the spring of 1924, the Bishops of Dublin, Galway, Tuam and Clogher simultaneously released Lenten Pastorals that attacked 'offenders against our standard of public decency'.[20] The ground for the Pastoral had been prepared by an article in the *Ecclesiastical Bulletin* in February of 1924 by a Fr Richard Devane, S.J., a veteran campaigner who had progressed from burning English Sunday newspapers a decade earlier to becoming the only individual invited to speak on his own behalf before the government-established Committee on Evil Literature, whose role was to prepare the ground for the Censorship of Publications Act. 'Indecency is indecency,' proclaimed Devane in a follow-up fusillade in 1925, 'even though the cunning hand of some degenerate artist pretends to hide its nakedness under the transparencies of a seductive style.'[21]

Robinson's story in *To-morrow* that August, 'The Madonna of Slieve Dun', provided exactly the kind of ammunition that figures like Devane needed if their campaign for censorship was to embrace literary works as well as advertisements for condoms. The story is simple, almost parable-like: an innocent young girl, living in an Irish village notable for its drunken debauchery, is raped one night by a tramp. She becomes convinced that she is going to give birth to the messiah who will redeem the village. One by one, the villagers come to believe her, and reform their lives; however, the story ends with the tramp, drunk in a pub in another town, boasting of the rape. It provoked one senior member of the Carnegie Committee in Ireland, Fr T.A. Finlay (whose credentials went back to the Land War in the 1880s) to resign. The story must, he wrote, 'give grievous offence to, and provoke just indignation in, every believer in Christ who may read it. With the writer I could not, without prejudice to higher interests, associate myself before the public in the work of the Committee.'[22] His resignation was quickly followed by that of the Provost of Trinity College, J.H. Bernard, and, ultimately, by that of Robinson himself.

Robinson's unpublished correspondence of the time shows that the incident upset him greatly. 'Forgive me for not having written to you before, I've been awfully busy and worried', he wrote to Lady Gregory on 23 December 1924. 'The Carnegie situation has resolved itself into the suspension of the Committee and my dismissal. It's a complete victory for the obscurantists but only a temporary one I think.'[23] Indeed, the incident also seems to have had its effect on Lady Gregory, at a time when she was all too aware of the precarious predicament of the Abbey's Protestant directorate, and their dependence on a subsidy from a notoriously stingy government with strong ties to the Catholic Episcopacy. In 1927, advising Robinson against producing a new play that she feared might give offence, she confessed that she may have been suffering from 'undue nervousness owing to the Carnegie business'.[24]

In the months immediately after this skirmish with 'the obscurantists' in 1924 and into early 1925, Robinson began work on his play with the 'Ibsenish' hero, *The White Blackbird*, and entered into his most intense period of public advocacy of Ibsen. While it is always slightly suspect to read a play as a kind of allegory, on the rare occasions that Robinson commented on his own work he often produced surprisingly political readings that border on the allegorical. For instance, he once wrote: '*The White-Headed Boy* is political from beginning to end, though I don't suppose six people have recognized the fact', moving on to argue that the play's prodigal son hero could be identified with Ireland, and his over-bearing mother with England. 'Our battles are only symbols', he wrote in an introduction to a collection of his plays, 'and parliaments and republics are shadows of a shadow.'[25] Again, this willingness to see symbols may well have been a product of his intimate absorption of Ibsen's dramaturgy, although his language, no doubt, also has something to do with his lifelong admiration for Yeats.

If we allow ourselves to see symbols, *The White Blackbird*'s inheritance plot becomes something more than a conventional device: the return of an awkward son to inherit the mine that was his father's lifework to create, while the rest of his family betray that inheritance, may well have seemed to Robinson to have had a very particular resonance in the Ireland of the 1920s. In the autobiographical work he published late in life, Robinson places particular emphasis on a series of epiphany-like awakenings into idealistic nationalism, whether finding 'hundreds of copies of the old *Nation* newspaper' in a neighbour's house, or cycling six miles through the darkened countryside to catch a train to see *Cathleen ni Houlihan* at the Cork Opera House as a young man.[26] As early as his 1918 play, *The Lost Leader*, Robinson can be seen defining an oppositional stance for himself against an Ireland in which 'Home Rule became merely the exchange of government by English shop-keepers for government by Irish gombeen-men', and 'the fight for the possession of a nation's soul' had been betrayed.[27] Having already rehearsed these themes even before the Irish state became a reality, it takes no great stretch of the imagination to see *The White Blackbird* as being at least as overtly political as *The White-Headed Boy* -- a play about reclaiming the squandered inheritance of the politics of ideals.

The *Irish Times* review of Robinson's 1928 production of *John Gabriel Borkman* suggests that he was once again exploring the possibility of an idealism that would escape orthodoxy in his staging of the play. Borkman, for the *Times* reviewer, is 'the idealist, the man obsessed with the desire for power, not for his own selfish gratification, but for the furtherance of his fellows'.[28] It is worth noting, however, that this reading of Ibsen in Ireland at the time was not confined to Robinson. In an essay entitled 'The Genius of Ibsen' that appeared in the *Dublin Magazine* in the summer of 1928, T.G. Keller concluded that audiences could draw 'no moral' from Ibsen's plays; instead, Ibsen was a 'seer ... who climbed instinctively to the towering summit of paradox where simplicity reigns.'[29] Behind it all, there was, of course, George Bernard Shaw's *The Quintessence of Ibsenism*, which had appeared in its revised version in 1913. 'Our ideals, like the gods of old, are constantly demanding human sacrifices,' writes Shaw. 'Let none of them, says Ibsen, be placed above the obligation to prove itself worth the sacrifices it demands; and let everyone religiously refuse to sacrifice himself and others from the moment he loses his faith in the validity of the ideal.'[30] This perhaps comes closest to capturing Robinson's understanding of the Ibsenite hero; it also maps the path he was to take in public life, as he sought to find a position in which he could both uphold and critique idealism, testing obscure ideals against the obscurantists.

The Opposite Extreme of Disillusion

There is, however, an ironic twist to this tale. Where reviews of the Ibsen productions at the Abbey in the mid-1920s convey a sense of excited relevance, towards the end of the decade the tone starts to change. By the time of the annual Abbey production of *A Doll's House* in 1929, the reviewer noted the empty seats in the stalls, and speculated that perhaps 'Ibsen has lost somewhat of his appeal to modern audiences.'[31] By the time of Robinson's 1932 production of *The Wild Duck*, the reviewer was more precise as to why Ibsen no longer matched the times. 'In this post-war world,' the reviewer maintained, 'there are few enthusiasts who, like Gregers Werle, go about presenting their "demands of the ideal" on humanity, and fewer still who would listen to them if they did. The pendulum, in fact, has swung almost too far to the opposite extreme of disillusion.' In the nineteenth century, the review continues, 'Ibsen's home-truths must have come as a salutary shock'; however, Irish audiences in 1932, having experienced civil war and the hardening of ideals into rigid orthodoxies, did not need to be reminded 'how a muddled idealism may have effects very far from those intended.'[32]

Perhaps the clearest indication that Ibsen had lost his shock value in Ireland by the late 1920s came when Anew McMaster's touring company, featuring the redoubtable Mrs Patrick Campbell, announced in December of 1929 that they were going to perform what had, in its day, been Ibsen's most notorious play, *Ghosts*, over a weekend at the Abbey. McMaster's touring company at that point was already a fixture in the towns and villages of rural Ireland, where they brought a rich mixture of Shakespeare and melodrama to audiences who seldom saw professional theatre of any description. To have secured for his fit-up company the services of (an admittedly aging) Mrs Patrick Campbell, (for whom Shaw had written the role of Eliza in *Pygmalion* in 1914) was the kind of incongruous *coup* that would characterize McMaster's career. 'It is difficult to see now why this play incurred the ban of the Lord Chamberlain for thirty years in England', puzzled the *Irish Times*, 'and difficult also to see why it should be regarded as prurient. It is in effect a sermon ... worked out in terms of false idealism in triumphant conflict with truth.' Unable to shock cosmopolitan Dublin, McMaster took the production to Limerick, where it was performed 'for the first time in the Irish provinces.' Instead of outraged locals, McMaster found a Limerick audience with a keen 'interest in the modern drama of ideas', suggesting, hinted a reviewer, that 'the possibilities for intellectual drama in the provinces ... are almost limitless.'[33]

The McMaster company tour of *Ghosts* in 1929 must lie somewhere in the background of Robinson's 1933 play, *Drama at Inish*, in which a touring company, headed by two slightly down-at-heel, but larger-than-life actors, Hector de la Mare and his wife, Constance Constantia, arrive in the seaside town of Inish with their repertoire of Strindberg's *The Father*, Tolstoy's *Power of Darkness*, and Ibsen's *A Doll's House*. In the published script, Robinson called the play 'an exaggeration in three acts', and this is worth keeping in mind. Initially, when the company play Inish the theatre is filled every night. 'It just bears out what I have always said,' announces Hector: 'give people the right stuff, well put on and intelligently acted and they will support it.'[34] However, before long the plays start to have a strange effect on the people of Inish:

Michael. Did you hear the awful thing that's after happening to Jim Clancy?
Annie. No, what is it?
Michael. Threw himself off the end of the pier.
Annie. For pity's sake! ...
Annie. Was he drowned dead?
Michael. No, ma'am. Bruised. The tide was out.
Hector. What was the reason for it?
Michael. No one knows, sir. He kem out of the Pavilion – he'd been watching the play – and he went to the end of the pier and stood there for a bit and then lepped over.[35]

1 **Lennox Robinson, *Dramaidheacht in Inis* [*Drama at Inish*], Taibhdhearc na Gaillimhe 1946: Walter Macken, Peig Ní Mhaicín, Neans Ní Laoi, Laim Ó Floinn, Idé Ní Mhathúna. Courtesy of Taibhdhearc na Gaillimhe**

Six months before Anew McMaster and Mrs Patrick Campbell played *Ghosts* in Limerick, the Censorship of Publications Act had been passed into law, on 16 July 1929. The Act outlined a number of different grounds under which material might be banned; however, by far the most important ground (and later the most widely used), was that which provided for the banning of printed material that was 'in ... general tendency indecent or obscene' with 'indecent' defined as 'suggestive of, or inciting to sexual immorality or unnatural vice or likely in any other similar way to corrupt or deprave.'[36] *Drama at Inish* asks: what does it mean to say that a work of literature (or theatre) could 'corrupt or deprave' its audience? Taken literally, it would mean precisely what happens in the play: people jumping off piers, entering into suicide pacts, throwing knives at partners in loveless marriages, or, in one of the play's funniest moments, inspiring an otherwise innocuous and reliable rural member of the Dáil to vote against the government. 'It was that play', pleads the poor distracted TD, '"An Enemy of the People."' '"An Enemy of the People", responds one of his outraged constituency supporters: 'Faith, that's you; that's your name from this out.'[37] Later, writing in the *Irish Press* on the eve of the 1954 General Election, Robinson archly suggested that all newly elected members of the Dáil should be marched up to the Gate Theatre *en masse* for a command performance of *An Enemy of the People* to 'listen to what Henrik Ibsen has to say about lies and corruption and gerrymandering in public life'.[38]

The point, of course, is that people do not, as a rule, throw themselves off a pier or vote against the government after seeing a play by Ibsen. By making explicit (even as an exaggeration) the absurdity of the fundamental premise of censorship – that its function was to save people from being 'corrupted or depraved' – *Drama at Inish* was as much a part of the campaign against the 'obscurantists' as the founding of the Irish Academy of Letters in 1932, in which Robinson was centrally involved, along with Yeats and Shaw. *Drama at Inish* thus shifts the ground of the censorship debate: literary censorship is not simply politically wrong, it is fundamentally misguided. But here lay the problem: while this admission was strategically important in context of undermining Irish censorship, in making it Robinson effectively boxed himself into a corner, and from that point onwards his work is marked by the kind of stasis that characterizes so many of his contemporaries. If the modernist theatre of Ibsen had lost the power to shock or to alter perceptions, if *Ghosts* could play Limerick without generating a ripple of anxiety – in short, if it was not worth censoring – what was its value? At one point in *Drama at Inish*, the actor-manager Hector de la Mare recalls seeing Ibsen performed in Cork when he was a young man. 'Those plays changed my life', he says. 'And did they change Cork?' he is asked. 'They did not,' is the emphatic reply. 'We played there two summers ago; the same miserable little audiences of cynical people, the same corruption, public and private.'[39]

In the 1920s, Ibsen had suggested to Robinson that it might be possible to be an idealistic nationalist in a culture in which nationalism and idealism were both fossilising into suffocating orthodoxies. After the passing of the Censorship of Publications Act, the possibility held out in Ibsen's plays diminished, and Robinson (like so many of his peers) increasingly found that the only viable stance was outright opposition to the 'obscurantists', from which he cautiously denounced 'the same corruption, public and private' in the name of realism. From that point onwards, while Robinson continued to rehearse his admiration for Ibsen's plays, he no longer produced Ibsen's work,[40] and he relaxed that 'vigilant open-mindedness' that Shaw had identified as the effect on anyone who took seriously Ibsen's self-critical idealism.[41] As such, Robinson's engagement with Ibsen at the time of the Censorship of Publications Act allows us to trace, in a kind of microcosm, one of the central cultural dynamics in the Irish culture of the period – one whose endgame is only now being played out.

---

[1] I am indebted to the New York Council for the Humanities, who provided funding that made possible the research used in this essay. Any views, conclusions, or recommendations expressed in this publication do not necessarily represent those of the National Endowment for the Humanities.

[2] *The Whiteheaded Boy*. dir. Gerard Stembridge, Barrabas, Project@The Mint, Dublin (September 1997); *The Big House*. dir. Conall Morrison. Abbey Theatre, Dublin (1 August, 2007); *Is Life Worth Living?*, dir. Jonathan Bank. Mint Theater, New York (19 August, 2009).

[3] Lennox Robinson, *Drama at Inish, Selected Plays: Lennox Robinson*, ed. Christopher Murray, Irish Drama Selections 1 (Gerrards Cross: Colin Smythe, 1981): 238.

[4] Lennox Robinson, *I Sometimes Think* (Dublin: Talbot Press, n.d. [1956]): 25.

[5] Robinson, *I Sometimes Think*, 25.

[6] Lennox Robinson, 'Ibsen's Influence on Irish Drama', *Irish Times* 31 March 1928: 6. The first book-length study of Ibsen's influence on Irish drama would develop this argument in the early 1950s. See Jan Setterquist, *Ibsen and the Beginnings of Anglo-Irish Drama I. John Millington Synge* (Dublin: Hodges, Figgis and Co.; Upsala: A.-B. Lundequistska Bokhandeln, 1951).

7 Luke Gibbons, '"Famished Ghosts": Bloom, Bible Wars, and "U.P. Up" in Joyce's Dublin', *Dublin James Joyce Journal* 2 (2009): 1.

8 The only other producer to produce a significant number of plays in the period was Michael J. Dolan; he produced *Juno and the Paycock*.

9 Lennox Robinson to Lady Gregory, 6 February 1926, MS Letter, Berg Collection, New York Public Library. This and subsequent citations from the papers in the Berg Collection reprinted by kind permission of the New York Public Library.

10 Robinson, *I Sometimes Think*, 16, 23-4.

11 'Ibsen at the Abbey Theatre' *Irish Times* 1 December 1926: 11.

12 Lennox Robinson to Lady Gregory, 4 October 1925, MS Letter, Berg Collection, New York Public Library.

13 'Abbey Theatre', *Irish Times* 25 Sept 1925: 8.

14 'Ibsen Centenary: '"John Gabriel Borkman" at the Abbey Theatre', *Irish Times* 4 April 1928: 4.

15 Lennox Robinson, *The White Blackbird*, dir. Lennox Robinson, Abbey Theatre (12 October 1925).

16 Lennox Robinson, *The White Blackbird* (Dublin: Talbot Press, 1926): 84.

17 Robinson, *White Blackbird*, 79.

18 Lennox Robinson to Lady Gregory, undated [*ca.* 1924/1925], MS Letter, Berg Collection, New York Public Library.

19 [W.B. Yeats],'Editorial', *To-morrow* 1 (August 1924) : 1.

20 *Problem of Undesirable Printed Matter: Suggested Remedies. Evidence of the Catholic Truth Society of Ireland Presented to the Departmental Committee of Enquiry* (Dublin: Catholic Truth Society of Ireland, 1926): 20.

21 R.S. Devane, *Indecent Literature: Some Legal Remedies* (Dublin: Brown and Nolan, n.d [1925]): 16. The article was originally published in the *Irish Ecclesiastical Bulletin* in 1925.

22 T.A. Finlay to J.H. Bernard, 30 October 1924, Lennox Robinson Papers, Berg Collection, New York Public Library.

23 Lennox Robinson to Lady Gregory, 23 December 1924, Lennox Robinson Papers, Berg Collection, New York Public Library.

24 Lady Gregory to Lennox Robinson, 7 November, 1927, Lady Gregory Papers, Berg Collection, New York Public Library.

25 Lennox Robinson, Introduction, *The Lost Leader: A Play in Three Acts* (Dublin: Thomas Kiersey, 1918): 5.

26 Robinson, *Three Houses*, 180 and 182.

27 Robinson, *Lost Leader*, 97.

28 'Ibsen Centenary: "John Gabriel Borkman" at Abbey Theatre', *Irish Times* 4 April 1928: 4.

29 T.G. Keller, 'The Genius of Ibsen', *Dublin Magazine* 3 (April-June 1928): 46.

30 George Bernard Shaw, *The Quintessence of Ibsenism. Now completed to the death of Ibsen* (New York: Hill and Wang, 1957): 154.

31 '"A Doll's House": Revival at the Abbey Theatre', *Irish Times* 13 March, 1929: 4. It is worth noting, however, that when a touring production of the play arrived in 1938, A.E. Malone argued for its relevance: 'The rebellion of Nora Helmer is an exciting thing, in which every generation will find itself mirrored.' A.E.M[alone], '"A Doll's House": Gwen Ffrangcon-Davies as Nora', *Irish Times* 26 July 1938: 8.

32 '"Wild Duck" Presented at the Abbey Theatre', *Irish Times* 1 November 1932: 6. There were other Irish productions of Ibsen at the time as well, including the Gate's *Peer Gynt* (1928), and a production of *The Master Builder* at the Northern Drama League's annual *feis* in 1930.

33 'Ibsen Play in Limerick: A Very Successful Production', *Irish Times* 20 January 1930: 4.

34 Lennox Robinson, *Drama at Inish, Selected Plays: Lennox Robinson*, ed. Christopher Murray (Gerrards Cross: Colin Smythe, 1981): 219.

35 Robinson, *Drama at Inish*, 222.

36 *Censorship of Publications Act, 1929* (No 21/1929); II:6, I:2.

37 Robinson, *Drama at Inish*, 249.

38 Robinson, *I Sometimes Think*, 28.

39 Robinson, *Drama at Inish*, 210.

40 *The Wild Duck* in 1932 was Robinson's last Ibsen production for the Abbey. However, this may have been partly because the Gate had started to perform Ibsen: *Peer Gynt* (1928), *Brand* (1936), and *Ghosts* (1938).

41 Shaw, *Quintessence of Ibsenism*, 154.

4 | Denis Johnston's Ibsen and Post-Revivalist Ireland

Irina Ruppo Malone

With the foundation of the Irish Literary Theatre in 1899, Ibsen entered Irish society – not as a controversial playwright, but as a rather misunderstood and frivolous deity. While Edward Martyn and George Moore had already been exposed to the power of Ibsen's realistic drama, W.B. Yeats laboured to create a different image of the Norwegian playwright. He championed Ibsen as the author of *Lady Inger of Østratt* (1854) and *The Vikings at Helgeland* (1857) – the great European figure who 'produced dramas founded on the heroes and legends of Norway', and took part in the movement 'which in almost every way resembled the national literary movement that was going on in [Ireland]'.[1]

Yeats's shuffling some facts of Ibsen's life (Ibsen did not gain international fame for his early romantic plays) was a failed attempt to block the spread of dramatic realism on the Irish stage. The success of such playwrights as Fred Ryan, Padraic Colum, and later the Cork Realists – Lennox Robinson, T.C. Murray, Seamus Kelly, and R.J. Ray – was evidence that *The Vikings at Helgeland* and *The Feast at Solhaug* (1855) were a great deal easier to ignore than *A Doll's House* (1879), *Ghosts* (1881), and *Hedda Gabler* (1890). Ibsen's plays were rarely seen in Ireland. Between 1890 and 1932, there were only twenty-two productions of Ibsen's plays in Dublin (of which only thirteen were by local companies). Yet his realistic dramas haunt the works of the period.

The last scene of *Ghosts* is evoked in Murray's *Maurice Harte* (1912) where a woman watches her seminarian son suffer a mental collapse. The ex-convict with a heroic vision, John Gabriel Borkman,

is transformed into an Irish revolutionary in Lennox Robinson's
Patriots (1912). Nora Helmer seems to be the inspiration for the
heroine of Robinson's *The Cross-Roads* (1909) and Sean O'Casey's
The Plough and the Stars (1926).[2] The echoes of *Hedda Gabler* in
The Player Queen show that Yeats too fell under the spell of Ibsen.
He started to work on the play after seeing Mrs Patrick Campbell
play Hedda in Dublin in 1907, and, over the long period of its
gestation, turned it into a dramatic exploration of the conflict
between realism and romanticism – *The Player Queen* (1922).[3]

'There will be a reaction against the realism of Ibsen and
romance will have its turn', Yeats said to Lady Gregory in 1898.[4] An
early draft of the *Player Queen* suggests that, a decade later, Yeats
had come to respect the contemporary audiences' desire for 'the
flavour of life' and [their] thirst for what exists, sheer life, the flame
that comes from us that are its fuel, people like themselves, pettish,
troublesome, ordinary people'.[5] Indeed by 1928 Lennox Robinson
could safely make a claim that Ibsen's discovery that a play can be
made out of the raw materials of everyday life is at the very
foundation of contemporary Irish drama.

Yet I am not content to tell the story of Ibsen's reception in
Ireland as a victory of the drama of everyday over national
romanticism. To say that would be to imply that Ibsen's influence on
Irish drama ended some time in the late 1920s – the twilight years
of the Irish Revival. Moreover, there are some moments in Ibsen's
plays that disallow the easy identification of Ibsen with realism that
such a view of his Irish reception implies.

In *Peer Gynt* a certain Strange Passenger tells the protagonist
that 'one dies not midmost of Act Five'.[6] Ibsen's nonchalance in
breaking the fourth wall near the end of his play and re-examining
the nature of his relationship with his audience is also notable in
later plays.

In *Master Builder*, Solness in a seeming moment of absurd grief
confesses that he blames himself for the house-fire, the illness of his
wife, and the death of his children because he failed to mend a crack
in the chimney – a flaw that had no connection to the outbreak of
the fire. Robert Brustein has demonstrated how this admission
turns *Master Builder* from a drama of guilt and retribution into a
modernist work that attempts to 'repeal the simple, fundamental
law of cause-and-effect which has been an unquestioned statute at
least since the Enlightenment – the law that ruled the linear, logical,
rationalistic world of literature, and, in particular, the Western

literature of guilt'.[7] In *The Wild Duck*, Hedwig confesses that she often thinks of a mock-forest assembled by her grandfather in the attic as the depths of the sea. She cannot conceive of the attic as simply an attic, nor does she take part in the game, pursued by her grandfather, which sees the attic as a forest. For her the attic is neither what it is nor what it represents. This subverts the play's exploration of truths and lies, pictures and their negatives, realities and metaphors. It uncovers the existence of a hidden value in the gap between language and the world it seems to describe.[8]

These moments do not merely suggest what some Irish disciples of Ibsen had begun to notice in 1928, that, as Robinson put it, 'Ibsen is not a realist at all'.[9] They are points which deliberately challenge the premises on which the plays are built. The words of Hedvig, Master Builder, and The Strange Passenger that so puzzled contemporary critics of *Peer Gynt* seem now to confirm Durbach's assertion that Ibsen is the progenitor of the theatre of the absurd.[10]

Ibsen's games with time and causality and language were ignored; I would risk saying that they went unnoticed by the first Irish realists. Ibsen's modernism is more apparent to us now because, as Errol Durbach points out, the flow of literary influence is bi-directional. 'After Beckett and Pinter', he writes, 'we are compelled to see Ibsen in a new and startling way and to acknowledge in the afterlife of his plays a mirror of our most urgent concerns.[11] Twentieth-century scientific discoveries and political nightmares did not only affect the development of new artistic forms, they also changed the ways we approach existing literary works.

My concern here is with the beginnings of the Irish engagement with this other Ibsen – not the social critic of the Cork Realists, nor the romantic nationalist of the young Yeats, but the playwright of paradox from whose drama 'we can draw no moral, political, social or any other-so called teaching'.[12] These are the words of Thomas Keller, whose 1928 article on Ibsen stands out from several retrospective comments occasioned by the playwright's centenary. Especially interesting is Keller's note on *The Wild Duck* ; for him the play 'exists chiefly in a unique world of inversion where anything might happen, and where everything, even the death of poor little Hedvig, belongs to the category of things which are not what they seem'.[13] Keller's article on Ibsen might be seen as a foreshadowing of two interrelated developments in Irish theatre.

One is the Gate Theatre's inaugural production of *Peer Gynt* in 1928, revived in 1932, and the other is the Gate's 1929 performance of *The Old Lady Says 'No!'*, an event that launched the playwrighting career of the twenty-eight-year-old Denis Johnston.

Johnston did not consider himself a disciple of Ibsen. Most contemporaries pointed to Georg Kaiser and Ernst Toller as the chief influences on the expressionist and richly allusive *The Old Lady Says 'No!'*. Johnston himself insisted that he owed far more to August Strindberg and Karel ?apek. Yet, *The Old Lady Says 'No!'* is inspired by the same interest in the dynamics of myth-making that made Ibsen turn the folk Peer Gynt into a self-deluding impostor. Like Peer, Johnston's protagonist, the Speaker, bases his identity on what he is not. He is an actor in a melodrama about the leader of the 1878 rebellion Robert Emmet. An accidental knock on the head during the performance sends him into a dream in which he believes himself to be Robert Emmet trapped in twentieth-century Dublin. Like the Peer Gynt of Act V, he is only intermittently recognized by the people for whom his assumed persona has become a legend. In the world of *The Old Lady Says 'No!'* the boundaries between illusion and reality are in constant motion – it is the Dublin of Joyce's 'Circe', which is in itself indebted to Act V of *Peer Gynt*.[14]

The folkloric elements of *Peer Gynt* make it possible to read the play on different levels. For Yeats, writing in 1897, it appeared as a superb example of romantic nationalist drama.[15] For the early stage interpreters of the play it was a beautifully wrought fable, a journey through Norwegian folklore.[16] The Gate Theatre founders, Micheál MacLiammóir and Hilton Edwards, however, discovered the play's expressionist qualities. The stage was Peer's play space: Aase's hut, mountain peaks, and the valley were suggested by two sets of steps, positioned at various angles (a design inspired by the work of Jurgen Fehling and Leopold Jessner). Dispensing with the pictorial realism of the earlier productions, MacLiammóir and Edwards relied on the interplay of coloured light and silhouette and made the audience participate in Peer's imagining his world into being.

The play's exploration of the interaction between poetic imagination and reality, highlighted in the Gate production, was particularly relevant in the cultural climate of Free State Ireland. It was a society that saw the nationalist dreams of the Revival turn into crude realities. The Easter Rising and the Irish Civil War had exposed the danger of the myth of Kathleen ní Houlihan – the female embodiment of Ireland rejuvenated through the sacrifices of her sons. For the Protestant literary elite, the increasing materialism and nationalist intolerance of the Free State seemed to mock the earlier idealizations of the country as Celtic fairyland, Tír na nÓg. The makers of the Irish Literary Revival were like Peer Gynt, who upon his return to Norway discovers the relics of his fantasies, illogically materialized in the real world of dirt, death, and dirty jokes.

The Old Lady Says 'No!' was one of the first dramatic explorations of the post-revivalist crisis. Kathleen appears in Johnston's play as a bloodthirsty and sex-crazed hag. She is also the alter-ego of the Speaker's lost beloved, Sarah Curran. As for the Celtic fairyland, that seems to be as easily accessible, for Dubliners, as Clontarf and Walsh Road. In one of the first scenes, the Speaker's revolutionary words are interrupted by the bus conductor's announcement: 'Next bus leaves in ten minutes. All aboard for Tir-na-n'Og. Special reduced return fares at single and a third'.[17] This trade in revivalist ideals is reminiscent of the auction scene in Peer Gynt, in which Peer puts up his imaginary palace and Kaiserdom for sale, along with a 'dream of a silver clasped book, /That you can have for an old hook and eye' (223).

While the Gate unintentionally transformed *Peer Gynt* into a play about Ireland and Irish culture, Johnston wandered into Ibsen's territory while writing about post-Revivalist Ireland, while playing with Yeats and O'Casey and Joyce. And just as Johnston's first play reflected, in its engagement with *Peer Gynt*, the change in the public perception of Ibsen in Ireland, so may his later work be suggestive of the roles that Ibsen was to play in the development of Irish drama.

Johnston's third play, *A Bride for the Unicorn* (1933), is a modern morality play in two parts. It traces the life of Jay (or Jason) from youth to the grave, or rather from the moment when he sets the time in motion to the discovery of the secret of his existence and disappearance into a tall grandfather clock. The clock, permanently positioned on the stage, divides Jay's life into hours, turning his life-journey into one day.

'Many great writers have tried to write the life of Man and have put their lives into it', Johnston said to the Massachusetts University students in 1951; 'Goethe – Ibsen – Joyce. All too verbose. All have a Walpurgisnacht scene'.[18] This is all true of *A Bride for the Unicorn*. The echoes of *Peer Gynt* are especially notable in the nightmare scene, in part 2. At eight o'clock in the evening of his life, Jay rebels against the futility of his existence: 'was it for this the clay was sanctified – to be a home for all the crawling creatures of the grass'.[19] Peer's discovery that 'dearly one pays for one's birth with one's life' (265) is echoed in Jay's question: 'Why should I love this thing called life – this thing that I have purchased from the clock?'(56). 'Sinister figures' point at Jay and threaten him from each side; they are his nurse, his wife, the sins of his fathers, his doubts, and his shadow. We are reminded of Peer's mad run across the withered heath in Act V, scene 6. There are syntactic echoes. Compare the reproaches of the unsung songs in Ibsen's play to the shadow's utterances in Johnston:

> We are songs; thou shouldst have sung us! ... Down in thy heart's pit we have lain and waited; we were never called forth. In thy gorge be poison (232).

and

> You willed your shadow to grow tall until it lay across the Earth. So now I stride in grisly majesty behind you (56).

At the heart of Jay's existential horror is regret for not having loved fully and for deceiving the woman he married. In the figure of a masked woman who came out of the clock in the first scene, life offered him a promise of paradise. Jay married Hera in the hope of 'identify[ing] her with the woman of his dreams'(44). In fact Jay carries the mask of that woman and hopes, one day, to place it upon Hera's face as a sort of affirmative experiment. But their marriage is a failure because, as Jay explains: 'There has not been any appropriate moment in married life to propose such a test, without a risk of an argument' (44). Besides, Jay knows that Hera would not pass the test: 'I married you, but I still love her' (55), he admits.

The man's double failure in love is central to many of Ibsen's dramas. Ingrid and the Troll-Maiden in *Peer Gynt*, Gunhild in *John Gabriel Borkman*, Rita in *Little Eyolf*, and Maja in *When We Dead Awaken*, all testify against the heroes of these plays for treating them as ersatz versions of their true love. 'You said you would take me up to a high mountain and show me all the glory of the world',[20] says Maja to Rubek. But instead, their relationship was only 'a tolerably amusing game'.[21] Hera accuses Jay of a similar crime: 'You married to mock me. You promised me that nocturnal gymnastics could create a permanent paradise' (55).

In the absurd world of *A Bride for the Unicorn*, Ibsen's words are subverted and the multidimensional allusions create the effect of parody. 'The sins of the fathers', for instance, that key phrase from *Ghosts*, are personified as angry creatures, reminiscent of the comic and angry trolls in Peer Gynt in Act II: 'We are the sins of the fathers. Cirrhosis – Gout – the pallid Blood of Gentility. For their pleasures we prick him. Burn him up!' (55). However, it is this very irreverence of approach that marks Johnston's similarity to Ibsen. Ibsen's plays are also richly allusive and greatly irreverent in their engagement with the text of the Bible. The Holy Scripture provides Peer with an excuse to don a troll's tail and drink bovine excrement. Much later he mistakes the trolls' egotistic motto 'to thyself be enough' for a verse from a psalm or Solomon's Proverbs (147). The characters of Ibsen's later dramas suffer from the same forgetfulness. Rubek promises Maya to take her to the highest mountain and show her all the glory of the world. Neither of them seems to be aware that this is an almost direct quotation from the Gospel. Rubek refers to it as 'sort of figure of speech ... a schoolboy phrase--the sort of thing I used to say when I wanted to lure the neighbours' children out to play with me'.[22] The Bible permeates the language of Ibsen's plays, yet it is a language of empty or erroneous referents. The word of God has become irrelevant for Ibsen's characters, yet they retain the instinct of quotation, as they struggle to come to terms with the chaos of their lives.

Johnston touched on this aspect of Ibsen when he pointed out, in his lecture on *Peer Gynt,* that the play makes us realize that '[w]e cannot go back to the God of the Middle Ages and we have not yet created another God that we can go on to'.[23] The problem he is describing is that the word 'God' is still operative in our engagement with the universe, in spite of its meaninglessness for the modern day atheist. This dissociation between the original meanings of a culture's myths and their usage informs the tragic-comic vision of *Peer Gynt*. Heaven, Hell, God, and the Devil are actual entities. Yet the spiritual world does not exist apart from the material one – rather it reflects it. God's heavenly kingdom is a bureaucracy; his justice is that of a financier. The Button Moulder is a well-trained clerk. He must melt Peer's soul because he has written instructions to do so. He explains the necessity of annihilation of individual consciousness by his Master's thriftiness. God 'flings nothing away' (238) and inadequately developed personalities must be recycled; 'We've done it already to plenty of folks. /At Kongsberg they do just the same with coin/That's been current so long that its impress is lost' (239). The Devil refuses to admit Peer to Hell on the strength of his account of his sins, saying: 'Who, think you, would care/ to throw away dearly-bought fuel in times/ like these on such spiritless rubbish as this?' (260). The Devil is busy; according to his records one Peter Gynt is a great sinner and him he must find. Officials, apparently, are prone to such mistakes.

Clerks and fraudulent financiers are the masters of the universe in *A Bride for the Unicorn*. In part two Hercules Limited is set up by Theseus (or Alix) and Hercules (familiarly known as Les); the company whose sole business is floating its shares on the market serves the role of God. Hercules Ltd, we are told, are 'unaffected by the deplorable conditions prevailing in the industrial world ... affected only by the immutable laws of higher mathematics. The issue is now open. Invest in the Big One' (39). As the costs of the shares inflate, and the company bosses are celebrating with crates of champagne, Jay shouts 'This can't go on! It can't go on forever'. At this stage the clock strikes twelve and someone cries: 'Noon! The voice of God!' 'All hats are doffed, Jay falls on his knees', and 'from somewhere in the crowd a voice starts to sing The Delphic Hymn to Apollo':

Sing, sing O children of triumphant Zeus ...
To him who tunes his lyre upon the snowcapped heights
Sing, fair-armed daughters of the trumpeting Gods.
Sing of your brother Phoebus of the golden hair
Who rules Parnassus and the Delphic Stream
Flowing from the fair Castalian Hill. (41-2)

And this is where Johnston breaks off the first part of the play. Its high lyricism suggests that this scene does not simply satirize the replacement of God with Mammon. Rather it suggests that God and banks are one and the same, and shifty financial dealings may lead to intimations of paradise.

Ibsen and Johnston dispense with the romantic habit of separating the metaphysical world from the material one. Other time-honoured boundaries, such as the one between the play and the spectators, are broken too. As mentioned above, Ibsen has the Strange Passenger reassure the drowning Peer in Act V: 'one dies not midmost of Act Five' in an unusual move for a nineteenth-century playwright (213). We are perhaps less surprised that Jay is asked in the closing movement of Johnston's play: 'How did you manage to get into this production?' To which he replies 'Oh just merit, I suppose. I was one of the Ugly Sisters in last year's Pantomime' (73).

I do not wish to suggest that Johnston needed Ibsen to learn the tricks of anti-illusionism. My point is that in the mirror of Johnston's plays we can see Ibsen's own fascination with the paradox of reality and his rebellion against the limitations of the contemporary language of the theatre. We begin to think of Ibsen less as a realist, a didactician, but as someone who as Johnston put it 'rises above the battle and views it humorously'.[24] Is it not possible, therefore, that Irish engagement with Ibsen expands beyond dramatic realism and may have informed the tradition which stretches from *Ulysses* to the absurdist works of Flann O'Brien?

---

[1] 'Dramatic Ideals and the Irish Literary Theatre', *Freeman's Journal*, 6 May 1899: 5.

[2] See Irina Ruppo Malone, *Ibsen and the Irish Revival* (Basingstoke: Palgrave Macmillan, 2010): 84-85 and 69-71 .

[3] Ibid., 43-51.

[4] Lady Gregory, *Our Irish Theatre: A Chapter of Autobiography*, ed. Roger McHugh (Gerrards Cross: Colin Smythe, 1972): 17.

[5] W.B. Yeats, *The Writing of the Player Queen: Manuscripts of W.B. Yeats.* Transcribed, edited and with a commentary by Curtis Baker Bradford (DeKalb: Northern Illinois University Press, 1977): 83 (version B, draft 8).

[6] Henrik Ibsen, *Peer Gynt*, trans. Charles Archer, *The Collected Works*, ed. William Archer, vol. 4 (New York: Charles Scribner's Sons, 1909): 213. Hereafter cited parenthetically.

[7] Robert Brustein, *Critical Moments: Reflections on Theater and Society 1973-1979* (New York: Random House, 1980): 109.

[8] Compare Toril Moi's discussion of this passage and its relation to her overall thesis of Ibsen's modernism; Toril Moi, *Henrik Ibsen and the Birth of Modernism* (New York: Oxford University Press, 2006): 256-58.

[9] Lennox Robinson, 'Ibsen's Influence on Irish Drama', *Irish Times* 31 March 1928: 6.

[10] Errol Durbach, 'Sacrifice and Absurdity in The Wild Duck', *Mosaic: A Journal for the Interdisciplinary Study of Literature* 7.4 (1974): 99-107.

[11] Errol Durbach, 'Ibsen and the Dramaturgy of Uncertainty', *Ibsen Studies* 6.2 (2006): 131.

[12] T.G. Keller, 'The Genius of Ibsen', *Dublin Magazine* 3 (April–June 1928): 44–47.

[13] Ibid.

[14] See Bjørn J. Tysdahl, *Joyce and Ibsen–A Study In Literary Influence* (Oslo: Norwegian Universities Press; New York: Humanities Press, 1968): 112.

[15] John Eglinton, W. B. Yeats, AE, and W. Larminie. *Literary Ideals in Ireland* (London: Fisher Unwin, 1899): 17.

[16] Frederick J. Marker and Lise-Lone Marker, *Ibsen's Lively Art* (Cambridge: Cambridge University Press, 1989): 13-24.

[17] Denis Johnston, *The Old Lady Says 'No!', The Dramatic Works of Denis Johnston*, vol. 1 (Gerrards Cross: Colin Smythe, 1977): 3-76, 42. Hereafter cited parenthetically. I have retained Johnston's spelling of the Irish expression.

[18] Denis Johnston, A Lecture on Peer Gynt (University of Massachusetts), the Papers of Denis Johnston, the Manuscripts & Archives Research Library, Trinity College Dublin, MS 10066/51/17. This and subsequent citations from the Papers of Denis Johnston are reprinted by kind permission of Rory Johnston and the Board of Trinity College.

[19] Denis Johnston, *A Bride for the Unicorn, The Dramatic Works of Denis Johnston*, vol. 2 (Gerrards Cross: Colin Smythe, 1979): 11-79, 57. Hereafter references are given in parentheses.

[20] Henrik Ibsen, *When We Dead Awaken, The Collected Works*, trans. William Archer, vol. 11: 325-456, 340.

[21] Ibid., 341.

[22] Ibid., 340-41

[23] Papers of Denis Johnston, the Manuscripts & Archives Research Library, MS 10066/51/17.

[24] Papers of Denis Johnston, the Manuscripts & Archives Research Library, MS 10066/51/18.

5 | Artists and Users in the Later Plays of Ibsen and Friel

Patrick Burke

W.B. Yeats's oft-cited distillation of a recurring human dilemma, the choice between 'perfection of the life or of the work'[1] reflects a concern, characteristic of the Romantic Movement, which, in varying permutations, was to become central for artists in the twentieth century – the relative moral superiority of calling versus duty. Modern cultural history is littered with instances of persons, usually men, of exceptional cultural stature, intensely committed to a calling, a credo or an undeniable social mission, whose lives in the domestic, emotional or sexual spheres were, in as much as may be understood of such matters without prurience, self-preoccupied, ruthless, even cruel: as Janacek, the protagonist in Brian Friel's *Performances,* puts it, 'Aren't all artists users?'[2] The conflict between calling and duty has featured in many novels and plays and in poems such as Tennyson's *Ulysses* (1833), in which Ulysses' son, Telemachus –'Most blameless ... centred in the sphere/ Of common duties, decent not to fail/ In offices of tenderness, and pay/ Meet adoration to my household gods' – is contrasted in his dependability with his wayward father: 'Yet all experience is an arch wheretrhough / Gleams that untravelled world, whose margin fades/ For ever and for ever when I move'.[3]

For purposes of this paper, I wish to focus on two plays by Ibsen – his last two, *John Gabriel Borkman* (1896) and *When We Dead Awaken* (1899), and on two plays of Friel, *Faith Healer* (1979) and *Performances* (2003), in each of which the implacable drive of male aspiration is challenged by complexities of the erotic. I have directed *John Gabriel Borkman* and *Faith Healer* only, but would emphasize that theatricality, anchorage in the practicalities of acting, directing, design, and movement, have guided my commentary on all four plays.

I

John Gabriel Borkman

The comment by the painter, Edvard Munch, that *John Gabriel Borkman* is 'the most powerful winter landscape in Scandinavian art'[4] has acquired proverbial status. The cold is everywhere in the play: outdoors, according to Ibsen's directions, 'trees are bent with snow', snow 'which makes the surroundings dimly visible'.[5] And while the new-fangled trams are becoming standard means of transport, the eloping *ménage a trois* of the beautiful Mrs Fanny Wilton, young Erhart Borkman, and the even-younger Frida Foldal is in a traditional snow sleigh, the exuberant speed of which knocks over Frida's father, Vilhelm. Indoors, Mrs Gunhild Borkman, introduced as 'an elderly lady of *cold,* distinguished appearance' (my emphasis) admits to her more warm-blooded sister, Ella, 'I'm always cold' (23-24). The three principal characters who assemble in the open courtyard at the beginning of the great fourth act, white-haired, grey-haired and bare-headed, are of a piece, in colour tones, with the heavily snow-covered ground on which they stand; they now inhabit their natural *milieu*. Such literal cold both magnifies and projects onto the landscape that cold of the heart which, as Ella seems to believe, kills Borkman at the ending of the play, but which, with characteristic frankness, Gunhild insists 'killed him long ago'. Ella's reply is frighteningly resonant: 'One dead man and two shadows ... is what the cold has made of us ' (94). In a brilliant transposition, as Borkman ascends further up the mountain to the heart of coldness, as it were, his killing of the capacity to love, for which Ella so irrefutably rebukes him in Act Two, is visibly reprised; following his most passionate utterances in the entire play, declaring his love for 'the veins of iron-ore stretching out their arms to me', Borkman's heart is gripped by what he initially describes as 'a hand of ice' and, as he dies, as 'a hand of iron-ore'. Borkman – chauvinist, philanthropic tycoon, Viking warrior out of time – now pays the price for his mortal sin in selling Ella's heart for 'the kingdom ... the power ... and the glory' (92-93), even if he is visited in his final moments by faint intimations of moral culpability.

Ultimately, it seems to me, if we wish to gain purchase on Ibsen's underlying moral and artistic concerns in *John Gabriel Borkman,* to weigh the significance of temporal processes from a dramatist whose next work was to be entitled *When We Dead Awaken,* we may usefully resort to the tragically short-lived German critic, Peter Szondi (1929-1971), and his brilliantly terse argument in *The Theory of Modern Drama* (1965) that the theme of *John Gabriel Borkman* is time – 'the past itself, the repeatedly mentioned "long years" and the "wasted lifetime"'.[6] At the conclusion of Shakespeare's *The Winter's Tale,* Leontes pledges to examine 'the wide gap of time since first/ We were dissevered' (V, iii, 154-55), 'gap' connoting unlived time, a death in life. Ibsen's play *is* that examination, in as much as it can be conducted on stage at all; as Szondi warns: 'Only something temporal can be made present in the sense of dramatic actualization'.[7]

Production

I directed *John Gabriel Borkman* for the Dublin Shakespeare Society, in the auditorium of St Patrick's College, in March 2001. My concerns at the time were threefold: to rehabilitate for the audience the power, not strikingly manifest in Ibsen since his early *Brand* and *Peer Gynt* (nor, post-Ibsen, in any mainstream Western drama), of poetic, intensely felt language,[8] to focus some of the more significant ambiguities of capitalist ambition in contemporary Ireland (the Ireland of 'the Celtic Tiger', in which philanthropy and reckless waste could be either allied or implacably opposed), and to highlight the intellectual pre-emptiveness of some so-called feminist discourse, particularly in the then burgeoning area of Women's Studies.

Some of the foregoing may be most readily weighed in terms of Ibsen's delineation of the title character: the driven prose made integral to the play Borkman can variously deploy for the kind of bombast and rodomontade his vainglory tempts him to use with the pathetic Foldal, whereas his love speech to the earth and the mountain spirits in the final act is charged with eloquence, albeit that of a dying man. His 'Napoleonic gesture' of thrusting his right hand into the breast of his coat, as Foldal is heard approaching, the solitary outrider for the vast numbers envisaged by Borkman as some day begging him to lead them, is at once ludicrous and oddly suggestive of visionary potential. And while Borkman's dismissal of the value of the female to society is even less worthy of debate now than in 1896, it cannot negate the play's final muted chords, a lament for 'the son of a mountain-miner' (94), beloved of two strong women.

I set Acts I and III, Gunhild's area, in front of the main proscenium-arch curtain, on a depressed 'apron' (about eighteen inches below the curtain line) using minimum furniture or *mise en scène*, except for the location, towards the centre, of the 'big iron stove', at once an indication of severe cold and a pointer towards social decline (a more affluent household would have had the kind of white-tile stove we observe in *Hedda Gabler*). For Act II, Borkman's domain, I put the apron back into direct alignment with the forestage. The motor sound that accompanied the raising of the apron conveyed something of the ascent to Borkman's world, including, as it were, its engineering features. Act IV, the biggest challenge to a director and designer, I approached as follows: I lowered the apron down to its limits, a distance of about six feet below auditorium floor level, leaving a substantial space between the audience and the stage, thus beginning the opening out and upwards of the action. I used that lowered area also as the sound-source for the departing sleigh of the lovers, its bells and the shouts of its excited passengers. The audience felt as if they were on a mountain slope, high above the action. I raised the main curtain, which, with skilled lighting, showed the snow-covered area immediately around the Borkman house. In the centre of the now enlarged space a very large mound-like structure had been constructed, the top of which could take the weight of a park bench; this, of course, imaged the copses and snow-covered slopes through which Ella and Borkman climb until they reach the vantage point from which Borkman pours out his love for his putative kingdom. That sequence includes my favourite stage direction in all of Ibsen – '*the house and the courtyard disappear!*' (90). It is, of course, a fascinating coincidence that within two years of the play's première, the first work of the Lumière brothers appeared. A virtually impossible challenge in stage terms was eminently feasible in the newly emerging medium of cinema.

The production was a success, with two strong contestants in Gunhild and Ella (Julie Shearer and Imelda McDonagh), a scene-stealing Foldal (Joe Jordan), two good-looking and sexually aware 'juves' (Nessa Power and Paul McCorry), and a Borkman (Ian Blackmore) who caught the frustrated power and vanity of the role with greater ease than he did the necessary visionary dimension.

II

Faith Healer

Implicit thematically in the foregoing is the scope, value and implacability of the so-called male dream. This links *John Gabriel Borkman* directly to Friel's *Faith Healer* (1979). Having stated categorically to Foldal, early in Act II, that '[women] distort and destroy our lives. Mock our destiny ... our progress to victory' (54), Borkman expands on the theme later with Ella: 'you must remember that I am a man. As a woman, you were the dearest thing in the world to me. But if the worst comes to the worst, one woman can always be replaced by another'(61-62). Paramount importance attaches to 'one's mission in life': 'the power to create human happiness in ever-widening circles around me' (72). For apparently similar reasons, bearing on his 'complete mastery' his 'private power ... that certainty that was accessible only to him', Frank Hardy, in *Faith Healer,* [9] regularly excludes Grace, his wife/mistress, from his sphere of intimacy:

> **Frank.** That very virtue of hers ... settled on us like a heavy dust. And nothing I did, neither my bitterness nor my deliberate neglect nor my blatant unfaithfulness, could disturb it. (335)
> **Grace.** And then, for him, I didn't exist. Many, many, many times I didn't exist for him. But before a performance this exclusion –no, it wasn't an exclusion, it was an erasion – this erasion was absolute: he obliterated me. (344)

In partial excuse for such neglect, Teddy refers to 'the strange gift [Frank] had' (365), and Frank himself, in his first monologue, acknowledges, with something allied to misgiving, his possession of 'a unique and awesome gift' (333), that of faith healing. Using the monologue form with brilliance of imaginative insight equal to anything in Beckett, Friel both interrogates and affirms the reality of faith healing. At one extreme, it is aligned by Grace's patrician father to the 'chicanery' (371) of an opportunist 'mountebank' (348) or by Teddy to theatrical show, to the 'fantastic' talents of legendary performance 'artists': Fred Astaire, Lillie Langtry, Houdini, Charlie Chaplin, Gracie Fields (355). At the other extreme, its metaphysical efficacy is attested to by the curing of the ten people in Glamorganshire or of the bent finger of the young man, Donal, in the pub in Ballybeg or by the memories of Frank himself: 'occasionally it worked – oh, yes, occasionally it *did* work' (333).

Thus, on occasion, a beneficent metaphysical otherness is in some way mediated by Frank – however unkempt, however drunk, however vain, however selfish – as a kind of Christ figure. Accordingly, his wait in the pub for McGarvey (who, we have been informed, is severely incapacitated) and his wedding-guest friends, becomes a kind of transposed Maundy Thursday, encompassing the Last Supper and Frank's comment that '[he] knew instinctively why [he] was being *hosted*' (372, my emphasis), as well as the pain of some of the recollections which haunt him, as he later 'walked that floor for a couple of hours' (374). If, then, his savage murder by McGarvey's men, when the attempted healing fails, is a form of crucifixion, the ultimate worth of *Faith Healer* revolves around its destined parallel with the resurrection, not of Frank Hardy but of the collective sensibility of the audience. It is the *play*, which is a 'faith healer'.

Production

I directed *Faith Healer* for the Dublin Shakespeare Society in June 1987. In contrast to the *Borkman,* it was presented in a small underground theatre, capacity of about fifty, at 50 North Great George's Street, which the Society had a lease on at that time. I found a pleasing congruence between the intimacy of the venue and the directness of the monologue format, although I quickly realized in rehearsal that that format was not uniformly deployed in respect of the three characters: Frank is hypnotic, somewhat forbidding, enigmatic, a strong-minded interviewee to an invisible interviewer, especially in his first monologue. (Readers of a certain age will recall the palpable power of the late Donal McCann in the role in the Abbey Theatre première in 1980). With Teddy we are in a music hall; he relates to and sometimes manages the audience, with an experienced trouper's *élan*. Technically, Grace's is not a monologue but an extended soliloquy, which James Fenton, in a *Sunday Times* review in 1981, found 'very badly written'.[10] A simplistic observation, though there's no gainsaying that Grace's sequence is the most difficult to put across.[11]

In one very important respect, *Faith Healer* may be seen as affiliated to a comparatively small body of plays, profoundly different from each other in form and structure, though united by a deeply-felt artistic concern that the author *write the whole performance,* not simply the dialogue or stage directions. With this approach, essential elements such as music, movement, setting, stage properties and, in particular, language, are repossessed by the author, whereas so often in modern drama, these become the remit of the director – a situation not at all to Friel's liking, as we shall see.

Examples of such 'through-written' plays would be some of the Greek or medieval drama (for example, *Oedipus Tyrannus* or the celebrated *Second Shepherds' Play)*, or, given that this is peculiarly a modern phenomenon, almost all of the later plays of Beckett, notably *Footfalls* or *Play*. Much of Richard Wagner's aesthetic philosophy *vis-à-vis* operatic form is predicated on writing the whole performance, notably the daunting *Ring* cycle. Such an approach appeals particularly to dramatists who are wary of directors or remain to be persuaded that they are necessary at all. That is the view of Brian Friel: 'I look on my manuscript as an orchestral score ... I look to the director and the actors to interpret that score exactly as it is written. It is not their function to amend ... or to rewrite, or to cut, or to extend'.[12]

Compliance with that stance makes the author, in a sense, a kind of 'director' from within the text, prescribing moves, rhythm, climaxes, conflict. In the light of the foregoing, it seems more than a little ironic that Friel leaves 'blocking' and movement in *Faith Healer* to the director, his own authorial voice focusing on *mise en scène* – on costuming (why the 'vivid green socks' for Frank?); on props such as the 'empty dog basket' in Teddy's monologue, tellingly evocative, congruently with the whole dynamic of the play, of both absence and presence; on the use of stage space so that, for example, the powerful upstage centre is dominated in three of the four monologues by 'the tatty banner' advertising Frank's faith healing, whereas for the fourth, Frank is existentially on his own; the position of the banner and, to a less obvious extent, of the chairs serves to dictate a kind of ambiguous dramatic choreography related to character impact; for example, Frank never sits (indicative of dominance?) and Grace rarely stands (of passivity?). In Frank's prospective encounter with him, McGarvey sits in his wheelchair, at once commanding (the wheelchair as throne?) and helpless. That is what Peter Brook meant when, in his seminal *The Empty Space,* he described the set as 'the geometry of the eventual play';[13] you cannot indicate authority from downstage right, especially if those to be commanded are upstage centre.

Friel's suggested lighting cues are expertly conducive to intimations of haunting and time displacement. Frank, a magus-like presence, 'with that special voice' (343) he used for intoning the

Welsh and Scottish place names, emerges from darkness at the start of the play, then, after a mesmeric pause of three to four seconds at the end of each of his monologues, abruptly disappears. Grace, 'found on', nervous and distraught, dully dressed, chain-smoking, gradually fades from our awareness at the end. Teddy, also 'found on', is initially an engaging intimate of the audience. By the end, he does 'not see ... them any more' (369); both extremes are 'placed' by what is virtually the 'theme tune' of *Faith Healer*, Jerome Kern's 'The Way You Look Tonight' (from the 1936 film, *Swing Time*), in many ways a metaphor for the play, not least in its distinction between appearance, as sponsored by Teddy, and bedrock reality, the somewhat elusive goal of Frank's whole life. The appeal of the lyrics is brought back to earth by the worn, scratchy surface of the recording Teddy used as 'atmospheric background music' (336) for Frank's healing sessions, the combined euphony and cacophony of which mirrors the combined transcendence and seediness of the play as a whole – Frank as faith healer or 'mountebank', Grace as honoured wife or self–debauching mistress, Teddy as acolyte or minor criminal?

My production, one of the first to be seen outside the Abbey Theatre, seemed to be successful, thanks largely to a talented cast, in which Gerard Stembridge played Frank, Cathy Lawler was Grace, and (in the best interpretation I have seen of the role) Val O'Donnell was Teddy.

III

The impact of some of the 'mid-career' work of Ibsen and Friel, in plays such as the former's *Hedda Gabler* (1890) or the latter's *Crystal and Fox* (1968), is closely bound up with mystery, with emphasis on ambiguity or elusiveness of motivation: what do Hedda and Fox actually want in their lives? Can we – or they – ever know? However, at least one other play by each dramatist, Ibsen's *When We Dead Awaken* and Friel's *Performances*, both coming late in their respective careers – Ibsen aged seventy-one, Friel, seventy-four – dispense with such willed imprecision. The shared theme of those latter plays, the life of the artist and the high price exacted from their lovers for that art to find expression, is also, by metaphorical extension, the situations of Borkman and Frank Hardy.

Performances is, to me, less achieved than *When We Dead*

Awaken, albeit posing challenges virtually unique in modern theatre. [14] *Performances* revolves around the passionate relationship between the Czech composer, Leos Janacek, and Kamila Stosslova, a married woman, forty years his junior, to whom, during the last eleven years of his life, he wrote over seven hundred letters. His String Quartet No. 2, which he christened *Intimate Letters,* composed in the last few months of his life, would seem to have been 'inspired' by the ardour of the relationship. The play contains two characters presented in quasi-realistic format, Janacek and a research student, Anezka Ungrova, whose doctoral topic is 'the relationship between the writing of that [string quartet] and those passionate letters' (22). Of a piece with the kind of strategy deployed by Friel in plays as thematically varied as *Lovers* (1967), *The Freedom of the City* (1973), *Faith Healer* and, pre-eminently, *Living Quarters* (1977), we are to understand that the interaction of Janacek and Ungrova reaches across the grave. We are told in the script that the 'time' of the play is 'the present' (8), even though Janacek died in 1928. This temporal elasticity frees the action to accommodate references to computer systems, to feminist ideology, and, more significantly, to posthumous comment on his work by Dvorak and Janacek himself. However, there are four other 'characters', about whose places in the unfolding drama all critics appear to have been silent since the play was first presented: this is the quartet of musicians who play extracts from *Intimate Letters* as part of the play's ongoing action, and two full movements, the *moderato* and the *allegro,* lasting about thirteen minutes, at the ending. While patently required to be very accomplished musicians,[15] they do not simply 'act' themselves or improvise dialogue but are named Ruth, Judith, Miriam, and John and assigned lines in the text. All of those names are Biblical (three of them, Ruth, Judith, and John, names of whole books in the Old and New Testament).

Performances reworks the kind of conflict already observed between the visionary male and the loving woman whom he abuses. In this instance Friel softens the polarity; the male project, to which the woman is sacrificed, is the musical expression of their *mutual* love. For Anezka, 'your passion for Kamila Stosslova certainly had a *determining effect on that composition* [Second String Quartet] and indeed on that whole remarkable burst of creative energy at the very end of your life'(22). For Janacek, however, the unfolding action of the play compels an articulation of his priorities: 'the work's the thing ... Everything has got to be ancillary to the work. And for all her naiveté in these matters even Kamila acknowledged the primacy of the work', work by which 'she was transformed into something immeasurably greater –of infinitely more importance than the quite modest young woman she was, in fact' (34). Despite Anezka's *Oleanna*-like rejection of that stance: 'I just know you're wrong... Every fibre in my body insists you're wrong. You don't know what the real thing is'(35), the composer insists, in a virtual quotation from Yeats: 'I never considered the life all that important. I gave myself to the perfection of the work' (37).

In such plays as *Volunteers* (1975) and *The Communication Cord* (1982), Friel not only deploys dramatic language to brilliantly fine effect but insinuates language as itself a theme of significance. The most intelligent, most accomplished and most celebrated example of that approach is, of course, *Translations* (1980). From as far back, however, as the use of Mendelssohn's Violin Concerto in *Philadelphia, Here I Come!* (1964) to the extensive use of Chopin in *Aristocrats* (1979), to the varied forms of dance music of *Dancing at Lughnasa* (1990), or the multiple music cues of *Wonderful Tennessee* (1993), Friel insists on the epistemological primacy of music as a form of expression, as the only medium adequate to expressing all the nuances of human feeling, as transcending the limitations of spoken language. With music, according to Janacek as presented in *Performances,* 'we reach into that amorphous world of feeling and sing what we hear in the language of feeling itself; a unique vocabulary of sounds created by feeling itself' (31), in comparison to which, 'the people who huckster in words merely report on feeling' (31). *Performances,* then, makes a double assertion in terms, one, of the paramount value of the aesthetic, so that love 'is the music in the head made real, become carnal' (34), and, two, of the supremacy of music within the arts. That is why Friel requires that *Performances* ends with the playing in full, for almost fifteen minutes, of the third and fourth movements of the *Intimate Letters* String Quartet[16], and this is why the members of the quartet are required to function in an acting as well as instrumental capacity; the contrast between their skilled 'performances' as musicians and their amateur 'performances' as actors gives onstage embodiment to the superiority of music over language.

IV

When We Dead Awaken can be seen as a resonant echo chamber to some of the issues sounded in this essay. In *Faith Healer,* Grace's nervous excess, eventual breakdown and suicide following the brutal death of Frank figure as a more muted version of the collapses in sanity of Irene, consequent on Rubek's leaving her. Irene's state is so severe as to require hospitalization in a straitjacket and, when free, the rather bizarre attentiveness of what most translations term a 'nun', David Rudkin calls 'a sister in black'[17], and Peter Watts insists was Ibsen's own term, 'deaconess'.[18] Similarly, Grace's recriminatory anger that she had 'debauched myself for [Frank]' (344) is enlarged by Irene into the recurring rebuke that, having stripped herself naked as artist's model for Rubek as sculptor, and then been denied his love, followed by years of sexual degradation, she now considers herself emotionally and spiritually 'dead'. Irene's accusation that that death was consequent on her giving '[her] soul'[19] to Rubek is matched by Ella Rentheim's accusation that Borkman, by killing in her 'the ability to love and be loved', had committed 'the deadliest sin ... a double murder... of your own soul and mine' (61).

In terms of the depiction of temporality, for the peculiar purposes his two last plays call for, Ibsen begins to move away from retrospection – in the stage realization of which he had for so many years shown such consummate mastery that some playwrights have not learned even yet to move beyond him – towards future address. In *John Gabriel Borkman,* such address is meagre, the muted reconciliation between characters whose deaths are imminent; Gunhild's 'Now we two can join hands, Ella' is met with Ella's 'I think we can ... now' (94). In total contrast is the powerful *liebestod* of the following in *When We Dead Awaken:*

> **Rubek**. Then let us two dead people live life to the full for one short hour before we go down again into our graves!
> **Irene**. Arnold ... Up into the light, where glory shines. Up to the promised mountain top.
> **Rubek**. Up there we shall celebrate our wedding feast, Irene, my beloved.
> **Irene**. The sun may look on us, Arnold.
> **Rubek**. All the powers of light may look on us. And all the powers of darkness, too.(*leading her*) First we must pass through the mists, Irene. And then –

Irene. Yes, through the mists. And then up, up to the top of our tower, where it shines in the sunrise.[20]

That sequence, followed almost immediately by the avalanche which sweeps Rubek and Irene to their deaths, is blessed by the Nun's 'Pax vobiscum', [Peace be with you] – a future-centred prayer which endorses freedom and truth, the same twin 'pillars of society' to which Ibsen had paid titular tribute more than twenty years earlier, here complicated, rendered free of easy definition. The ending of *Performances* is constituted wholly by the backward look; as Janacek listens to the music of the *Intimate Letters* Quartet, '*he opens the book* [his *Intimate Letters* to Kamila], ... *pausing now and then to read a line or two. Now and then he leans his head back and closes his eyes*' (39).

In its treatment of time, the conclusion of *Faith Healer* is of a piece with the overall dramatic richness of the play; Frank Hardy, made *present* to the audience by dramatic artifice, since he is already 'dead' [the past], recalls his fateful meeting with McGarvey, the 'cold certainty' (340) of his intimation [future-directed] that 'nothing was going to happen' (375) and the unstated inevitability of his *imminent* killing. Where Borkman and Rubek make their final ascents with the loving women whose love they had thitherto failed to reciprocate, Frank Hardy, alone on an empty stage, confronts a destiny in which familiar definitions of identity are transcended: the sense that 'in all existence there was only myself and the wedding guests' is superseded by the quasi-mystical insight that 'even we had ceased to be physical and existed only in spirit, only in the need we had for each other' (376).

If, then, the parallels to Jesus, referred to earlier, extend significantly the resonances of *Faith Healer*, here, by an audacious broadening of the whole field of force of the play, Frank Hardy figures as a flawed embodiment of archetypal cosmos, McGarvey of chaos, locked in elemental struggle of *being*. Ultimately, Frank's sacrifice vindicates a logocentric reading of experience: 'At long last I was renouncing chance' (376).

Conclusion

Friel's attempt, in *Performances,* to redefine the essence of the theatre experience by interweaving music with play-text is in logical continuity with Ibsen's concern, as he aged and as the twentieth century dawned, that established strategies in plot realization – to do with setting, music, lighting, language – might no longer be congruent with the overall action of a given play. This is what Strindberg had in mind, in the Preface to *Miss Julie,* when he observed that the 'new wine has burst the old bottles': 'we have not succeeded in adapting the old form to the new content'.[21] Hence the theatrical boldness of *When We Dead Awaken*, the first Ibsen play to be set exclusively outdoors. The second act requires no less than 'a *vast treeless plateau ... a long mountain lake ... a range of mountain peaks ... a stream*'.[22] It poses formidable challenges, moreover, in the incipient poetry of its awkwardly heightened prose, in the unprecedented brevity of the third act (a mere fifteen minutes), in the insinuation that an as yet unavailable acting style, neither wholly naturalistic nor stylized, be required for the six characterizations. In a well-known communication to Moritz Prozor, Ibsen declared: 'I shall not be able to absent myself long from the old battlefields. But if I return, I shall come forward with new weapons, and with new equipment'.[23] The contrast between the forthright militariness of Ibsen's 'new weapons' and the flexibility of Strindberg's 'new wine' may be instructive. Friel, I suspect, is closer to Strindberg. At any rate, all three circle around the recurring question: whether life, under the remit of the *mores,* laws, morality and social structures that Christian, bourgeois positivism has put in place, is ultimately unlivable. The logocentrism of Friel is one way towards an answer. The other, as Harold Bloom reminds us, confronts us with Ibsen's trolls, with whom we do constant battle, who tempt us with both the promise of authenticity and the excitement of wilful destructiveness: 'Most simply, trolls are *before* good and evil , rather than beyond it'.[24]

---

[1] W.B. Yeats, 'The Choice' (1933), *The Collected Works of W.B. Yeats,* vol.1: *The Poems*, ed. Richard J. Finneran (London: Macmillan, 1983): 246-47.

[2] Brian Friel, *Performances* (Oldcastle: Gallery Press, 2003): 25. Hereafter references to this source appear in parentheses.

[3] Alfred, Lord Tennyson, 'Ulysses', *Norton Anthology of Poetry*, 1st edn (New York: London, 1996): 896-97.

[4] Cited after Michael Meyer, *Ibsen* (Garden City: Doubleday, 1971): 747.

[5] Henrik Ibsen, *John Gabriel Borkman*, in English version by Inga-Stina Ewbank and Peter Hall (London: Athlone Press, 1975): 82. Hereafter references to this source appear in parentheses.

[6] Peter Szondi, *Theory of the Modern Drama* (Cambridge: Polity Press, 1987): 15.

[7] Ibid., 16.

[8] Apart from some of Ibsen's early work, together with that of some of the founder-figures of the Abbey Theatre, verse had largely been abandoned as a dramatic medium since the eighteenth century, while reality had not yet been given to Jean Cocteau's notion of *poésie de théâtre*.

[9] Brian Friel, *Faith Healer, Selected Plays* (London and Boston: Faber 1984): 343. Subsequent references to this source are in parentheses.

[10] *Sunday Times* 5 March, 1981: 41.

[11] In a recent interview (March 2011) with Ingrid Craigie, one of the finer interpreters of the role, she informed me that Grace was the most difficult part she had ever played.

[12] Brian Friel, 'Self-Portrait', *Brian Friel: Essays, Diaries, Interviews: 1964-1999*, ed. Christopher Murray (London: New York, 1999): 44-45. This originally appeared in *Aquarius* in 1972.

[13] Peter Brook, *The Empty Space* (Harmondsworth: Penguin, 1968): 113.

[14] The play nearest to *Performances* in structure and tone would appear to me to be *Every Good Boy Deserves Favour* (1977) by Tom Stoppard.

[15] The musicians for the première production were the distinguished Alba String Quartet.

[16] During the actual run at the Gate Theatre, for reasons never made clear, the amount of time given was severely reduced. Friel was therefore never given an opportunity to test his methodology against performance.

[17] See *When We Dead Awaken; Rosmersholm: Two Plays by Henrik Ibsen*, trans. David Rudkin (Bath: Absolute Classics, 1990): 8.

[18] See Henrik Ibsen, *Ghosts and Other Plays,* trans. Peter Watts (Harmondsworth: Penguin Books, 1979): 299.

[19] Henrik Ibsen, *When We Dead Awaken, Plays: Four*, trans. Michael Meyer (London: Methuen,1980): 235.

[20] Ibid., 266.

[21] August Strindberg, *Plays: One*, trans. Michael Meyer (London, Secker & Warburg,1975): 1.

[22] Ibsen, *When We Dead Awaken*, 237.

[23] Meyer, *Ibsen*, 785.

[24] See Harold Bloom, *The Western Canon: The Books and School of the Ages* (London: Macmillan, 1994): 354.

6 | Frank McGuinness's 'Only Ibsen of the Western World'

Helen Heusner Lojek

From 1987 to 2010, Frank McGuinness produced stage adaptations of twenty-seven works by other authors – adaptations that provided income and, particularly in the early years, a sort of playwriting tutorial. His nine versions of Ibsen plays stand out as the largest block of adaptations, and Ibsen's name comes up frequently when McGuinness discusses his own plays. Internal and external evidence indicates McGuinness's affinity for Ibsen and his belief that Irish accented versions of Ibsen will speak powerfully to English language audiences. Clearly he shares with Ibsen a varied approach to play structure, convictions about the handling of stage space, and a world view.

His adaptations have occasionally struck critics as what Stephen McKenna (writing to J.M. Synge in 1903) described as 'frieze-clad Ibsens'.[1] They have also earned both popular and critical praise. His adaptation of *A Doll's House* won four Tony awards in 1997. Benedict Nightingale declared he had seen 'some good' *Ghosts*, but 'none better than' the 2010 production of McGuinness's adaptation.[2] And the Abbey Theatre's 2010 production of McGuinness's adaptation of *John Gabriel Borkman*, which travelled to the Brooklyn Academy of Music in 2011, attracted full and enthusiastic houses. It also caught the wave of public outrage about the misconduct of financiers. Fiona Shaw, who played Gunhild Borkman, described the play as 'wonderfully pertinent',[3] and the night I saw the production names of financiers who seemed as culpable as Borkman echoed throughout the Brooklyn lobby.

Like Marina Carr, who numbered Ibsen among the 'poets of the theatre' whose works 'thrill' her and from whom an apprentice playwright may learn 'many things',[4] McGuinness praises Ibsen's influence on both the form and the content of his own work:

> I think he is an extraordinary mind and an extraordinary mentor, armed with a terrifying capacity to reach into a terrible darkness. He does so and he helps you to do so by reason of the sheer skill of his construction ... I do these versions for instruction and I do them for pleasure.[5]

2 *John Gabriel Borkman* **in a version by Frank McGuinness, Abbey Theatre, October 2010, directed by James Macdonald Cathy Belton (Mrs Wilton), Marty Rea (Erhart Borkman), Lindsey Duncan (Mrs. Ella Rentheim), and Fiona Shaw (Mrs Gunhild Borkman). Photograph: Ros Kavanagh**

One strand of Ibsen's appeal for McGuinness is the Norwegian's presentation of social critiques in recognizable naturalistic realms. Speaking and behaving in familiar ways, Ibsen's middle-class characters reveal anxieties about status and sex and refute any lingering notions that serious issues may be discovered and discussed only in relation to the privileged. Especially in McGuinness's early plays (*The Factory Girls, Observe the Sons of Ulster Marching Toward the Somme, Carthaginians*), he too offers dramatic worlds that are ordinary and characters for whom privilege is something others enjoy. And, like Ibsen, McGuinness presents characters confronting dilemmas of class, gender, and sexuality that are issues not only for them but also for their nation.

Ibsen's importance is evident in McGuinness's early work. In *The Factory Girls* (1982), Rebecca's name and interest in horses derive from Ibsen's *Rosmersholm*, and McGuinness specifically linked the play to his admiration of Ibsen; bringing the shirt factory workers to life was a political act, and Ibsen is a favourite playwright 'because his politics have a passion and they're not just based on intellect'.[6] Passion and intellect are informing principles in McGuinness's own drama, and McGuinness's willingness to present (with increasing directness throughout his career) issues of sexuality that impact both characters and society parallels Ibsen's willingness to be equally direct. McGuinness's openness about sexuality includes direct presentation of homosexuality (illegal in Ireland until 1993). If such subject matter opens him to charges that he, like Ibsen, writes 'morbid sex-obsessed drama'[7], he seems untroubled.

In *Someone Who'll Watch Over Me* (1992), the 'movies' which the prisoners invent owe debts not only to actual films from Hitchcock to Attenborough, but also to the fantastic events of *Peer Gynt*.[8] They constitute another tribute to Ibsen's powerful influence without being direct references or adaptations.

In the late 1980s, when McGuinness adapted *Rosmersholm* (1987) and *Peer Gynt* (1988), he was teaching at what was then St. Patrick's College Maynooth and beginning to establish himself as a playwright. In 2002 he noted that working on adaptations helped to bridge the world of academia and the world of playwriting.[9] Trained as a medievalist at UCD, McGuinness had selected Old Norse as a required language[10] and developed a friendship with Fevronia Orfanos, a Finnish student studying at UCD. In 1986 he wrote to tell her he was working on *Rosmersholm* and promised: 'Should it ever be published, I promise to dedicate it to my favourite Finlander. (Yes, yes, I know Ibsen is Norwegian, but for God's sake, woman, he's Northern European too!)'.[11] Those connections with the Nordic countries may seem incidental and unimportant, and McGuinness's conflation of Finland and Norway is surprising, given his keen awareness of national borders in his own part of Europe. Such connections, however, illustrate the reality that for McGuinness there is never 'just one trigger for a play', and his sense that he must have a 'passion', an 'obsession' with any play on which he works.[12]

The adaptations also provide McGuinness with an opportunity to insist on the value of Irish English – to demonstrate his belief that English or American accents are neither superior nor sufficient. Stephen Rea has made the same point:

> Because I've worked in England, I had the notion imposed upon me that you had to speak in a particular way if you were working in English theatre. Particularly if you were doing translations of foreign classics ... I resented it very much and it robbed me of all the colour and emotion in my own accent.

Rea praised McGuinness's adaptation of Chekhov's *Uncle Vanya* (1995) as 'very uplifting ... wonderful for actors'. [13]

Translating Ibsen into English is generally acknowledged to be difficult, with results that 'often come across as flat-footed'.[14] Discussing the challenges in 1998, translator Inga-Stina Ewbank noted that 'an Ibsen translation into English is still expected to sound as if Ibsen had written in a standard English idiom, when in fact the Norwegian of his dramatic texts is more inventive than standard'.[15] McGuinness's knowledge of Norwegian is limited, and mine is non-existent. I am not arguing that his adaptations/translations are somehow more 'accurate' than others. His affirmation of Irish accents and idioms, though, has earned the gratitude of Irish actors, emphasized connections between nineteenth-century Norway and twentieth-century Ireland, and brought critical praise.[16] Praise for his versions has not been universal, of course, and English or U.S. critics sometimes dislike the same Irish idioms that have earned praise in Ireland. A U.S. commentator, for example, protested that phrases like 'God above, do you not understand me now?' and 'Who's had the brass neck to tell you that?' were 'antique-sounding phrases' that do not help 'collapse the distance between Ibsen's era and our own'.[17]

Irishisms like 'God love you' or 'Himself alone' – a play on 'Ourselves Alone'[18] – often enrich the adaptations in ways that arguably *do* 'collapse the distance' between Ibsen and the contemporary world. Fintan O'Toole has pointed out, for example, that because McGuinness possesses a 'cultural reference point for Ibsen's satire on linguistic nostalgia' he was able in *Peer Gynt* to adapt Ibsen's language into a 'come-all-ye' that encouraged Irish audiences to hear the lines with particular acuteness:[19]

> But the strangers mixed the language and disaster's what we saw.
> In the old days lived a people, we call them Orang-Utang.

They possessed the forest freely ...
... till the foreigner said, your ways you must mend....
Four centuries of oppression fell upon the monkey tribe ...
Men like me shall fight for our right to roar our hearts off ...[20]

I have shortened the quote and thus maimed the 'come-all-ye' form in order to emphasize themes likely to resonate forcefully in the Irish psyche: foreigners referring to the natives as apes, destroying native language and 'ways', and instituting four centuries of oppression.

More recently O'Toole has explored the fact that 'watching an Irish play in Ireland is very different from seeing it in Minneapolis'.[21] The cultural gap is an unexplored reality behind McGuinness's adaptations of Ibsen. McGuinness adapted *Peer Gynt* for Irish audiences. Other adaptations were written and performed first in England, and many have crossed the Atlantic to encounter U.S. audiences. Varying audiences have produced varying results, and that overlay impacts both McGuinness's work and its reception.

A striking aspect of all the adaptations is McGuinness's ability to work the formal structure and language of standard academic translations into dialogue with the rhythms of actual speech. Here, for example, is Rolf Fjelde's translation of Wangel's offer of freedom to his wife in *The Lady from the Sea*:

Wangel. Now you can choose your path – in full freedom.
Ellida. [*stares at him briefly as if struck dumb*]. Is that true – true – what you are saying? You mean it – with all your heart?
Wangel. Yes, I mean it – with all my miserable heart.
Ellida. Then you *can* – ? You can let this *be*?
Wangel. Yes, I can. Because I love you so much.
Ellida. [*her voice soft and tremulous*]. Have I grown so close – and so dear to you?
Wangel. With the years and the living together, yes.
Ellida. [*striking her hands together*]. And I – who've been so blind![22]

Jens Arup and James Walter McFarlane translate the same passage this way:

Wangel. I set you free. I cancel our transaction.
Ellida. Is this true what you say, Wangel? Do you mean it with all your heart?
Wangel. Yes, from the very depths of my heart I mean it.
Ellida. But can you!
Wangel. I can because I love you.
Ellida. Have you come to love me so truly and so dearly?

Wangel. It has come from the years we have lived through together.
Ellida. How blind I have been not to see it.[23]

McGuinness's sparer, more playable dialogue is roughly half as long, with a syntax more familiar to contemporary English language audiences and actors:

Wangel. Choose your path. You're free – absolutely free. *[She stares at him, astonished.]* I mean it – in my heart – my breaking, broken heart. I can let it happen because I love you. *[She is quiet and trembling.]* You have become my heart, beating through all our life together.
Ellida. And I was deaf to it.[24]

The appropriate role for translator or adaptor is complex. Colin Teevan, who adapted *Peer Gynt* in 2007, expressed a desire to

> make the classics work as living, breathing theatre, reinventing the shock they had when first performed and making them accessible with all their complicatedness ... The intention was not to rewrite the play but to re-contextualize it so that the audience could experience the radical force of Ibsen's vision in the present, not preserved in a Nordic *aspic*.[25]

Teevan's summary fits McGuinness's work and underscores McGuinness's recognition that his adaptations necessarily have a 'short life. They will last ten, fifteen years ...'.[26] Like the outdated satire imbedded in Ibsen's plays, McGuinness's idiomatic adaptations work to meet audiences where they are, preserving the essence of the plays while making them more speakable for contemporary actors. He is particularly adept at matching the rhythm of his adaptations to the rhythm of Irish speech and allowing actors and audiences to find the humour in lines from plays that are intensely serious – something particularly evident in *John Gabriel Borkman.*

Translation and adaptation are inherently difficult. Michael Meyer, who translated *Peer Gynt* in 1962 and worked with the Royal Exchange Theatre's 1999 production, has argued vigorously that only a bilingual person can adequately confront translation's challenges. To illustrate, he points to the fact that in English there is no term meaning '"self-sufficient" in a negative sense', and thus English versions of the line *Troll vær deg selv-nok* [Troll, be thyself enough!] are extremely difficult, because it is hard to render an English equivalent of the Norwegian negativity. Meyer quotes several solutions[27] and notes that in 1999 'Troll, be thyself – and to hell with the rest of the world' seemed best to him.[28] McGuinness's adaptation plays with the Shakespearean 'to thine own self be true' and then encapsulates the negativity in a line echoing the Irish slogan 'Ourselves alone', with its ambiguity of positive and negative: 'be your self alone'.[29] Despite his limited understanding of Norwegian, then, McGuinness has happened on a solution that works for Irish audiences. Espen Skjønberg, who delivered the line in 1999, convinced Meyer to endorse 'Troll, be thyself – and thyself alone.' Meyer argues that the phrase should not appear in a printed translation, but agreed that since the actor would be hugging himself and laughing, it would work for that production.[30]

McGuinness does not re-site Ibsen's plays, which remain set in Norway. He is not, in other words, producing concept adaptations like Mustapha Matura's *Playboy of the West Indies*. He is not translocating but translating. On the other hand, he describes his adaptations as aiming at creating 'the conditions by which the audience is transported into the world of the play', experiencing it 'organically, and not in any fragmented or piecemeal way'.[31] The language of McGuinness's adaptations and often the accents of the actors situate the plays in Ireland. Occasionally production choices suggest an Irish setting, but McGuinness has noted that for him, adaptations in the language allow for 'making the text my own. Much more than setting it in Durham or in Mullingar'.[32]

The adaptations thus mediate between Norway and Ireland. Occasionally productions emphasize the Irish connection, so that Anne Bamborough (from whose literal translation McGuinness was working) noted in the programme for *Peer Gynt* that 'as it says in the play, "we all have Peer Gynt's blood inside us"; my guess is that in Frank McGuinness's version he will also be taken for a typical Irishman'.[33]

Occasionally McGuinness's Irishisms do not work so well. At the end of *The Lady from the Sea*, for example, McGuinness has Ballested observe: 'Soon snow will be general all over, as the man says'[34] – a somewhat laboured and artificial anachronism that raises Joyce's 'The Dead', with its parallel examination of marriage, as an Irish work thematically connected to the Norwegian play.

Above all, McGuinness has produced playable scripts that are, in his own terms, 'speakable'.[35] As David Johnston puts it in relation to McGuinness's adaptations of Spanish drama:

> The translator ... must possess sufficient irreverence to allow his or her own creativity to come into play with the text ...

McGuinness's sense of fidelity to the spirit of these [Spanish] plays derives not from a thesaurus-inspired devotion to lexis but from a performance-aware recreation [that] establishes the distinctive Irish voice of his stage language ... the plays remain undeniably Spanish, but not in a loosely exotic or impenetrably linguistic way ... and McGuinness ... brings speakability and concision to his idiom.[36]

Producing adaptations supplemented McGuinness's modest income from teaching and writing his own plays. Asked in 2004 about the 'top seller' status of his version of *A Doll's House*, he praised the published text as 'a great little money-spinner'.[37] The adaptations also (like McGuinness's early work acting and directing) served as advanced schooling in the art of dramatic structure. Continental dramatists, McGuinness has noted, 'teach you more about your craft ... you have to go and look at other theatres and know at least what you're rejecting'.[38] Ibsen plays like *A Doll's House* and *An Enemy of the People* are often praised – or excoriated – for their naturalism, and naturalism is also a frequent mode in McGuinness's own plays. Naturalism is not the only mode for either playwright, however – and not the only mode for which each received both praise and condemnation. Ibsen's plays also provided models for McGuinness's ventures into the non-naturalistic dramatic world.

McGuinness's version of *Peer Gynt* was produced in 1988, shortly after his play *Innocence* (1986) appeared, and while he was workshopping *Mary and Lizzie* (1989) with the Royal Shakespeare Company. In the introduction to the 1990 publication of his *Peer Gynt* script, McGuinness describes Peer as

Liar, blaggard, louse, drunk, violent, then shockingly, pitifully tender, mad as a tree, good, occasionally, to his mother, cracked about women, afraid of men, sorely needing his absent father, crazed with ambition, sick from failure, this creature I wouldn't let into my house, but I welcomed him charging into my head, for the pain, the terrible pain of Peer Gynt must be endured as well.[39]

Dominic Hill, who directed the 2007 National Theatre of Scotland/Dundee Rep production of *Peer Gynt,* described Peer in similar terms:

An outsider, a poet, a womanizer who doesn't fit into the local community, who is publicly despised but privately envied for being 'different'. A guy who longs to escape to make something of himself, who loathes the idea of mediocrity and who in chasing celebrity tramples on and destroys the only people who love him.[40]

Those descriptions fit not only Peer, but also Caravaggio in *Innocence* – and many would regard large portions of them as accurate descriptions of McGuinness himself.

In his introduction to the published play McGuinness also notes the 'formidable energy' of Ibsen, 'rampaging forward, taking the classic five-act form and inflating it beyond repair, planting dynamite beneath the unities of time and place, risking artistic suicide'.[41] That description brings to mind both Ibsen's sense that the play should be read, not produced, and Willy Russell's *Educating Rita*, in which – asked how to solve the staging challenges of *Peer Gynt* – Rita replies 'put it on the radio'. In 1999 McGuinness specifically connected the 'structural ambitions' of *Peer Gynt* with *Mary and Lizzie*'s 'sprawling nature, its ability to cross continents, its ability to go anywhere that it wanted to go'.[42] That description also fits *Mutabilitie* (1997), a play McGuinness began working on at least as early as 1986 and one he mentions frequently in the same interview.

Like most creative inspirations, of course, the influences that produced the *Peer Gynt* adaptation were multiple and complex. In 1988, writing again to Orfanos, McGuinness described his feelings at the opening of *Peer Gynt*:

> I have been praised for being close to Ibsen. Little do they know who my guide to the great man is. You know the length of the original play. I knew that it was more than a marathon, but you know how Finns have such a good record of long distance races.[43]

The Gate's 1988 production of McGuinness's *Peer Gynt* was a fitting part of its sixtieth year celebration, a re-staging of a play Hilton Edwards and Micheál MacLiammóir had mounted during the Gate's first season and a reminder of the Gate's commitment to innovation and internationalism. Those connections are also reminders of the varied influences that animate McGuinness's creations. He has cited MacLiammóir's touring production of *The Importance of Being Oscar*, which he saw as a youth, as a seminal influence. His appreciation of and identification with the gay couple who founded the Gate is intense and led in 2002 to *Gates of Gold*, a play loosely based on the lives of the couple and featuring a disappearing wall that surely owes a debt to Ibsen's symbolic use of architecture in *The Master Builder*.[44]

Twenty years after the opening of *Peer Gynt*, McGuinness's adaptation of *The Lady from the Sea* opened in London, and the playwright completed an adaptation of *The Master Builder*. In a classic McGuinness interview – lively, engaging, perceptive, and a helpful preparation for readers he hoped would become audiences – the playwright lamented the end of his twenty year focus on adapting Ibsen's major plays: 'I've lost my Henrik ... I've lost him surely, I've lost my only Ibsen, my only Ibsen of the Western World'.[45] Though the production of *John Gabriel Borkman* two years later indicates that McGuinness had not then totally lost his Ibsen, the channelling of Synge emphasizes McGuinness's passion for Ibsen and for the connections he has explored between Ibsen and the tradition of Irish drama to which he himself has contributed so much.[46]

Parallels between Ibsen and McGuinness are easy to find. Both come from small, ethnically homogeneous countries on the margins of Europe, partly colonial and partly post-colonial and characterized by extensive seacoasts. Both are sensitive to women's lives and challenges, concerned with the role of the artist, direct in approaching sexual issues. Each creates both naturalistic and fantastic plays and explores issues of metatheatricality. Both Ibsen and McGuinness also manage to create characters who illustrate national issues without becoming symbols or losing individuality. And in their explorations of the particular, Ibsen and McGuinness reach a remarkable generality. Seamus Heaney has described Brian Friel's connections with non-Irish writers as resulting in a 'sense of writerly responsibility drawn from the far horizons'.[47] The same quality is evident in McGuinness, and it is no wonder that he, like Joyce, admires Ibsen and celebrates connections between Ibsen's drama and Ireland. There may not be only one Ibsen of the western world, but McGuinness has created a powerful one, and it is no surprise that he lamented concluding twenty years of adaptations.

[1] Stephen MacKenna to Synge, January 1904, *The Collected Letters of John Millington Synge*, ed. Ann Saddlemyer, vol. 1 1871-1907 (New York: OUP, 1983): 75.

[2] 'Ghosts at The Duchess', *The Sunday Times* (London) 24 February 2010.

[3] *The Late Late Show*, RTE, September 25, 2010.

4 'Dealing with the Dead', *Irish University Review* 28.1(1998): 195. Carr also mentions Chekhov, Williams, Wilde, Beckett, and Shakespeare, but Ibsen receives more attention than the others.

5 Maurice Fitzpatrick, 'Interview with Frank McGuinness', 18 March 2009. http://www.mauricefitzpatrick.org, accessed January 2011.

6 Quoted in Sarah O'Hara, 'Productive Lives', *The Irish Press* 17 March 1982.

7 *Synge, The Collected Letters*, vol.1, 75.

8 I am grateful to Christopher Murray for pointing out this connection to me.

9 Radio interview. *Rattlebag*, RTE, 30 April 2002. McGuinness made similar remarks in a 1999 interview, observing that the Ibsen translations were 'enormous help for teaching. They've always been the bridge between teaching and writing – and, you know, I'm still learning, still very happy to learn from those who stretch the boundaries, who still stretch the boundaries, when they're properly realized'. 'Frank McGuinness in Conversation with Joseph Long', *Theatre Talk: Voices of Irish Theatre Practitioners*, eds Lilian Chambers, Ger FitzGibbon and Eamonn Jordan (Dublin: Carysfort Press, 2001): 306; first published as 'New Voices in Irish Theatre', *Études Irlandaises*. CCXLIV (Spring 1999): 9-19). In 2004 McGuinness returned to the notion that the adaptations bridged his two worlds: 'for every [adaptation] I've done my teaching purposes and my writing purposes will be combined in this slog to get this play into my head and to know it' ('Frank McGuinness', *Faber Playwrights at the National Theatre* (London: Faber, 2005): 115).

10 He is fond of repeating the story that, told of his work on Old Norse, his mother replied, 'Oh that's great, son, you'll never be out of a job with that skill'. And of his regret that she was no longer alive when his version of *A Doll's House* won four Tony awards; *Faber Playwrights*, 115.

11 Quoted in Helen Lojek, 'Letters from Frank', *Irish University Review* 40:1 (Spring/Summer 2010): 30.

12 *Faber Playwrights*, 106, 115.

13 Carole Zucker, 'Interview with Stephen Rea', *Canadian Journal of Irish Studies* 26.1 (Spring 2000): 91. Rea appeared in McGuinness's adaptation of Chekhov's *Uncle Vanya* (1995), which he praised as 'a very uplifting translation, wonderful for actors'.

14 Toril Moi, *Henrik Ibsen and the Birth of Modernism: Art, Theater, Philosophy* (Oxford: OUP, 2006): 328.

15 Quoted in Moi, 328.

16 Mel Gussow noted that the 'rhetorical excess' of *Rosmersholm* was 'somewhat alleviated in Frank McGuinness's translation', *New York Times* 14 December 1988: C21. Commentary about McGuinness's adaptation of *The Lady from the Sea* (2008) has been positive: 'a forceful, often Irish-sounding new version' (Paul Taylor-Indy); 'an

elegantly pungent, Irish-inflected new version' (Sam Marlowe), an 'admirable new translation' (Michael Billington).

[17] Charles Isherwood, 'At the Top of the Ladder, Confronting His Demons', Review of *The Master Builder New York Times* 24 October 2008. Michael Meyer objected to the language of *Rosmersholm* as 'stilted and obscure' ('The Weight of Tradition', *New York Times* 14 December 1988: C21) and John Peter described it as *'speak-able'* but full of 'odd discrepancies' ('The Pitfalls of the Creative Translator', *Sunday Times* 7 June 1987).

[18] Henrik Ibsen, *Peer Gynt*, a version by Frank McGuinness (London: Faber, 1990): 47 and 74. There is also language from the Bible, Shakespeare, and Catholicism.

[19] Fintan O'Toole, 'Judged by Its Peers', Review of Peer Gynt, Theatre Ireland (December 1988/March 1989):17.

[20] *Peer Gynt*, 73.

[21] 'In the theatre, the audience makes the play' (*Irish Times* 31 October 2009: Weekend Review 9).

[22] Henrik Ibsen, *The Lady from the Sea, The Complete Major Prose Plays*, trans. Rolf Fjelde (London: Faber, 1978): 685.

[23] Henrik Ibsen, *The Lady from the Sea, The Oxford Ibsen*, ed. James McFarlane vol. 7 (New York: OUP, 1966): 163-64.

[24] Henrik Ibsen, *The Lady from the Sea*, A new version by Frank McGuinness from a literal translation by Charlotte Barslund (London: Faber, 2008): 89.

[25] 'Making the Classics Live', Programme note, *Peer Gynt*, Barbican Theatre (bite festival), 2009:10-11.

[26] *Faber Playwrights*, 116.

[27] 'Be true to your self-ish' (Kenneth McLeish) and 'To thine own self be-all-sufficient.' (Christopher Fry and Johan Fillinger).

[28] Royal Exchange Theatre 'Resource Pack.' http://www.royalexchangetheatre.org.uk.

[29] McGuinness, *Peer Gynt*: 28.

[30] Royal Exchange 'Resource Pack'.

[31] Royal Exchange 'Resource Pack'.

[32] Frank McGuinness, 'I'm not entirely respectable. I couldn't be', Interview with Charlotte Higgins, *The Guardian* 18 October 2008.

[33] McGuinness worked with Bamborough on both *Rosmersholm* and *Peer Gynt*. On other adaptations McGuinness worked in other ways, but always with one or more literal translations in hand.

[34] Henrik Ibsen, *The Lady from the Sea*, 115.

[35] *Faber Playwrights*, 115.

[36] David Johnston, '*En otras palabras*: Frank McGuinness and Spanish Drama', *The Dreaming Body: Contemporary Irish Theatre*, eds Melissa Sihra and Paul Murphy (Gerrards Cross UK: Colin Smythe, 2009): 183-98.

[37] *Faber Playwrights*, 113.

38 'Frank McGuinness in Conversation with Joseph Long', 305.

39 McGuinness, *Peer Gynt*, vi.

40 Director's Note, Programme, *Peer Gynt*, Barbican (bite festival) 2009: 6.

41 Ibid.

42 'Frank McGuinness in Conversation with Joseph Long', 301.

43 Quoted in Lojek, 31.

44 The *Peer Gynt* production also allowed McGuinness to work with Michael Colgan, Patrick Mason, and Shaun Davey, collaborators with whom he has had enduring relationships.

45 'A Happy Marriage', Interview with John O'Mahony, *The Guardian* 24 April 2008.

46 See Irina Ruppo Malone, *Ibsen and the Irish Revival* (Basingstoke: Palgrave Macmillan, 2010): 163 for a discussion of connections between Christy's wounding of his father in *Playboy* and Peer's abduction of Ingrid in *Peer Gynt*.

47 *Stepping Stones: Interviews with Seamus Heaney*, ed. Dennis O'Driscoll (London: Farrar Straus, 2008): 178.

7 | Directing Ibsen in Ireland: Round-table Discussion with Máiréad Ní Chróinín, Lynne Parker, and Arthur Riordan

Our people – let me make this clear –
The clothes we wear are all made here.
Nothing gets in from the world outside,
Except these silky ribbons tied
Around our tails ...[1]

tá saol ár bpobal suite ar talamh atá
truaillithe le bréig'[2]

The following roundtable discussion took place on 7 November 2009. It was moderated by Kurt Taroff and Irina Ruppo Malone and featured Lynne Parker and Arthur Riordan, co-founders of Rough Magic, and Máiréad Ní Chróinín, co-founder of Moonfish.

Moonfish was established in Galway in 2006 by the sisters Máiréad and Ionia Ní Chróinín. Their 2009 production of *An Enemy of the People* in Irish was highly praised, not least for its use of surtitles allowing non-Irish speaking audiences to understand the show. The production was directed by Máiréad Ní Chróinín and starred Brendan Conroy as Dr Stockmann, Bríd Ní Neachtain as his wife Caitriona, Ionia Ní Chróinín as Petra Stockman, Donncha Ó Crualaí as Peadar Stockmann, Peadar O Tresaigh as Mortan Cíl, Dara Ó Dubhláin as Hovstad, Séamus Ó hAodha as Billing, Padraic Ó Tuairisc as Aslasken and Morgan Cooke as Captaen Horster.

Established in 1984, Rough Magic is one of the leading independent theatrical companies in Ireland. It is based in Dublin. The translation used for their production of *Peer Gynt* was carried out by Arthur Riordan, actor and playwright.

On the date of the conference, Arthur read from his translation of *Peer Gynt*. He chose Peer's imaginary fight with a tree in Act III, the madman Huhu's tale of the campaign for the language of the apes in Act IV, and finished with an acted version of Peer's monologue on the devil and the pig from Act V.

Arthur's reading of scenes from *Peer Gynt* delighted the audience, not only because it brought to life the comic, controversial, and metatheatrical aspects of this play; in the context of the conference, this short performance momentarily bridged the gap between the past theatrical productions and the productions yet to come.

Peer Gynt was performed at the Dublin Theatre Festival of 2011, two years after the conference and the discussion took place. In June 2011, Lynne Parker provided a short addendum outlining her thoughts on the production. It is found at the end of this section.

Irina Ruppo Malone: Máiréad, could you tell us about your production of an Irish language translation of *An Enemy of the People*?

Máiréad Ní Chróinín: It was a labour of love that began in 2007 when we first began to think seriously about producing a show in Irish. And the main catalyst for this was that in 2007 an EU regulation came into force that granted Irish the status of the 21st official language of the European Union, which put it on a par with 'majority languages' like German, French, and so on. But of course we're not used to thinking of Irish as a 'majority' language, so for us this new status prompted the question: what does it mean for Irish to be at the same level as other European 'first languages'? Does it challenge our preconceptions of Irish, which are often of a language that is old-fashioned, not suited to the themes of today, difficult to present work in because it makes us think in certain ways, only allows us to tell certain stories, and, most importantly, doesn't allow us to communicate directly with the same number of spectators?

With this in mind we wondered if we could tackle the perceived 'limited' scope of themes and stories that could be told through Irish by presenting a European classic through Irish. European classics have been produced in many different languages all over the world; they have shown that they transcend translation to become relevant to all sorts of different times and societies. To push the question of whether *Irish could really be a language of modern Europe we decided to produce an Irish-language translation of a classic along the lines of the revivals of Chekhov and Ibsen that we had seen coming out of mainland Europe in recent years – productions that moved beyond 'period' approaches, and made the themes relevant and challenging to their modern audiences. We were thinking along the lines of productions like Thomas Ostermeier's *A Doll's House* and *Hedda Gabler*,[3] and Kretakor's *The Seagull*.[4]

3 *Namhaid don Phobal* [*An Enemy of the People*], **Moonfish Theatre 2006, directed by Máiréad Ní Chróinín: Brendan Conroy (Dr Stockmann), Padraic Ó Tuairisc (Aslasken), Dara Ó Dubháin (Hovstad). Courtesy of Moonfish Theatre.**

As I discovered once I started to research the translation of classics into Irish, the question we were trying to interrogate with our production was actually a question that had been asked decades ago, during the period of the Gaelic Revival. From the beginning of the project of a national Irish theatre, people asked the question what role Irish should have in Irish theatre. Should the primary focus be on promoting the language through theatre, or should the primary focus be on promoting theatre through the language? It is a fascinating question, and the debates that happened in the Abbey, the Gate and Taibhdhearc na Gaillimhe – which was for a time directed by Mícheál MacLiammóir of the Gate, who had excellent Irish – are all debates we could still have about the relationship between theatre, national identity, and language.

Personally, I have sympathy for the views of Liam Ó Brian, one of the original members of the board of Taibhdhearc na Gaillimhe, and of Mícheál MacLiammóir, both of whom saw Irish-language theatre as an opportunity to further the art form of theatre, as opposed to using theatre to simply promote the Irish language. According to Pádraig Ó Siadhail, in his *Stair Dhrdmaiocht na Gaeilge*, MacLiammóir and Ó Brian felt that by putting examples of the classic European plays on stage through Irish, for the benefit of the general public and, particularly, for the benefit of potential playwrights, they would encourage the highest standards in writing and reviewing, which would, in turn, place Irish-language theatre on the same footing as European theatre. Their purpose then, in staging translations of European work in Irish was first and foremost to put *the best* plays on stage in Irish, be they original Irish-language works or works from abroad, and in this way to set the standard for theatre in Irish.

This was not too far removed from MacLiammóir and Hilton Edwards's project with the Gate Theatre, which was set up in reaction to the perceived insular programming of the Abbey at the time. MacLiammóir and Edwards argued that Ireland must be outward-looking and open to the influence of the wider world, and so the Gate produced translations of leading European playwrights such as Ibsen, Chekhov, and Strindberg.

For me, the question of Ireland's openness to outside influences, in particular the influences in Europe, remains open. So it is interesting to think beyond this particular project, to wonder if there is a role for Irish in mediating between Europe and Ireland. I think it is notable so far that theatre from Ireland, when it tours internationally, tends to tour to countries like the US, the UK, and Australia and that, I think, is directly linked to the fact that we are linked linguistically – through English – to these countries. Of course we could tour theatre in English to countries where English is not the main language, but we do not tend to. So Irish theatre is not in constant dialogue with mainland Europe as matters stand. At a symposium the Dublin Theatre Festival held just this year on how Irish theatre might 'break into' the European scene, one of the questions the European promoters there from Germany and Finland asked was: 'Where is the theatre in the Irish language, why do we never get theatre in Irish?'. But what they want is not *Playboy of the Western World* in Irish, or a version of *Diarmuid and Gráinne*, or even Ibsen in Irish. What they want is contemporary new productions in Irish that are aware of, and respond to, the styles and themes of contemporary European theatre.

That is the challenge that we saw when we first started thinking about this project, and which we tried to address by creating an Irish-language version of Ibsen that responded to contemporary European directorial re-interpretations of the classics. We aimed at a successful production that would showcase Ibsen's brilliant play. But a more long-term result we hoped to achieve was to show that Irish-language theatre can be contemporary and can reach out to audiences beyond fluent Irish speakers, and, like MacLiammóir and Ó Brian, to give potential playwrights the possibility of seeing a classic through Irish.

But to come back to Ibsen, I think it is significant that the first Irish-language translation staged in the Gate, and later in Taibhdhearc na Gaillimhe, was *Peer Gynt,* and that almost a century later we again found ourselves looking to Ibsen for a story from the European canon that resonates in Ireland, and that allows us to stage *the best* of theatre in Irish.

Irina Ruppo Malone: But why this particular play?

Máiréad Ní Chróinín: When we were thinking of doing a classic play through Irish I went looking at the catalogue of the archives of Taibhdhearc na Gaillimhe. I came across the name of Henrik Ibsen, a playwright I admire greatly, and a play I did not recognize – *Namhaid don Phobal – An Enemy of the People.* I was curious, and I happened to find a copy of the English language translation by Christopher Hampton, which was produced in London in 1997, so that is the version I read first in 2007.[5]

At the time Galway had just come out the other end of the cryptosporidium water crisis, so the play spoke to me on a very local and immediate level. But by the time we came to produce the show, in 2009, events had overtaken us, and the play had taken on wider resonances with the implosion of the Celtic Tiger, which exposed to many people just how much the 'boom' had been built on unethical and unscrupulous activity – as the Doctor says *'tá saol ár bpobal suite ar talamh atá truaillithe le bréig'* [our public life is resting on land that is polluted by lies]. Not only that but the gaps exposed by the sudden lack of public funds called into question, to my mind, our values as a society during the boom times. It seemed that, in its pursuit of riches, people had chosen the wealth over the health of society. And the figure of the Doctor, in this context, reminded me of the people who had spoken out during the boom time, the Cassandras – like George Lee – who had been attacked and vilified for raining on the parade.

But of course Ibsen's genius is that he does not simply give us a black-and-white story of 'good Doctor' versus 'evil establishment'. The Doctor has right on his side, certainly, but he is also vain, jealous of his brother's status in the town, and dismissive of other people's intelligence. He is right to be worried about the health threat to the town, but he does not appreciate that the threat to the town's economy is also a valid concern.

So despite the anger he might have felt after *Ghosts* (and which prompted the writing of *An Enemy of the People*) it seems to me that Ibsen looks beyond his own personal opinions and tries to capture the paradox between the loud, uncompromising, campaigning voice that is such a powerful political tool, and the voice of the constant complainer, the haranguer, that people just either tune out or turn against.

There is one more reason why I felt that the play would resonate particularly well in an Irish context, and that is to do with the private side of the play – the relationship between the two brothers. There is nothing more Irish, I think, than a story of families falling out over little slights that slowly gather until one day there's a fight and one side of the family never speaks to the other again. I do not know how often it has been depicted in Irish plays, but it is certainly a story that many people have in their families.

What makes the play so powerful is Ibsen's understanding of human psychology – that whatever the ideals we profess, ultimately we are also motivated by our relationships with the individuals around us, so that in fact it is impossible to 'unweave' the public from the private.

Pat Burke: It is a pity that the whole question of drama in Irish remains a closed book to so many people. A former colleague of mine, Alan Titley, wrote a sequel to *Waiting for Godot* called, *Tagann Godot*, (in which Godot turns up)[6] ... Speaking in terms of your future planning or current policy, what would you see as criteria for choosing another translation or another classic?

Máiréad Ní Chróinín: We would probably be very interested in doing something that is more contemporary, possibly something that is not just a translation of a script but is in itself devised through Irish. That is how we are thinking at the moment, but we don't really have clear, definite ideas. Originally, I planned to stage a trilogy of classic plays translated into Irish: Ibsen, Shaw, and Brecht, drawing from Taibhdhearc na Gaillimhe. But we moved away from that, pretty much because it was such a mammoth undertaking to do the Ibsen in the first place, so to do the trilogy would take an awful lot of time. And in the end translation probably is not what we are going to be focusing on.

Pat Burke: Have you any writers?

Máiréad Ní Chróinín: We do not, and that is one of the things we would like to find: writers working through Irish. We are particularly interested in working with playwrights who are interested in exploring ways of using Irish.

Irina Ruppo Malone: There have been several points made during this conference about the Hibernization of Ibsen and the problems incurred when plays travel from language to language. Do you think this Hibernization is more apparent in the English-language than the Irish-language translations of Ibsen?

Máiréad Ní Chróinín: I noticed a marked difference between how one perceives Gearóid Ó Lochlainn's translation and a version by an English playwright, Christopher Hampton, which was produced in 1997 in London. Irish has not changed as much as English has. When you read Hampton's translation you are very much aware that you are reading old-fashioned English. It sounds strange and very unwieldy sometimes; it certainly does not sound like a contemporary text. When you read the Irish translation, you do have a more modern feeling. Possibly because you cannot really shorten Irish, you have to say the whole sentence, and that does not sound wrong or unmodern to an Irish speaker.

Irina Ruppo Malone: You mentioned that there were large parts you had to cut. Could you comment on that?

Máiréad Ní Chróinín: We were working with the old translation carried out by Gearóid Ó Lochlainn for Taibhdhearc na Gaillimhe, which I think was the one that was produced at the Gate as well. Gearóid Ó Lochlainn had translated it directly from Norwegian into Irish, and we really liked the idea of working with the script that had not gone through the medium of English, that had not been translated and re-translated. I would probably not do that again, because you do underestimate the amount that language has changed. The play originally was produced in 1932.

4 *Namhaid don Phobal* [*An Enemy of the People*], **Moonfish Theatre 2006: Brendan Conroy (Dr Stockmann), Séamus Ó hAodha (Billing), Peadar Ó Treasaigh (Mortan Cíl), Dara Ó Dubháin (Hovstad) Courtesy of Moonfish Theatre.**

The translation is a three and a half hour play, and we wanted to bring it down to two and a half hours. We did find that there were some characters we did not want to include, such as the two Stockmann sons. There is also one scene with the journalist and Petra which we felt could be removed without doing too much damage to the story line of the play. We also cut some of the doctor's argument, which is really long and reflects the ideas of Ibsen's time. Stockmann makes a strong argument which is almost Darwinian that we also cut. Even though it is an interesting argument in the sense that it reveals something about the doctor, we felt that in the context of society now and our understanding of science it would maybe make people have a stronger reaction against the doctor than Ibsen had intended. He certainly intended the doctor making a scientific argument, but I am not quite sure that he would have meant it quite so negatively as we might interpret it today.

Irina Ruppo Malone: Could you tell us about the set?

Máiréad Ní Chróinín: We wanted a contemporary version. We wanted the play to reflect what was happening economically and socially. One of the images that really stuck in my mind while driving through Ireland was the amount of half-built places with scaffolding still up – half-finished projects that were abandoned when the economy ground to a halt. The idea that they were just standing at midpoint where things were frozen reminded me of the baths in *An Enemy of the People*. They are up and running at the start; they are a spanking new investment, yet if the doctor reveals what he is going to reveal everything will grind to a halt. That's the end of the economy; that's the end of the development of that town. We constructed the set which was a kind of a scaffolding model. Acts I, II, and III, set in the doctor's house, were on the ground floor. You had the printing press up above, for Act III, and then the ground floor was transformed into the house where the doctor makes his speech.

We were working with surtitles as well, which is something we wanted to try out in the context of European theatre being brought to Ireland. I see a lot of productions in the Dublin Theatre Festival or in opera where you see surtitles used with no questions asked. The surtitles allow Irish audiences to understand plays in languages they would not be familiar with, and I suppose our argument was that Irish audiences are not familiar with Irish, and there are many people who would like to see this play who might feel that they would not understand it all the time, if it was purely in Irish. So we decided to project surtitles. We used the upper tier of the set to project the surtitles onto. According to the audience feedback, it worked much better for act III, when the actors were also there. It

did not work so well when the actors were on the lower part of the
stage.

Irina Ruppo Malone: I remember a wonderful moment in Act IV
in the scene where the crowd attacks Stockman, at which stage the
cellophane cover of the set was lit in blue. There was almost a
folkloric feel to it, there seemed to be an echo of the troll scene in
Peer Gynt with the clamouring of the trolls. Was that intentional?

5 *Peer Gynt*, **translated by Arthur Riordan, Rough Magic Theatre
    Company, October 2011, directed by Lynne Parker: Fergal
    McElherron (Dark Self) Rory Nolan (Peer Gynt), Karen Ardiff
    (Aase/The Green Clad One), Peter Daly (Light Self). Photograph:
    Ros Kavanagh. Courtesy of Ros Kavanagh and Rough Magic.**

Máiréad Ní Chróinín: I did not have *Peer Gynt* in my mind. I
suppose it was a happy coincidence. I think it was born out of a need
to budget to a certain extent. We did not want to do a large-scale
production. This can be done if you plant people in the audience,
which then becomes a crowd and descends on the stage. We did not
want to do something which was so realistic an interpretation. We
wanted to go in the other direction: make the play theatrical and use
light and shadow.

Christopher Morash: It is worthwhile to remind ourselves of the
first Irish production of *Peer Gynt*. Micheál MacLiammóir, in his

autobiography, *All for Hecuba*, recalls how he and Edwards had at the Peacock theatre a stage not big enough to swing a cat, so they decided to throw caution to the wind and do *Peer Gynt*.[7] But that particular production was extremely influential, because what he did was a cyclorama that he lit with sky-blue light and two props that were shaped like stairs. They were valleys, mountains. Put them together, and they became a pyramid. And that idea that you could do a lot with a little was really the founding idea for the way that the Gate kicked off in those early years. [8]

Kurt Taroff: At this point I would like to put a question to Lynne, to ask her about Rough Magic's forthcoming production of *Peer Gynt*.

Lynne Parker: The thing you have to bear in mind is that we have not produced the show yet, so all I can describe is the intention or intentions behind the production and what ideas we have at present. If you come to see the show and it does not bear any resemblance, don't blame me; it's a work in progress. Listening to Grieg's music for *Peer Gynt* one Christmas, I just started thinking about the play; and that was a good few years ago. And this is a fascinating piece. But you never arrive at a production by just one route; there are always several ideas that kind of factor in.

I've always been quite interested in the Nordic psyche. We produced a Jon Fosse play a few years ago [*Dream of Autumn* in 2006] and introduced ourselves to contemporary Norwegian writing, but *Peer Gynt* is the great classic. Yet it is kind of vulgar; it does not bear any resemblance to Ibsen's other stuff which is all so clear and disciplined. *Peer Gynt* is a fantasia. Strictly speaking this is not a play but a dramatic epic poem. In order to catch the essence of it you have to deliver it in verse. And Arthur happens to bleed verse. You may have seen his musical play *Improbable Frequency* (2004) which is mostly in verse as well. But it is one thing to have a verse skill and another to marry that to a classic text. The first thing we did was commission a literal translation from Kari Dickson. Arthur has used the literal translation, working on chunks of the text, not necessarily all consecutively, so you'd be getting these big gaps in the middle, and now it's more or less ready to be joined up.

We have adopted a practice of developing productions through workshops and public presentations in the past few years. That certainly got *Improbable Frequency* off the ground. When you are dealing with something that is quite difficult, it is a really good idea to do these presentations in front of audiences, sometimes of friends, sometimes the wider public. You can gauge from their response how well you are doing. At the Theatre Festival last year we did a workshop. Loughlin Deegan, the director of the Dublin Theatre Festival came to see what work we had done. This was only a couple of days with some actors, and he thought it was very jolly indeed and encouraged us to do this piece as our presentation for the Dublin Theatre Festival last year. And the response was really terrific.

We were very keen that this work would have an Irish context as well as a Norwegian one, because there is so much connection between the cultures. Arthur has been working with a percussionist called Robbie Harris who is a genius Bodhran player; he made tracks for us with various rhythms. He does not just deal with Irish rhythms, but world rhythms. Robbie is very attuned to the music of North Africa, which is such a big location in the play as well. Robbie has been working in the workshops, playing with us and playing along with a saxophonist called Brendan Doyle. They had really been improvising; first Robbie would set down the rhythm, but Arthur was very conscious of Ibsen's rhythms, comparing his translation with the Norwegian original. Not that you know Norwegian, Arthur, but you could tell by looking at the original how close you were. And in fact the rhythms are quite similar

Arthur Riordan: Not all the passages. It's great to write against the rhythm. It reads very badly, because generally when you are speaking to a rhythm the last thing you want to have is each stressed syllable falling on the drum beat. This just kills it off, so having somebody play a rhythm there gives me a chance to syncopate.

Lynne Parker: So we divided the parts between six actors. There are so many parts like 'this boy', 'another boy', 'yet another boy'. They are not exactly characters, they are tones and voices. They are part of an orchestration, so whatever you end up doing in terms of characterization, it's really going to be almost song. The actors worked with the musicians for the first workshop, which consisted of readings. We actually just repeated that performance earlier this year when we did a presentation of work in progress as part of Rough Magic 25th birthday celebrations [4-5 April 2009]. And each time the response had been really positive.

Later in the summer, I felt that I needed some time to work out how I would actually present the play on stage. There were a few ideas that started to take root then. The strangest things influence you. For instance, I was struck with the self-obsessed character in *Synecdoche New York*. I hated the film, but it reminded me of Peer as well as the question of the self explored in the play. That threw off a few ideas.

Now Arthur had written an extraordinary piece a number of years ago which was based on Eamonn de Valera. It was called *The Emergency Session* (1992). It is a series of songs and one of them is a song called *Mé Féin*. This suggested to me an idea of treating the central theme of *Peer Gynt* in an Irish context. Not that we want to remove *Peer Gynt* from the Norwegian context, rather we need a way of fusing both cultures. So I got a bunch of actors again, and this time we did not concentrate so much on the musical side. We knew we could do that; we knew what our approach was. What I had to discover, though, was how to present the play in a way that makes sense of its non-naturalism. So there are two things that I tried, and one was a setting which was essentially a pub.

The whole play is almost like a night in a pub. It is a series of stories; it's not necessarily dialogue, although there is dialogue in it, but there are long descriptions and story-telling. You can almost imagine being part of a boozing night where people are singing songs, and each one catches the attention for a while. And that began to shine with an idea of a metaphor for the Irish condition. Sorry for the unavoidable cliché, but setting the play in a pub is a very Irish mechanism. Besides, we thought that this play, so often done as a vast epic with an enormous kind of staging, would benefit from a microcosm approach. The play would become an epic drinking session, where a character actually changes in the course of the night (as indeed I believe happens – and certainly there is an ageing process). So we got the actors and put them in a small box-like space and began to move them in abstract ways. In fact you get a lot of bang for your buck, if the space is small. A very little movement can go a very long way.

The second thing I tried was dividing Peer into three selves. This is often done with three actors playing young, middle-aged, and old Peer. But our approach is different. Peer is constantly pulled in both directions. One actor played Peer, with two more playing the good voice and the bad voice in his head. These two actors walked around like the heads on his shoulders. Sometimes they adopted different characters within the head; one would become the Boyg, for instance, while the other one might reveal the connection between Peer's good intentions and his feminine side.

6 *Peer Gynt,* **Rough Magic Theatre Company, October 2011, Sarah Greene (Solveig/Female Troll), Rory Nolan (Peer Gynt), Will O'Connell (Writer/ Troll), Hilary O'Shaughnessy – (Ingrid/Green-Clad One), Arthur Riordan (Mountain King). Photograph: Ros Kavanagh. Courtesy of Ros Kavanagh and Rough Magic.**

There are also three women, who were positioned just at the line with their arms folded. Being the elements of the pub, they became a chorus, a very funny one actually, with the shrill voice of the mother echoed by the beguiling voice of the girlfriend. Sometimes they would be speaking in chorus. Choral work may be wonderfully sombre and melancholy, but when you speed it up it is very amusing. I got this idea from seeing a show by the Volksbühne Berlin earlier this year in which a woman was followed by a chorus of fifteen other women, all of whom are voices in her head. They kept bothering her, she kept screaming at them, and they were screaming back at great speed.

Some of the ideas we have now might be completely wiped out in the end. However, what we are planning to do now is create a bar as a central stage icon image; around this small area, there would be an imaginary world. Peer is such a fantasist, he needs space to go off and indulge in this epic journey. In the space around the bar, we could get a mixture of mechanical and possibly projected filmic images. Actors would be able to get outside the pub and move within that limbo-land. We have a couple of designers who are working on ideas for that, but it has not taken any real form yet.

I saw a very impressive *Peer Gynt* co-produced by the Dundee Rep and the National Theatre of Scotland.[9] That was a really successful show that was transferred to the Barbican. They also staged it as a descent into alcoholism (again it is a very Scottish story), but they did it in an epic way. They had a whole society built around it, including fabulous trolls. We have something different in mind. I think our production is going to be more about the psychological journey, which is the real fascination of the play. Besides, Ibsen seems to have his finger on exactly what's going on at the minute in the Irish economy and Irish political life. So we will give it a contemporary context, and there is plenty of room to manoeuvre there. Take the whole notion of trolls – there are plenty of those walking around. Also quite Irish is the idea of the guy with a rural past who gets ahead of himself, is a bit of a scamp and a scoundrel, and then starts to travel the world and get ideas well above his station, and suddenly comes to face himself in his later years.

Arthur Riordan: Also pretentiously self-justifying it.

Kurt Taroff: On the issue of translation and textual interpretation, could you comment on the troll king explanation of the difference between the men's motto and the trolls' motto: 'å være seg selv-nok'.

Arthur Riordan: The standard translation of the phrase is an elegant 'to thyself be true enough' which is I think quite close to the Norwegian. What I went for to give it an Irish flavour is 'be yourself, sure'.

Kurt Taroff: What do you think this encapsulates in the play for Peer?

Arthur Riordan: I think Ibsen cleverly always skirts around the notion of the self rather than attacking it directly. It is introduced by the trolls. Obviously their version is a skewed version of being yourself, and they are wrong. So I suppose the best way to approach it is in the trollish sense which is be yourself, be selfish and that's no more, rather than being fully rounded, rather than trying to achieve your full potential. Be just what you are and not what you could be.

Kurt Taroff: That's what the trolls are saying?

Arthur Riordan: That's what the trolls are saying: be what you are instead of fulfilling your potential. This constant banter you hear in all Reality TV, how 'at the end of the day you have to be yourself'. This is used exactly the way it is used in *Peer Gynt*, as a licence and justification for the most knuckleheaded things you can think of doing. So it is a very twenty-first-century notion – the Gyntian self.

Lynne Parker: Absolutely. There are plenty of parallels that we can push here with the celebrity culture, and the X Factor generation. We are aiming to produce the show within the next two years, hopefully next year, but we have a bit more investigation to do of the play itself and what form it is going to take. We need to gauge the scale of production, so we can budget. We are also very interested in the musical side of it. Robbie has been working with rhythm at the minute, but there also needs to be a melodic input. Robbie also works with the fascinating band called Tarab, an Irish Arabic fusion band. As so much of the play happens in Africa, we would love to work with them to see how that musical influence would affect the story-telling. The other missing component is Norwegian musicians. I had the pleasure of going to a Norwegian traditional band a few weeks ago. To me they sounded so Irish. There are really strong parallels and similarities, there have just got to be more connections there; that's as much as we can say for the moment.

Kurt Taroff: Your translation features rhyming couplets.

Arthur Riordan: Really it just happened, I don't know what percentage. As I progressed, there were more and more abab couplets, and I was trying to fit as many feminine rhymes as I could to give it that flavour. I thought that Ibsen's own rhyming scheme and metre are loose enough, so I could allow myself some licence, and I tried to stay pretty close to the sense of it.

7 *Peer Gynt,* Rough Magic Theatre Company, October 2011:
Fergal McElherron (Dark Self/The Devil).

Lynne Parker: Another time the rhythms change within speeches, you get a variation, and it's part of the fun of it as well. And it is seriously enhanced when you have the Bodhran working with it as well, and the music.

Kurt Taroff: It seems to be having that effect already of getting you to a place where the rhythm becomes natural at some point, and then, once you have it, you can let it go and see where the production takes it.

Lynne Parker: Yes. Some of the pieces are much more lyrical than others; some of them are really rhythm driven; some of them are almost like rap; and then there are much more melodic lyrical passages as well, depending on the mood and situation.

Kurt Taroff: One of the things I find interesting about staging *Peer Gynt* was that Ibsen did not initially think about it as either stageable or as something that he wanted to stage. I always found that Ibsen imagined his readers staging the play in their minds like a romantic closet drama sort of way, and that becomes one of the major obstacles to staging it. How you are going to stage this massive epic? Are you intending to make cuts to the playscript, and if so what would be your motivations?

Lynne Parker: We have not cut anything yet. Arthur's translation is based on everything that Ibsen wrote.

Arthur Riordan: I believed it was necessary to go through the whole thing first and work out myself what each line was. My next step, if I have the luxury of having the time to do it, would be almost to try and re-write all that I have done, almost from memory, just to see what stands out as important, just as a way of seeing what might be cut.

Lynne Parker: It is a seriously weird work, and we don't know enough about it yet to make those decisions. We have to find out more about it, we have to do this forensic science. You would not presume to cut things without really understanding why Ibsen loved it, so we cannot be cavalier about it.

Kurt Taroff: One of the things we were talking about today is that there is an image of Ibsen. If you ask an average playgoer what sort of plays Ibsen wrote you are very likely to hear that he produced realistic, political plays. You are less likely to hear about the much more mythical Norwegian Ibsen. You mentioned earlier that you saw echoes in the Irish context within that mythical facet of the play, so I wonder if you could talk about that.

Arthur Riordan: I was in a gym a couple of weeks ago and saw an Irish politician who has not distinguished himself unusually, except that his career has been a litany of colourful and easily avoided disasters. I saw him in the dressing room in the gym – stark naked, holding court – fabulous. And it struck me as, well, if not Peer Gynt, well then a troll. What's so attractive about Peer is that he goes from one apocalyptic disaster to the next and justifies it to himself and works out that this was for the best after all. This is just what I saw in this TD, the same unembarassability for the start, but a sort of indestructibility as well.

Lynne Parker: I think the idea of going around something is so Irish. That's exactly why we are in a mess; we keep going around the problem, never facing it head on. So I think there is plenty of work we can do with the whole idea. The idea of the troll as well is a fascinating one: something that looks human but is not quite, you can just tell by the tail. The whole subculture of the trolls and their court, which is a super-culture really; there are obvious parallels to, yes, Fianna Fail, but not just them.

Arthur Riordan: Also those passages of the play which deal with parochialism born out of the turn-of-the-century nationalist revival offer obvious parallels to Ireland. And it's quite easy to highlight them.

Lynne Parker: It could be so attractive to set it at the Shelbourne Hotel, where so many of these deals are made, and so many lives get pissed down the toilet. The idea of using a political satire is quite attractive. Again there is more research that we need to do. We need to explore who Ibsen was satirizing in these characters. You really feel that these are portraits, and parallels could easily be done in images such as the one Arthur just brought up.

Irina Ruppo Malone: Have you had a chance to look at other politicized productions of the play?

Lynne Parker: It is funny for a play that has so many challenges, *Peer Gynt* is done very often. I saw a production in Scotland and the very successful Icelandic one which seemed to have been set in an operating theatre, using an abstract idea. It was quite a small set in contrast to the Dundee Rep epic scale production with big scaffolding and a rock band. I suppose part of you is aware of the productions, but part of you does not want to see them. You do not want to be unduly influenced.

In June 2011, Lynne Parker supplied the following addendum on the state of the production which allows further insight into the development of the Rough Magic Peer Gynt *(Dublin, 27 September – 16 October 2011).*

Lynne Parker: Over a year has passed since that conversation took place and our ideas have moved on considerably. We now have firm dates for the Dublin Theatre Festival this year, so the production is really starting to take shape.

The more time you spend with a text the more you get down to the fundamental questions. Why is this story told in this way? What is the function of the verse? What world do we need to create?

Some ideas we hold on to, some have been jettisoned. The idea of setting the piece in a pub became increasingly limiting. Even metaphorically, the night-long drinking odyssey doesn't offer the scope needed for this cosmic piece. It became clear that it is a dream-play within a surreal universe and I tried looking at it through the prism of memory; and then it started to acquire a certain logic. The musical nature of the verse and the fantastical elements of the story are clearly drawn from the landscape and mythology of Ibsen's childhood, which can be read as a psychological state from which his protagonist seems unable to escape. It struck me that we should see the whole thing as a cyclical, rather than linear narrative, and that we should join Peer at the end of his story, as an old man. But in the opening seconds of the performance something should happen to trigger his memory and take him right back to the beginning, to his youth. One of our designers had been talking about a documentary he was making about Irish mental asylums. I realized that the perfect setting for this story was a large room in a modern mental institution, not a threatening or grim environment, but somewhere serene, apparently safe. The intrusion into this supposed sanctuary of psychological demons and the tricks of memory, in their most surreal form, is therefore logical, understandable, and terrifyingly limitless.

The music can be seen as one of those tricks of the mind, the fairytale rhymes of childhood returning to torment and seduce their victim; so Peer the escapologist extraordinaire is forever entangled by the fantasies that have been his refuge. The music ensemble I mentioned, Tarab, have now become a crucial part of the production. Their superb blend of Irish and Arabic traditional melody sits perfectly with the long, bejewelled passages of Ibsen's verse, particularly of course, in Act IV. In the end we felt that the mix was rich enough, and that to add Norwegian musical motifs was something we could do for fun but that did not have to be part of the strategic scoring. What had been a purely percussive score was now infused with melody and myriad colours, and the actors are now able to take energy from the music as well as the text. The music also forms the basis of the key theme of the play, the seductive quality of the imagination, which leads to fantasy and delight, but also to delusion and paranoia.

One idea we have retained is the three-sided Peer (a mischievous reference to the three-headed trolls in Act II). The plan is to have a central Peer who takes us through the play from youth to old age, but accompanied by his alter egos, Angel and Demon, who are both himself. This split of the Self seems to offer many possibilities to explore Ibsen's theme. And it gives us some very entertaining performance strategies, where the two alter egos converse with Peer by joining in his speech and thought processes, and vie with each other for control of his impulses.

I was encouraged to learn, when I visited the Ibsen Museum in Oslo, that Ibsen regarded a company of eight as the perfect size, because that is exactly what we have. So three of the actors are Peer. Of the others, two male actors play the people who refuse to leave Peer's memory, the self-contained man who cuts his finger off to avoid enlistment, and the Aslak figure, the bully who is always at his shoulder, in whatever manifestation. The three female actors take on the women in his life, the Mother, the True Love and the Abandoned Lover, virgin, whore, witch, harpy, nurse, etc. But, for example, the same actress will play both mother and seductress, just to make sure that the ambiguities are sustained. And all of these characters, who are also inmates and workers in the asylum, mutate into new entities onto whom he projects his memories.

On my trip to Oslo – kindly sponsored by the Norwegian Embassy – I met with a number of highly informed academics and dramaturges. They assured me that there are no rules to Ibsen and to *Peer Gynt* in particular, and that the only thing I needed to guard safely was that vital ambiguity, right up to and including the ending.

So, some distance has been travelled. But we have not yet started rehearsals. That's when the real journey, which in our case has a very linear progression to opening night (and then almost certainly in a cyclical pattern, to the pub) will begin.

---

[1] Henrik Ibsen, *Peer Gynt*, trans. Arthur Riordan.
[2] Henrik Ibsen, *Namhaid Don Phobal* [*Enemy of the* People], trans. Gearóid Ó Lochlainn (Dublin: Oifig an tSolathair, 1947): 10.
[3] Thomas Ostermeir's *Nora* [*A Doll's House*] was first produced at the Schaubühne in November 2002; Ostermeir's *Hedda Gabler* was produced at the Schaubühne in October 2005; *Hedda Gabler* featured in the Dublin Theatre Festival International in 2006.
[4] Kretakor Theatre took part in the Ulster Bank Theatre Festival in 2007; *The Seagull* was first premièred in 2003 and was directed by Árpád Schilling.
[5] Henrik Ibsen, *An Enemy of the People*, trans. Christopher Hampton (London: Faber, 1997).
[6] Alan Titley, *Tagann Godot: Coiméide Thraigeídeach Dhá Ghníomh* (Dublin: An Clochomhar Tta, 1991).
[7] See Mícheál MacLiammóir, *All for Hecuba: an Irish Theatrical Autobiography* (London: Methuen, 1947): 65-69.
[8] For a detailed account of this production and its reception see Irina Ruppo Malone, 'Ibsen and the Irish Free State: The Gate Theatre Productions of *Peer Gynt*', *Irish University Review* 39:1 (Spring-Summer 2009), 42-64.
[9] Directed by Dominic Hill, using a translation by Colin Teevan, premièred on 24 September – 13 October 2007, on tour in the UK 30 April – 27 June 2008.

CHEKHOV IN IRELAND

1 | Making foreign theatre or making theatre foreign: Russian theatre in English.

Cynthia Marsh

At the festival of Russian theatre, 'Revolutions', initiated in Stratford-upon-Avon in August 2009,[1] two young representatives of the new drama in Russia, the Durnenkov brothers (Mikhail and Viacheslav) participated in a panel[2] on the contemporary arts scene in Russia. The brothers' play *The Drunks* [*Pianye*] had been commissioned by the Royal Shakespeare Company (RSC) for the festival. To the question whether or not the play would or could be staged in Russia, the brothers commented that the play would have to be readapted for Russian consumption from the version that was currently being staged in Stratford. Answers to other questions revealed that the play had gone through substantial changes in the process of translation and modification for British staging. A subsequent private conversation with one of the translators working on the commissions revealed that this process of translation and adaptation was still operating during the runs of the plays themselves. This practice is common in British theatre for most new plays, as seen in the variations between fast-published scripts and their subsequent editions.

From further discussion on the panel it became clear that the establishment theatre in Russia does not know how to deal with the 'new drama' and is therefore very unlikely to stage it; that there are very few 'fringe' theatres in Russia; and that student groups though often interesting for their experimentalism have so far only staged the Durnenkovs' plays badly, and sometimes only in far-flung places (Kazan' was cited). So the accolade of performance in Stratford-upon-Avon, one of the great theatrical centres of the West, was an opportunity not to be lost for the Durnenkov brothers, however ferocious the changes. They were also speaking from the august stage of the Courtyard Theatre, currently central to all theatrical activity in Stratford during the re-building of the main house, and perhaps felt it might be discourteous to speak any more openly than they had. However, there is significant material to unpack here for the topic of staging foreign theatre in Britain.

This issue is about choices, and raising awareness of those choices, when a play is transposed from one culture to another through the medium of translation. The first part of the title of this contribution to the debate is an attempt to encapsulate the key choice: making foreign theatre or making theatre foreign. It impinges on the type of choice made by the initiators of a production, who can be any one or two of a complete chain of people or institutions. Let us say to begin with perhaps a translator and adaptor, working with a theatre and/or a potential director. Is the aim of the production to make a piece of foreign theatre intelligible to an English-speaking audience or is it to diversify repertoire by performing foreign dramatists? In fact by asking only these two questions it is quickly evident that it is almost impossible to pin down any rationales for this process of enabling theatre to migrate.

The examples of Ibsen and Chekhov present special conditions in themselves. Both dramatists are frequently present in Irish and British repertoires. For Chekhov (where I have access to the original language) audiences seem quickly to forget, unless reminded, that these plays were not written in English; while for Ibsen I suspect I might do the same, as I know nothing of Norwegian. We are not dealing with living writers here, but what pulls me up sharply are the experiences articulated by the Durnenkovs with regard to the fate of their text in migration, and the realization that this is happening to every text in migration. The last thing I would wish to do is to set an agenda for the migrating text. However, I would like to note some of the shaping processes to which the migrating text is subject, from the points of view of modern translation theory, modern directing and design practice, modern marketing, and review responses. There is also a further issue latent in the title, especially apposite to the topic of Ibsen and Chekhov in Ireland: 'Russian theatre in English'. The word 'English' was used without further modification. The meaning of 'English' is a central issue too. There are many Englishes, each with its own cultural baggage and expectations, which must affect every stage, every turn of the migrating text towards its destination reception.

Jatinder Verma is founder and artistic director of Tara Arts, a company dedicated to the development and exploration of British Asian theatre. A defining feature of Tara Arts productions is their use of texts from the scripted theatre of cultures other than the domestic British. Among his productions is an adaptation of Gogol's *The Government Inspector*. Not only did Tara Arts reset their *Government Inspector* of 1990 to 'a tin pot town in India' but 'using traditional Eastern performance forms' they imported 'a bizarre mix of English and Indian quotations from sources as diverse as Shakespeare, Kipling, Tennyson and Eliot'.[3] Verma called his approach 'Binglish', a gloss on the term Singlish for Singaporean English.[4] He uses this term to capture the ambivalence of Asian and black life in modern Britain which is regarded as 'not quite English', but at the same time striving to 'be English' in his words (194). His theatre in this respect is a challenge to the unthinking conventions of the British English stage. Perhaps developing a term 'Tringlish' to accommodate English translated from other cultures might prove useful? Translated English raises many issues, and one of our aims is to alert practitioners and spectators alike to its distinctive properties. But even that will not get at the essential differences that must exist between Chekhov or Ibsen translated for example into Irish and British, or even English English. And yet we all claim access to the vehicle of English.

From the point of view of translation theory, and to simplify the discussion, I have identified three different approaches with, admittedly, many variations. In the field of drama translation, I would categorize these as collision, hybridization and acculturation. These categories have been adopted for the sake of convenience and to bring some structure to the observations to be made. They are not intended to be prescriptive. As they stand, each will produce a different type of translation and subsequent production, and will operate to degrees of intensity which are different in the translation process from that of production. Indeed, the infinite variety of production possibility often entails an overlapping of these three categories.

With collision, there is a deliberate attempt to allow the awareness of translation to remain uppermost, to allow the two cultures, the source and the host, each to enact their differences.[5] This approach is likely to be the least frequent of the three identified. It entails knowledge of the source culture; it entails careful research; it entails persuasion of the value and significance of difference; and it entails the fostering of a sense of alienation. All these aspects are either not easily attainable, or arguably off-putting to an audience, not only the arbiters of the production, but also the source of crucial revenue. At its best, the collision approach respects an 'ethics of difference' (as Lawrence Venuti defines it) [6] in that attention is paid to both sides of the cultural divide. However, when the agenda is to bring change to the domestic culture, on one level I might place Trevor Griffiths's *Cherry Orchard* (1977) in this category, except for a lingering sense of his appropriation of the text to domestic concerns which have little to do with the source context. At a more extreme level, Declan Donnellan's Cheek by Jowl production with Russian actors of *Three Sisters* (2007), utilizing surtitles in English, achieved a different form of collision, almost entirely enriching in its authenticity and difference.

The second approach is termed hybridization.[7] There is much discussion among translation theorists themselves as to what the term 'hybrid' implies, from the notion that all translations are by definition composite of two cultures (the source and the target) to the notion of the 'mutant' text which deliberately 'mimics the linguistic spontaneity of the target culture' (281). A broad definition might be that the hybrid text is the type of translation where a conscious effort is made to retain elements of the source culture, but to ensure explanatory aspects of the home culture are sufficiently present to smooth reception and understanding, so as to avoid a sense of alienation or collision as described in the first category above. The result is that the source culture is mapped on to recognizable aspects of the host culture in an honourable effort to increase accessibility. But frequently the result is only to mask or downplay the potency of the source culture, leading to a sense of appropriation. In drama with its additional 'texts' and the practitioners who achieve performance, sometimes explanation or accommodation is offered at the textual level of dialogue (using Russian names or a halfway house towards them), and sometimes at the level of design, in costume, sound effects or set design. The materialization of Moscow as a doll's house type model in the Olivier National Theatre production of *Three Sisters*, at least in the filmed version,[8] emphasized the British (probably not solely British) stereotype of Moscow as the exotic turrets of buildings, rather than the familiar and family-centred memories of the sisters. I also wondered if there is some lateral contamination from Ibsen here? Chekhov's play (1901) can be seen as an inverted contemporary response to Ibsen's drama of family dynamics in *A Doll's House* (1879).

Finally, there is acculturation: the source culture is tamed, the domestic host culture is inscribed into the text, and at the extreme the text may be utilized for domestic purposes. In some senses, acculturation begins with the notion of the 'mutant' mimicking extreme referred to just now. Much of Chekhov production in Britain might be said to fit this category, so domesticated have Chekhov's plays become. Many productions subscribe to existing British views on Chekhov and are mounted to ensure the continuation of the tradition, embedded frequently in drama school where Chekhov is the standard vehicle for training in the System developed by Konstantin Stanislavsky. In this type of production, a diva plays Madame Ranevskaia *(Cherry Orchard)*,[9] or three actual sisters play the three sisters.[10] Translocation of setting is the extreme in this approach: an example would be the Mustapha Matura's West Indian *Three Sisters*,[11] or Janet Suzman's *Cherry Orchard* set in South Africa,[12] or indeed a resetting to Ireland, a trend begun by Thomas Kilroy and his *Seagull*.[13]

Even before the adoption of these processes, the selection itself of texts is fraught with problems concerning canon and censorship. Both Ibsen and Chekhov have their histories with regard to these issues. Both are located firmly within the canon of foreign dramatists, central to British and Irish repertoires, and indeed probably internationally, and so likely to be selected. Other writers are subject to censorship; they are not firmly within the canon and so rarely performed. Chekhov is certainly guilty of having prevented many other Russian writers from gracing British stages; on the other hand, his works have inspired others to be performed (Turgenev), and inspired original British and Irish plays. And Ibsen, banned in the early years, has now had similar effects.

What makes the canon is a matter of much current debate. Just like the shapers of reception, the factors which construct canon are infinite and variable, depending on fashion, taste, politics, chance and much else. What is clear is the need to argue for greater recognition of these undoubted shapers by default of public taste in foreign theatre, and make the selectors aware of the criteria they may sometimes unwittingly be applying. Equally, however, subverting the canon can be a risky business especially in these commercially uncertain times. Sometimes, the censorship exerted by the canon may be for the valid reasons of inadequacy or absence of translation; at others, the plays may be inconvenient ethically or politically for the receiving culture, and so it is in the receiving culture's own interests to suppress them. As a result, perception of the foreign culture rests on relatively few texts which are recycled continually. The outcome is a reliance on a few tired stereotypes. It is not solely translators or adaptors or their texts which produce this site of restricted communication.

On a practical level, performance and reception of a drama text on a foreign stage obviously require a text accessible to the audience. However, when the process of *mise en scène* is begun, then the translated text must negotiate a whole new set of conditions. It is a commonplace of communication theory that words are the least effective modes of communication, and that it is the visual aspects such as body language, facial expression, and aural aspects such as vocal tone, pitch and intonation which affect how information is transmitted. Translated into theatrical terms these issues bring us to the processes of gesture, set design, costume and sound effects among many others: what kinds of choices are made here? What are the shapers? It is at least halfway to acceptability that an adaptor of a foreign text now works with a translator, often a native speaker, or at least a literal translation, but far less common for such expertise to be available to the design team. I would like to argue that it is here that the process of domestic inscription is at its most potent, whichever approach is used by the translator whether collision, hybridization or acculturation. These factors are rarely considered by translation theorists as such, who would tend to include drama translation under the broad genre of literary translation, which assumes readership rather than spectatorship. It should also be remembered that published play texts are targeted at the reader as much as at performance. While editing a script for publication, dramatists frequently elaborate beyond the script used in performance, or may incorporate details of the première staging in their scripts.

To return to the work of the practitioners, the design team and so on, in their respective areas: these are precisely the places where the respect for 'difference' might be at its most effective. However, these are the aspects of a production least likely to be recorded, especially given the short-run productions of drama prevalent in the British repertoire system. The reliance in these practical stages seems to be on widely accessible stereotypes, however much there may have been an attempt to avoid them in the translating and adapting work.

As an example, let us take seagulls. One of the best known plays in the Russian repertoire translated into English is Chekhov's *The Seagull*. The implied view in Chekhov's play is of a bird flying free, alone, over an inland lake, indifferent to human life, until it is shot down unnecessarily by human agency. A British audience (and perhaps an Irish one) brings quite a different view of this bird in coming to watch a performance. This wall plaque in a well-known seaside town for example is related to the same bird:

West Dorset District Council
SEAGULLS
Seagulls are encouraged into
the town by being fed.
They cause nuisance by noise,
excrement, ripping open refuse
sacks and can display
aggression for food.
PLEASE REFRAIN FROM
FEEDING THE GULLS [14]

or this emotive headline from the *Daily Mail* in 2006: 'Pensioner is left bloodied from attack by seagulls'.[15] These two examples perhaps sum up the stereotypical British view of this bird. It suggests that in many respects we would be better off without them and that many British could cheerfully shoot them. How does this affect the British response to Konstantin's killing of the bird?

A stereotype is a complicated form of representation. At first glance it would appear to be a very efficient method of cultural shorthand.[16] Representing seagulls to ourselves as vicious polluting creatures captures their unavoidable noisy presence at seaside sites but which, importantly, are themselves places of pleasure. However, it denies or represses seagulls' role in the natural order of things as creatures of sea and land, and oversimplifies their complex relationship with humans ranging between dependence on us for food to nuisance. At its heart the stereotype contains a paradox in foregrounding one view while at the same time concealing others. Problems arise when a stereotype or recognized symbol in one culture is transferred to another. In Russia, a much less seashore-based culture, the seagull is a creature of the wild; and, I might add, the seagull has also acquired a stereotypical function as the symbol of Russia's first internationally acclaimed theatre (the Moscow Art

Theatre) on the basis of Chekhov's play; in Britain seagulls are reviled. Such are the depths of 'difference' that texts must negotiate.

A strong counter argument might rely upon what the translation theorists define in Lawrence Venuti's words as the 'remainder' of the text in translation.[17] 'Remainder' refers to those aspects of the text so embedded in their cultural origins as to be thought impossible to translate at any level. Russian texts provide endless examples; they usually stimulate footnotes in editions of Russian plays for foreign consumption. They include names; quotation from the national literature, unlikely to be known abroad; [18] others might be behavioural: why does Ranevskaia in *The Cherry Orchard* at the moment of departure say 'Let's all sit for a moment';[19] and what is patchouli (Gaev with oblique reference to Iasha, Act I)? [20] As in these examples, they are not always directly verbal issues, but in their cultural difference imply 'othervoicedness' or some culturally unmediated moment of action. Here the director, adequately informed, or others in the design chain, can release those remaindered moments in the modes of the gestural, the visual, and the aural which most concern them, rather than the automatic recourse to the shorthand of stereotype. Retaining an element of the alien enhances the sense of other and respects the source culture. The 'remainder' can also be regarded as threatening, possibly even destabilizing to the domestic culture, and as such, strong grounds are sometimes found for denial of its existence.

Reviewers are the acknowledged barometers of a production. For better or for worse they bridge the gap between stage and public, in the English sense of that word (i.e. not simply audience). Where the given performance is of a foreign or translated text they give voice to common perceptions of other cultures. With some noble exceptions (for example, where a critic may be a specialist in the repertoire of a specific foreign culture), the majority especially in Britain displays a spectacular ignorance of specific foreign contexts. Their position is understandable; they are speaking to or for the majority who make up the readerships/spectatorships of their individual media channels or outputs. And acknowledgement of these target reader-, listener- or viewerships, is valuable in itself, since it produces the variety of different critical views we have access to, at least in Britain. However, what strikes me across these different reviews is again the prevalence of stereotype. The reviews tell us about perceptions of a production, particularly design, accent and other aural material. There is nothing new about this function of the review.

To identify examples of stereotype from British reviews of Chekhov, reviews of the 2001 production in Chichester of *Three Sisters*,[21] in Brian Friel's adaptation, directed by Loveday Ingram, were examined. *Theatre Record* reproduced eleven reviews from the major dailies all published within a couple of days of each other.[22] So narrow is the reference that you would quickly understand that Russia and Russians are 'gloomy',[23] prone to 'self-inflicted unhappiness',[24] and that the play is marked by its lack of action. [25] Paradoxically, while recycling these stereotypes of Russian culture, several reviewers also point to cultural confusion, another frequent theme in reviews of Chekhov's plays. Here, they home in on the Irish setting to the production, commenting on Natasha and the servants' Belfast brogue,[26] while noting a 'confusing' 'post-modern Japanese'[27] or 'Oriental'[28] touch to the design, also described as reminiscent of 'Chekhov's Scottish contemporary Charles Rennie Mackintosh'[29] and 'too demure, contained, English'.[30] By this time, confronted by this cultural soup, I wondered what newspaper readers, contemplating a first Chekhov, would make of the theatrical experience in front of them!

Finally, the material aspects, particularly the visual, of marketing foreign or translated theatre and their role as shapers of interpretations of a production and creation of general images of other cultures yield much more evidence. Nowhere is the stereotype more central perhaps than in advertising. Its shorthand is essential; its graphic imagery fundamental to communication; and its text, reduced to the sound bite, punches home to the reader. Advertising materials include posters, flyers, adverts, publicity shots and write-ups, and programmes. In the media, only the review offers any counter to this wealth of communicative material.

If some programmes for productions of Russian theatre in Britain are compared, then recurrent images are found. For example, a doll's house version of Moscow and its domes featured in Tolstoy's *Fruits of Enlightenment* (1979) and Gorky's *Philistines* (2007). There is the ubiquitous tree cliché. They proliferate on programmes for *The Cherry Orchard*: Aldwych (1989); RSC (1995); Sheffield Crucible (2007). One treatment was slightly more refreshing but in fact borrowed from another cliché, colour: if it is twentieth-century Russian, it must be red, as in Griffiths's *The Cherry Orchard* (Nottingham, 1977). Trees actually spread everywhere in marketing representations of Russia; as well as The Cherry Orchard, Three Sisters gets the trees treatment: Manchester Royal Exchange (1986) had silver birches on its front cover. Although there is a mention of silver birches in the text, the trees specific to the Prozorov garden are mentioned by name and include maples and firs.[31] In the wake of this arboreal treatment of Chekhov, we also find what might be referred to as the 'Chekhovization' of Gorky, perhaps to increase establishment appeal. The cover of the programme for the Peter Stein and Botho Straus production of Gorky's Summerfolk from Berlin which visited the National Theatre in 1977 is a vista of spindly birches; and for their in-house production of Summerfolk (1999), an arcadian photograph, taken by Leonid Andreev of two Russians lounging in a flower meadow, graces the programme cover.

Culturally different Englishes bring some relief: The Cherry Orchard (South Africa and Birmingham, 1997) is represented by a modern windmill in a South African landscape sparsely treed, and for the Three Sisters, set in the West Indies (2006), a frieze of cartoonish palm trees sets off the black sisters, elegantly costumed 1940s style. A final stereotype derives from the endless fascination of an alien alphabet, even if wrongly transliterated: Cheek by Jowl's 2007 programme for its British tour of Cymbeline and Three Sisters. (The programme emphasizes the Russian, with the name of the company transliterated as ЧИК БАЙ ДЖУЛ). In Britain and probably elsewhere Russian theatre has its own visual language, as these materials demonstrate, and a sign system within that language has developed, peculiar to Chekhov. It is probably possible to determine the targets of a production by reading these signs.

It is much harder to get at the aural aspects of a production. There is a whole discourse around accent, concerning range, appropriateness and so on. However, rarely are sound effects given similar attention. Fortunately, the BBC has various productions of Russian plays in its archives, and collection and analysis of them is the next stage of my research. For our present purposes, just think of the range of possibility here: not only, for example, is there frequent reference to contemporary song, operetta and musicals both Russian and non-Russian in Chekhov's plays themselves, but the habit of adding music to productions opens up the whole world of Russian music itself. What shapes the choices? What is the effect of these choices on perception? It may not in the end be possible to find much detailed material in this area, but my guess is that stereotype plays an equally potent role here too.

The conclusions in this research seem to be tending in a negative direction; this kind of analysis shows what a hazardous and slippery affair transposing plays is. Picking over the bones of stereotypes and marketing motives brings the observer up against the cynicism of the demands for commercial success. It also exhumes the skeletons in the cupboard of colonialism: appropriation of cultural difference, even cannibalism,[32] rather than a happy celebration of such distinctiveness. Trigorin's cynical repeated response when Shamraev first mentions and then produces from a cupboard the stuffed seagull in Chekhov's play is: 'Don't remember. (*Thinking about it.*) Don't remember!'[33] Did Chekhov himself perceive the vacuity of stage and theatre symbolism ending in a stereotype, and make a joke at his own expense as long ago as that?

To come full circle, some will say that the most important point is that the Durnenkovs' play *The Drunks* has received an airing in Britain, if not yet in Russia. And the RSC must be praised for its zealous enthusiasm for supporting young Russian dramatists. The performance was moving, but the text had been negotiated to that position in adaptation. I read an earlier version of the text in Russian (produced who knows at what stage!) which was marked by a cynical continuing intertext with Gogol's bureaucratic Russia; which was angry about the destructive prevalence of alcoholism in Russia; and which was angry about the effects of war (both Afghanistan and Chechnya) on the individual and their loss of roots in a Russia still struggling to survive itself. It was raw and lacerating. It seems to me the play had been manipulated through the common stereotypes of British views of Russian culture, high emotion, long-term suffering and individual despair, with the perhaps laudable aim of achieving understanding and acceptance. This fate of *The Drunks* can probably tell us a great deal about the existing reception of Chekhov, and I guess of Ibsen and the many other foreign dramatists in translation/adaptation on the British stage.

And to return also to the title: 'making foreign theatre' still stands at one end of the spectrum, and translated theatre is a very welcome and important addition to any national repertoire, but it is, perhaps surprisingly, the least challenging mode. 'Making theatre foreign' is an important issue further along the scale from collision, engaging with hybridization and acculturation to different degrees. It can mean the foreign text is utilized to displace a dominant use of the

British English of existing translations, as the Irish and American examples remind us. Importantly, this aspect also teaches us to be aware of how we react to other cultures. The 'remainder' of the source culture can be a rich source of access to it; paradoxically, it can also remind us of the dangers of colonialism and cannibalism, which the Irish, American and other examples seek to attack, but in so doing they in fact adopt precisely the methods they decry.

---

[1] The Festival is set to evolve over four years from 2009 and is the inspiration of the Royal Shakespeare Company artistic director, Michael Boyd.

[2] One of a series of public 'brunch sessions', this panel took place on 20 September 2009.

[3] Nick Curtis, *Time Out*, 28 March 1990 (*Theatre Record*, 12-25 March 1990: 397).

[4] Jatinder Verma, 'The Challenge of Binglish: Analysing Multi-Cultural Productions', *Analysing Performance,* ed. Patrick Campbell (Manchester University Press, 1996): 193-202. This composite term also reminds one of 'Bollywood', the colloquial name for the massive Indian film industry dedicated to turning out hundreds of films annually in a popular Asian style with all the glamour of an erstwhile Hollywood.

[5] See Cynthia Marsh, 'Whose Text is it Anyway? On Translating and Directing Gorky's *Egor Bulychev'*, *Drama Translation and Theatre Practice,* eds Sabine Coelsch-Foisner and Holger Klein (Frankfurt: Peter Lang, 2004): 137-49.

[6] Lawrence Venuti, *The Scandals of Translation: Towards an Ethics of Difference* [1998] (London and New York: Routledge, 2003): 82-83, refers to a translation project following an ethics of difference.

[7] The debate about the hybrid text was focused on in *Across Languages and Cultures*, 2. 2 (2001) (Budapest: Akademiai Kiado, 2000-). The concluding article, Christina Schäffner and Beverley Adab, 'The Idea of the Hybrid Text in Translation Revisited': 277-302, outlines the diversity and complexity of the issues.

[8] *The Three Sisters*, National Theatre Company of Great Britain production, directed by Laurence Olivier, trans. Moura Budberg (Alan Clore Films, 1970).

[9] Any number of 'Cherry Orchards' have proceeded along this path. The result is that the stardom or diva-status, its centrality, is transferred to Ranevskaia herself, producing a particular and perhaps predictable reading of this play.

[10] Among examples are those of some famous theatre dynasties, the Redgraves (Queen's Theatre, London, 1990) and the Cusack sisters (Royal Court, and the Gate, Dublin, 1990).

[11] For example, Nottingham Playhouse staged Mustapha Matura's version of *Three Sisters* (*after Chekhov)* in 2006 on its tour round

England, not the whole of the UK. The action was relocated to the West Indies; the period was changed to the second world war; the characters' names were changed, as were their status, professions where applicable, and so on.

12 Janet Suzman's up-front, free adaptation of an adaptation by Roger Martin, staged at the Market Theatre, Johannesburg and called: *The Free state: A South African response to Chekhov's The Cherry Orchard* (1995), was staged at Birmingham Rep, in 1997.

13 Thomas Kilroy, *The Seagull*, 1981, adapted for the Royal Court Theatre (London: Eyre Methuen, 1981).

14 Lyme Regis Town Council, prominently displayed in several places along the promenade.

15 Luke Sakeld, *Daily Mail*, 28 June 2006: 7.

16 Michael Pickering, *Stereotyping: The Politics of Representation* (Basingstoke: Palgrave, 2001) provides a helpful study of this complex area which covers a number of disciplines.

17 Venuti, 10, and in passing.

18 Quotation may also have particular functions beyond textual reference, especially in a dramatist such as Chekhov alive to the minutiae of theatricality: see Cynthia Marsh, 'The Implications of Quotation in Performance: Masha's Lines from Pushkin in Chekhov's *Three Sisters*', *Slavonic and East European Review*, 44.3 (2006): 446-459.

19 Ranevskaia: 'Let's all sit for a moment' (I posizhy eshche odnu minutu) Act IV. Translation from Laurence Senelick, *Anton Chekhov: The Complete Plays*, (Norton, 2006), 1041. His footnote (n70) locates the basis of this remark in the old Russian custom of sitting for a moment before embarking on a journey.

20 Gaev: 'It smells of cheap perfume in here', *The Cherry Orchard* Act I (A zdes' pachuliami pakhnet). Senelick has omitted the reference to 'patchouli' in favour of 'cheap perfume', and added a footnote that 'patchouli', made from an Asian plant, is a perfume prized in the East but disliked in the West (989). Only by association do we discover that it is Iasha who is wearing it, and it becomes a hallmark of Gaev's distaste for him.

21 Chichester Festival Theatre, 26 August-29 September 2001.

22 *Theatre Record*, 27 August – 8 September 2001: 1103-06.

23 Patrick Marmion, *Evening Standard*, ibid., 1104; Simon Edge, *Express*, ibid., 1105.

24 Brian Logan, *Guardian*, ibid., 1106.

25 Charles Spencer, *Daily Telegraph*, ibid. 1103; Georgina Brown, *Mail on Sunday*, ibid., 1106.

26 Spencer, ibid., 1104; Michael Coveney, *Daily Mail*, ibid., 1104; Susannah Clapp, *Observer*, ibid., 1105; Jeremy Kingston, *The Times*, ibid., 1105; John Gross, *Sunday Telegraph*, ibid., 1105-6; Brown, ibid., 1106.

27 Kate Bassett, *Independent on Sunday*, ibid., 1105.

28 Logan, ibid., 1106.

29 Marmion, ibid., 1104.

30 Alastair Macaulay, *Financial Times*, ibid., 1103.

31 Natasha refers to cutting them down in Act IV.

32 See for example Else Ribeiro Pires Viera, 'Liberating Calibans: *Antropofagia* and Haroldo de Campos' Poetics of Transcreation', *Post-Colonial Translation*, eds Susan Bassnett and Harish Trivedi (London: Routledge 1999):95-113, where an argument is put forward (98) for cannibalism as a form of respect.

33 Trigorin: 'Ne pomniu. (*Podumav*) Ne pomniu!' (Act IV). Shamraev first mentions it just before Treplev and Nina meet in Act IV, and then actually produces the stuffed bird, provoking Trigorin's repetition, when the house guests return from supper, just before Treplev shoots himself (See Senelick, 797 and 802). There is a minute change in the punctuation between the utterance and the repetition. There is only one exclamation mark in the first uttering, after the second 'Don't remember!', but one after each element in the repetition.

2 | Rehearsing the 1916 Rising: Theatre Politics and Political Theatre

Robert Tracy

> During the early years of the century, Dublin was drama-mad
> ... In Dublin poets, writers, artists, revolutionists, were all
> interested in the theatre.
>
> (Máire níc Shiubhlaigh, *The Splendid Years*, 140)

In April 1914 Edward Martyn founded the Irish Theatre Company to stage his own plays, new work by other Irish playwrights, and plays from contemporary Europe. Martyn was a Galway landowner, an admirer of Ibsen and Wagner, a reformer of church music – he endowed the Palestrina choir at the Dublin pro-cathedral. A cultural nationalist with European sensibilities, he learned Irish, owned a Degas, a Monet, and a Corot, and was briefly President of Sinn Féin (1904-1908), Arthur Griffith's movement for an independent Ireland. With W.B. Yeats and Lady Gregory, he had founded the Irish Literary Theatre in 1899, guaranteeing money for its first performances: Yeats's *The Countess Cathleen* and his own *The Heather Field*. George Moore made Martyn the central figure in his memoir of the Irish Literary Revival, *Hail and Farewell* (1911-14), where he is depicted as naïve, clumsy, and constantly anxious about his soul. Moore's Martyn is a great comic creation, but underrates the real man and his accomplishments.

Martyn resigned from the Irish Literary Theatre in 1902, after Yeats and Moore revised his play *The Tale of a Town* into *The Bending of the Bough* (1900). As the Literary Theatre evolved into the Abbey he disliked the prevalence of peasant plays, usually by Synge or Lady Gregory, and plays about ancient Irish heroes, usually by Yeats. Martyn wanted plays that would recognize that Ibsen's middle-class characters and their problems existed in modern Irish life. Resentful because Yeats rejected his plays, he founded the Irish Theatre Company to produce them himself.

Looking for collaborators with practical theatrical experience who agreed that Irish audiences deserved access to avant-garde drama, Martyn chose two poets: Thomas MacDonagh and Joseph Mary Plunkett. Martyn was to be financially responsible for the new Theatre Company, and the Articles of Agreement specified that 'at least one half' of the plays performed 'shall be plays written by Mr. Edward Martyn, if so many be available'. Tom MacDonagh was in charge of productions, assisted by his brother John. Plunkett, like Yeats a student of the new performance theories of Gordon Craig and Stanislavsky, contributed the use of a Hardwicke Street building with a small stage and room for an audience of about a hundred.[1]

Martyn and his co-directors were genuinely committed to bringing revolutionary new dramas to Dublin. But while managing the Irish Theatre, MacDonagh and Plunkett were simultaneously planning a different revolution. Both were close friends of Patrick Pearse, and, like him, already members of Eoin MacNeill's Irish Volunteers, an armed militia organized to defend Irish Home Rule. Like Pearse they had also joined the Irish Republican Brotherhood, a Fenian organization committed to establishing an Irish Republic. As IRB members they would work secretly to prepare the Volunteers for an insurrection. With Pearse they would sign the 1916 Proclamation of the Irish Republic, take part in the Easter Rising, and face British firing squads in May 1916. In MacDonagh's case especially, I believe there is more than a merely chronological relationship between his theatrical and his revolutionary activities.

Martyn announced the advent of the Irish Theatre Company in Plunkett's *Irish Review* with an ill-tempered attack on the Abbey Theatre and its directors. Aware that he had become irrelevant, he charged that Yeats and Lady Gregory attracted 'silly little people with silly little plays' like *Cathleen ni Houlihan* and *The Pot of Broth*. Thanks to Yeats's 'weird appearance, which is triumphant with middle-aged masculine women, and a dictatorial manner which is irresistible with the considerable bevy of female and male mediocrities interested in intellectual things', the Abbey now defined Irish theatre. Peasant plays 'do not interest me', Martyn announced, 'in that the peasant's primitive mind is too crude for any sort of interesting complexity in treatment'. His new Irish Theatre Company would present 'native works, dealing with the lives and problems of people more complex ... requiring performers who can create characters of complexity and intellectuality' like those in his own plays. The new venture would encourage 'native Irish drama, other than the peasant species ... however depressed and ruined we may have been by English government and our own inept acquiescence by often playing into the hands of the enemy, we have still some inhabitants left in Ireland besides peasants. ... We will not expect to make money', he added.[2]

The first production, Martyn's *The Dream Physician* (2-7 November 1914), ridiculed George Moore, Yeats, his peasant visionaries, and the Kiltartan dialect spoken at the Abbey. A press release, probably written by Martyn, promised that the play would make its audience 'see in a new light – of sanity, many things in recent Irish movements which, under the hypnotism of a few clever writers, we were beginning to take for granted as having a real relation to life'.[3] *The Dream Physician* was not a success, though its audiences enjoyed the caricatures of Yeats and Moore. In December 1916 the Irish Theatre would present *Romulus and Remus*, another Martyn satire about Yeats, Moore, Lady Gregory, and the Abbey.

Though he was easily distracted with these vendettas, introducing Chekhov's plays to Dublin audiences was part of Martyn's project from the start. 'Our plays would be society plays in English, heroic plays, Ibsen and Strindberg', Tom MacDonagh told his brother John in May 1914, 'and possibly Tchekov plays, translations of course, and some Irish plays'.[4] In February 1915 Tom MacDonagh directed Chekhov's *The Swan Song*, himself playing the Prompter, in an evening of one-act plays: two by Irish, two by continental playwrights, in keeping with the Irish Theatre's mandate. *Swan Song* introduced Chekhov to Dublin audiences, preparing them for *Uncle Vanya*, also directed by MacDonagh, which ended the Irish Theatre's first season, running for a week (28 June-4 July 1915), to a mixed reception. Together with Martyn's 1919 *Cherry Orchard*, these productions began Chekhov's Irish career.

Martyn was brave to present Chekhov plays in Dublin when he did. In London they had provoked derision and even anger. The plays were called boring, the characters listless and incomprehensible. Shaw had persuaded the Stage Society to present

The Cherry Orchard (1911) and *Uncle Vanya* (1914), and the Adelphi Play Society to offer *The Seagull* (1912). Stage Society members were interested in the new dramaturgy, but half this select audience walked out during *The Cherry Orchard*, 'feeling that they were being insulted in their intelligence or that their legs were being pulled'. 'If our people won't stand it, it has no chance, because we have the pick here',[5] a Stage Society director commented. Chekhov had his defenders, but most reviews of these early productions were negative. English and even Irish audiences had learned to appreciate Ibsen by the end of the nineties, primarily as a social critic of middle-class hypocrisies. They assumed that Chekhov would also be a social critic, and found his refusal to judge his characters puzzling. Chekhov would only become popular in England after the Great War, when English self-confidence had weakened, and his characters' sense of failure, their aimless talk, and their inability to act decisively were recognized as the realism they are.

Tom MacDonagh directed the 1915 *Uncle Vanya*, with his brother John as Vanya, and Martyn sitting in on rehearsals. 'He sat long hours in our cold and drafty hall', John MacDonagh later recalled, 'interfering little, but glad when any problem of interpretation came up, so that he felt he was being useful ... he was a pathetic figure, sitting hunched up near a radiator but we all knew the keen enjoyment he experienced as he saw the play taking shape'.[6]

In the spring of 1915, then, Tom MacDonagh was running the Irish Theatre, lecturing on English literature at University College Dublin, but he was also planning the 1916 Rising. He had imagined an Irish insurrection in his 1908 play *When the Dawn Is Come*,[7] and had been Patrick Pearse's assistant at St Enda's school, where armed rebellion and dying for Ireland were almost part of the curriculum. MacDonagh played a central role in distributing smuggled rifles to the Volunteers in July 1914. A month after *Uncle Vanya* closed, he commanded the Volunteers at the funeral of O'Donovan Rossa, an old Fenian, where Pearse delivered a speech that was almost a declaration of war against British rule. Plunkett, equally if more secretly active, was not involved with *Uncle Vanya*, because when the play was rehearsing and performed he was in Germany arranging a shipment of rifles for use in the coming insurrection. The Irish Theatre was at once a serious theatrical enterprise and, from the start, a centre of revolutionary activity.

We can get some notion of how MacDonagh and Martyn handled Chekhov's dramaturgical innovations and dialogue from contemporary reviews of *Uncle Vanya*, or reviews of John MacDonagh's 1917 revival, which re-enacted the 1915 production with most of the original cast, including himself as Vanya. Since he probably used his brother's prompt copy, we can consider the 1915 and 1917 *Uncle Vanya* as the same production.

Reviewers note the Irish Theatre's inadequate space and scenery – green curtains suggested the garden of Act I. Máire Níc Shiublaigh was 'much too lovely' for Sonia, who refers to her own plain looks. Comments about 'long, wordy, and affected speeches' indicate that the directors clearly understood the indirect nature of Chekhovian dialogue that reviewers found rambling and incoherent: 'If ever the mirror of social life in its especial inanity has been held up to us with the sure hand of a genius, it is in this curious drama', Martyn wrote in 1919, discussing *The Cherry Orchard*,

> where [Chekhov] appears to have pushed his theories to their extreme possibilities ... listen to the general conversation that goes on at parties ... and hear the incoherent nonsense that flows in rivers from the mob around one ... Since ... the drama of ideas finds but scant favour among us, we can only hope for a better future from this venture where realism seems to have found its extreme ... Tchekoff is the delineator of incoherence ... his method, when carefully examined, will be found remarkably coherent ... he seems to have reduced the incoherence and absurdity of average humanity to a system. He is not concerned with the psychology of remarkable minds which the great masters of drama have made so fascinating ... You will not find ... in him those inevitable developments of soul action that lead to a most interesting climax ... He is a photographer of ordinary humanity ... we are often touched with their pathos as with their primal sadness of life ... the work of Tchekoff among the moderns seems to me second only to that of Ibsen. Both ... invented a new form of drama.[8]

Joseph Holloway, whose diary records many years of Dublin play-going, complained that the 1915 Astrov 'spoke like a talking machine and behaved like a marionette throughout the play', but MacDonagh replied that he had deliberately chosen a comic actor, and directed him to act the role in a stylized and uninvolved way, as a kind of talking machine.[9] While this is not necessarily the only way to perform Astrov, it is a plausible reading. Astrov has repeatedly given his speeches about preserving the forests, and his commitment to the woods is a way of avoiding his own uncertainties.

Holloway saw *Uncle Vanya* again in 1917, this time complaining that Vanya 'moped about monotonously throughout the whole evening uttering jerky sentences every now and then and never shaking off his mechanical monotonous ways'. Elena was 'rather still and cold of manner'. Both are defensible ways of acting the parts. Willie Pearse – shot after the Rising – emphasized Serebriakov's goutiness in 1915, when Martyn was suffering from severe gout. The 1917 Serebriakov, rather cruelly, imitated the 'voice tones and manners of Edward Martyn'. Holloway praised only Astrov, who 'tried to put life' into the role, as the 1915 Astrov had failed to do. *The Irishman*, more perceptively, thought this Astrov 'too spirited for the part'.[10]

A more significant response was the recognition of what the *Freeman's Journal* (12 February 1917) called 'comparisons ... between Irish and Russian character'. *New Ireland*, a Republican/Sinn Féin journal (10 February), declared that in both countries 'we meet like characters – people of lively imagination and soaring ideals, struggling for expression and life in a bog of uncongenial surroundings and vanished hopes'. More obliquely, *The Irishman* hinted at an Irish resonance: 'the mission of the author was to show wasted lives, capable of great effort, but choked by a system which restrains mental activity as effectively as it hampers civil liberty'.[11] At a time when the savage repression of the Rising had, in Martyn's words after Easter Week, destroyed 'such great talents and such high ideals',[12] Chekhov's characters, unable to break out of the oppression of circumstances to bring about the change they so desperately craved, must have seemed unbearably poignant to the Irish Theatre audience, many of whom would have known Tom MacDonagh, Plunkett, and Willie Pearse, and would have remembered the 1915 *Uncle Vanya*. The dead young leaders of 1916, some of them so intimately associated with the Irish Theatre and its mission to discover new dramatic forms, and with this play, had tried to break out of a political stasis in Ireland analogous to the emotional and social stasis of Chekhov's characters. Like them, they had been defeated. Sonia's effort to comfort Vanya with a promise of better things to come, as she and Vanya sit among their shattered hopes, might well have been spoken by the mothers and widows of the Rising's dead. The Irish

Theatre's 1917 revival of *Uncle Vanya* can be seen as homage to those dead and their aspirations.

Chekhov's first Dublin audiences were small, composed of people actively interested in new forms of dramaturgy, but also expecting another Ibsen. Dubliners were used to new forms of drama at the Abbey, plays dependent on language rather than action or plot, but they did not take to Chekhov. In the aftermath of the Rising, Ernest Boyd argued that the Irish Theatre had tried too hard to be Ibsenite, and praised John MacDonagh's *Weeds* (1919), arguably the first attempt at a Chekhovian play in English. *Weeds*, never published, drew on *The Cherry Orchard* to portray an Ascendancy landlord who hopes to win the loyalty of his tenants by wearing kilts and learning Irish, and the son of an evicted tenant who eventually buys the Big House. MacDonagh saw that the world of Chekhov's plays was familiar. Ireland too had decaying country houses whose inhabitants had seen better days and deplored their isolation, many talkers who preferred monologues to conversation. *Weeds* evaded 'the bloodless symbolism of pseudo-Ibsenite reincarnators' without lapsing into Kiltartan dialogue,[13] and developed a new form for 'plays dealing with' Irish rural life.[14]

As in Russia, there were peasants, a class that had disappeared in England. Many Irishmen, like many Russians, felt themselves to be ruled arbitrarily and unjustly. In the years after Parnell's fall, as during the reign of Nicholas II, there seemed little possibility of political progress. After 1916, Irish reviewers were soon noting Russian/Irish parallels. In 1919 'Measadóir' (assessor, appraiser) implicitly compared the 'pessimism' of Chekhov's characters to the loss of hope for political progress in Ireland after Parnell's fall: 'the patriotic efforts of the younger generation ... had suffered a defeat'.[15]

The Russia/Ireland parallel soon became a cliché in discussing Chekhov. St John Ervine urged that *The Cherry Orchard* be imagined 'in the Irish way', identifying 'the circumstances of Madame Ranevskaia' with 'any lady of the governing class in Ireland during the last thirty or forty years'.[16] In the thirties, Theodor Komisarjevsky, Russian-born, assured Peggy Ashcroft that Ranyevskaya was outside the range of any English actress. Only an Irish actress could play her.[17]

The Russian/Irish parallel recurs as Irishisms in Hubert Butler's version of *Cherry Orchard* for Tyrone Guthrie's 1933 Old

Vic production: 'he was a great hand with a stick'; 'write a good fist'; 'I will to be sure'; 'a bit of land'; 'a decent quiet fellow'.[18] Tom Kilroy's 1981 version of *The Seagull*, set in the West of Ireland at the time of the Land League, brilliantly utilizes the Irish parallels,[19] as do some of Natasha's speeches in Brian Friel's 1981 *Three Sisters*: 'God but that's a wild big crowd, Olga'; 'That's grand'; 'I'm as thick as poundies'; 'You put the heart across me!'.[20] In *Living Quarters* Friel even borrowed the personnel of *Three Sisters* – three sisters, their brother, an unreliable family friend, a dead soldier – adapted to contemporary Ireland as well as to his version of Euripides's *Hippolytus*.

Martyn's Irish Theatre in Hardwicke Street was at once an *avant-garde* theatre, a centre of cultural nationalism – the Dun Emer Guild shared part of the building – a drill hall for MacDonagh's Volunteers, and a regular meeting place for the IRB committee that was taking control of the Volunteers. Martyn and MacDonagh were serious about their mission to bring contemporary European drama to Dublin, but their theatre work was inextricably mixed with planning an uprising. 'I did all that I could to dissuade those unfortunate volunteers from their folly', Martyn wrote after the May executions. 'But they simply looked at me. From the very first I told them what would be the end of the volunteers.'[21] Under what circumstances did he issue these warnings? How much did Martyn know in the days leading up to the Rising? The MacDonagh brothers were rehearsing Strindberg's *Easter*, often in Martyn's flat, until the play opened on 3 March 1916, seven weeks before the Rising.

Despite his grief and increasingly poor health, Martyn was able to keep the Irish Theatre going after the Rising. With John MacDonagh's help, he presented Chekhov's *The Jubilee* in December 1917 and even *The Cherry Orchard* in June 1919. Briefly revived in January 1920, *The Cherry Orchard* was the Irish Theatre's last play. Dublin reviewers understandably saw Irish analogies as members of the Ascendancy left Ireland and Big Houses burned in 1919-1921. The Russian Revolution suggested other comparisons; the *Freeman's Journal* (25 June) saw the 'land question' as similar in both countries. *Young Ireland* noted that 'there are many Madame Ranevskys and Leonid Gayevs even in Ireland, whose only boast is some sire's deed and only care to keep what they hold'.[22]

Again reviewers' objections suggest that John MacDonagh and Martyn understood Chekhov's methods and intentions. Reviews still deplore a lack of action and 'inconsequential' dialogue,[23] the characters' addiction to 'talking piffle and doing nothing',[24] the absence of 'revelation'[25] and climax, all evidence that the directors and actors knew what they were doing. Some reviewers recognized the mixture of tragedy, gaiety, bravery, and incompetence in Ranyevskaya, and the difficulties of playing Lopakhin, at once sensitive and a boorish upstart; Paul Farrell seems to have made him too boorish. *The Irish Program* called him an Irish type: 'one could imagine him shouting for a Shellilah and Donnybrook'.[26]Holloway, misjudging as usual, condemned 'the impossibly silly ass' reading of Epikhodov, and Varia for her lack of animation.[27] Like *Uncle Vanya*, *The Cherry Orchard* was neither popular nor profitable in the politically distracted Dublin of that time.

'When I see a play of Tchekoff's I want to tear my own up', Shaw declared in 1914, after *Uncle Vanya*.[28] Instead he wrote *Heartbreak House*, his '*Fantasia in the Russian Manner*', a play he called Chekhovian despite its inevitable didactic content. He also spotted the resemblances between the Big Houses of Ireland and the country houses of Chekhov's plays. *Heartbreak House* owes something to the Big Houses of Somerville and Ross and Coole Park's aesthetic preoccupations as well as to England's leisured complacency before the Great War.

Yeats persuasively argued that a theatre could define and embody a nation unable to establish itself politically. The Easter Rising was political theatre, a dramatic performance in the centre of Dublin implicitly connecting the resurrection of Christ with the resurrection of Ireland that the Rising represented. Pearse's 1911 passion play in Irish,[29] his pageants about the Fianna and about Cuchulain's battle against overwhelming odds, and his 1915 play *The Singer*, with its endorsement of blood sacrifice, anticipated the heroic and sacrificial themes of the Rising. 'Did that play of mine send out/Certain men the English shot?' Yeats would ask, thinking of his *Cathleen Ní Houlihan*. In Pearse's *Singer* the hero 'will go into battle with bare hands' to 'stand up before the Gall as Christ hung naked before men on the tree' and die for his people.[30] Such phrases indicate Pearse's thinking as he felt his way toward armed and probably futile rebellion.

The Irish Theatre plays Thomas MacDonagh directed until just before the Rising are talky rather than heroic. Martyn's *Dream Physician*, with its schoolboy mockery of Yeats and Moore, of peasant drama and endless Home Rule debates, portrays a static and self-absorbed – and loquacious – Irish intelligentsia. In MacDonagh's own *Pagans: A Modern Play in Two Conversations* (Irish Theatre, 19-24 April 1915), performed a month before he directed *Uncle Vanya*, a middle-class couple recognize the failure of their marriage and agree to separate. It is a civilized discussion about individual freedom, of the sort engendered by *A Doll's House*. But it ends with a hint of the Rising MacDonagh was already planning: the husband, interested in 'revolutionary societies', intends to work for Ireland, asserting: 'My writings have been only the prelude to my other work ... a great opportunity is at hand ... politics will be dropped here, and something better will take their place.'[31]

What about *Uncle Vanya*, the play that MacDonagh directed after *Pagans*? Reviews indicate that director and cast understood how Chekhov's plays are about stasis, about talk rather than action. Chekhov's characters have lost their way, as he perhaps felt the Russian intelligentsia had. Inhibited from meaningful action, Vanya imagines himself a thwarted Schopenhauer or Dostoevsky. The three sisters talk of a Moscow they will never reach, Vershinin and Tuzenbach philosophize about what life might be like in a hundred years. They are part of the endless speculative conversation of 'cultured, leisured Europe', in the years before the Great War, that Shaw reacted to so forcibly in his preface to *Heartbreak House* after seeing the Stage Society's *Uncle Vanya*: 'nice people' but 'utter futility' because they ignored the fragile nature of their world: 'They took the only part of our society in which there was leisure for high culture, and made it an economic, political, and, as far as practicable, a moral vacuum'.[32] That speculative conversation, and the violence that would end it, are recorded in *Heartbreak House*, in Thomas Mann's *The Magic Mountain*, in Chekhov's plays. Then 'Something' happens, in *Heartbreak House* a zeppelin raid and a dynamite explosion. Hans Castorp crouches in the mud of the Western Front. In *The Seagull, Uncle Vanya*, and *Three Sisters* the conversation is interrupted by pistol shots, in *Cherry Orchard* by axes attacking the beautiful but unproductive cherry trees, and the ominous breaking string. In each of Chekhov's plays, the interminable conversation is violently interrupted, and the fragile order it represents will not survive that violent interruption and the departures that follow. A pistol at Sarajevo and the guns of August 1914 interrupted Europe's interminable conversation; the Easter Rising interrupted Ireland's. 'O but we talked at large before/The sixteen men were shot', Yeats remembered, in 'Sixteen Dead Men':

> But who can talk of give and take,
> What should be and what not
> While those dead men are loitering there
> To stir the boiling pot?[33]

Having worked to depict the indeterminate and ineffective conversations of leisured Europe in directing *Uncle Vanya*, Tom MacDonagh abandoned Ireland's literary, intellectual, and political discussions about changing Ireland, and the futility of Martyn's attacks on Yeats and Moore, and took up the gun, as *Pagans* predicted. MacDonagh's *Uncle Vanya* risked boring its audience by admitting it was about inaction and endless futile talk. It did not pretend to entertain. Can we connect MacDonagh's experience of this and other 'talky' Irish Theatre plays with his readiness to participate in an armed rebellion that seemed doomed to fail, but had the potential, perhaps, to shock Ireland into self-awareness, to end Ireland's stasis, to change everything? Did that play as well send out certain men the English shot?

---

[1] See William J. Feeney, *Drama in Hardwicke Street: a History of the Irish Theatre Company* (London and Toronto: Associated University Presses, 1984): 49-51 and Geraldine Plunkett Dillon, *All in the Blood*, ed. Honor O Brolchain (Dublin: A. & Farmar, 2006): 171-72.

[2] Edward Martyn, 'A Plea for the Revival of the Irish Literary Theatre,' *Irish Review* 4 (April 1914): 79-84.

[3] Feeney, 60.

[4] Dillon, 172. See also Edd Winfield Parks and Aileen Wells Parks, *Thomas MacDonagh: the Man, the Patriot, the Writer* (Athens: University of Georgia Press, 1967): 42.

[5] Arnold Bennett, review of *The Cherry Orchard*, *New Age*, 8 June 1911; *Books and Persons* (New York, 1917): 322.

[6] Denis Gwynn, *Edward Martyn and the Irish Revival* [1930](New York: Lemma, 1974): 328.

[7] Parks, 100-106.

[8] Edward Martyn, 'The Cherry Orchard of Tchekoff', *New Ireland* 8 (21 June 1919): 108-109.

[9] Feeney, 101-103.

[10] Feeney, 161-62.

[11] Feeney, 159-61.

[12] Madeleine Humphreys, *The Life and Times of Edward Martyn: An Aristocratic Bohemian* (Dublin: Irish Academic Press, 2007): 236.

[13] Ernest A. Boyd, 'The Work of the Irish Theatre', *Irish Monthly* 47 (February 1919): 71-76.

[14] Measadóir, 'Weeds', *New Ireland* 7 (18 January 1919): 181. Cited after Feeney, 221.

[15] Measadóir, 'New Forms in Drama', *New Ireland* 8 (21 June 1919): 109-10.

[16] St John Ervine, 'Review of The Cherry Orchard', *Observer* 18 July 1920.

[17] Interview, July 1987.

[18] Anton Chekhov, *The Cherry Orchard*, trans. Hubert Butler (London: H.F.W. Deane, 1934): 31, 61, 58, 9.

[19] Thomas Kilroy, *The Seagull* (London: Methuen, 1981).

[20] Brian Friel, *Three Sisters* (Dublin: Gallery Press, 1981): 33, 63, 71, 111.

[21] Humphreys, 235.

[22] *Young Ireland,* 5 July 1919. Cited after Feeney, 247.

[23] *Irish Times* 24 June 1919. Cited after Feeney, 242.

[24] *Independent* 24 June 1919. Cited after Feeney, 243.

[25] *Evening Telegraph* 24 June 1919. Cited after Feeney, 242.

[26] *Irish Programme* 3 July 1919. Cited after Feeney, 245.

[27] Feeney, 247-48; 260-63.

[28] H.W. M. [H.W. Massingham], 'The Sigh of Failure', *Nation* 16 May 1914: 265.

[29] Robert Hogan with Richard Burnham and Daniel P. Poteet, *The Abbey Theatre: the Rise of the Realists 1910--1915* (Dublin: Dolmen, 1979): 157-59.

[30] Ruth Dudley Edwards, *Patrick Pearse: the Triumph of Failure* [1977] (Dublin: Poolbeg, 1990): 130-31, 172, 262.

[31] Thomas MacDonagh, *Pagans: A Modern Play in Two Conversations* (Dublin: Talbot, 1920): 16, 39-40.

[32] Bernard Shaw, *Complete Plays with Prefaces*, vol. 1 (New York: Dodd, Mead, and Company, 1963): 449-50.

[33] W.B. Yeats, *Poems,* ed. Richard J. Finneran (New York: Macmillan, 1983): 162.

3 | Chekhov and the Irish Big House

Nicholas Grene

In October 1933 *The Cherry Orchard* opened at the Old Vic with a star-studded cast – studded, that is, with what were to be stars of the future: Charles Laughton as Lopakhin, Flora Robson as Varya, Marius Goring playing Epikhodov and even a young James Mason in the part of Yasha. It was directed by Tyrone Guthrie in a newly commissioned translation by his brother-in-law Hubert Butler. Both Guthrie and Butler were Irish; both had grown up in Irish country houses that might have suggested similarities to the cherry orchard estate of the Gayevs, Guthrie in Annaghmakerrig, County Monaghan, Butler in Maidenhall in Kilkenny. Butler had lived in St Petersburg through the winter of 1931-1932 and his later preoccupations as a writer were with Ireland and Eastern Europe. But there seems to have been no hint of Irishness in Guthrie's production and there is certainly no trace of characteristic Irish English in Butler's translation.[1] On the contrary, the dialogue is very much the English English of the time. Gaev considers Lopakhin a 'cad', an 'upstart' and a 'bounder'.[2] The appalling Yasha, complacently accepting the swooning adoration of Dunyasha, moralizes on her forwardness: 'if a girl gets sweet on a chap it means she's no better than she should be'.[3]

From the earliest productions of Chekhov during the First World War, parallels between the Russian and Irish situations had been referred to in reviews.[4] By 1968, fifty years later, an Irish inflected *Cherry Orchard* seemed obvious at least to Seamus Kelly, reviewing the famous production by Moscow Art Theatre director Maria Knebel at the Abbey. The production, Kelly wrote, might serve as a 'blue-print for future presentations of Chekhov's classic, based securely and credibly on the sort of Irish situation that was once as real to this country as Ranevskaia's was to the Russia of 1903'. It served as a blue-print, however, by what it might have done but did not do; it was not so much a blue print as a photographic negative. Knebel's might be *The Cherry Orchard* 'as in Russia'; what was needed was Chekhov as in Ireland:

> the truth of Chekhov's thesis would be more strongly emphasized if it were interpreted in terms of the decaying Irish Great House, with Gombeen-men taking over, and good old Somerville-and-Ross-type slaves left behind to die instead of Firs. No dramatist translates to an Irish scene and idiom of our very recent past more accurately than Chekhov.5

That self-consciously Irish Chekhov only finally arrived on the stage in 1981, and in two versions of Chekhov plays, neither of which was *The Cherry Orchard*. In April of that year Thomas Kilroy's adaptation of *The Seagull* opened at the Royal Court in London, and in September Brian Friel's *Three Sisters* premièred as Field Day's second production in Derry's Guildhall. Friel's decision to write a version of *Three Sisters* may have been, in an indirect way, a tribute to Tyrone Guthrie, who directed the play in the Minneapolis season where Friel had been an observer in 1963. His 'translation' of the play into a Donegal-accented English was very much part of the Field Day agenda to give Irish audiences drama that spoke to them in their own language. However different from Derry the Russian provincial city might have been where the Prozorov sisters languished for Moscow, the sense of stagnant stuckness and the progressive dying of hope might well have struck a chord when the play toured Ireland in 1981. Friel Irished up the language of his Chekhov characters, but they remain Chekhov's Russian characters – Tusenbach, Solyony and the rest. Kilroy's is a much more radical adaptation, re-locating *The Seagull* to the West of Ireland in the late nineteenth century and making the characters into Irish men and women: Arkadina becomes Isobel Desmond, Trigorin is Aston, Nina appears as Lily. And for the first time, we have an Irish Big House in a Chekhov play.

Kilroy disarmingly explains his reasons for undertaking the adaptation in his essay in the *Cambridge Companion to Chekhov*: 'The first reason why I did this was, quite simply, because I was asked to do so by Max Stafford-Clark, then artistic director at the Royal Court Theatre'. He goes on to say that both he and Stafford-

Clark felt that Chekhov needed to be rescued from 'a very English gentility' to which standard English productions were prone. So, in a sense, he and Friel were in the same business, re-appropriating Chekhov from a specifically English tradition. However, there was more to it than that. For, Kilroy continues, 'when I began to think about them, the parallels between Chekhov's Russia and nineteenth-century Anglo-Ireland became, for me, extraordinarily vivid and apt'.[6] This historical analogy is elaborated in the persuasive Introduction to the 1981 text of the play by Rob Ritchie, the Literary Manager of the Royal Court.[7] But Kilroy's adaptation brings out the contrasts as well as the similarities between the 1890s Russian world of *The Seagull* and the 1880s West of Ireland situation in which he places it.

To start with, in order to foreground the Russian/Irish parallels, Kilroy reads *The Cherry Orchard* back into *The Seagull*. *The Seagull* is set in Sorin's country house, a house perhaps a bit like Chekhov's own Melikhovo where the play was written in the summer and autumn of 1895. But there is no indication in Chekhov's text that the family is in financial trouble or the house in danger of being sold. Arkadina, temperamentally the opposite of the spendthrift Ranyevskaya, is mean with money and keeps her son Konstantin on short commons; all of her brother Sorin's resources go on supporting the estate and he cannot afford the metropolitan life for which he yearns. There is nothing out of the way in all this. By contrast, Kilroy's stage direction makes it clear that the set for the house 'should suggest the shabby-genteel state of the Desmond fortunes'(26). In Act II there is an added speech for Pauline (Chekhov's Polina) who is married to Cousin Gregory, Kilroy's version of Shamrayev, the manager of the estate. The place, she tells Dr Hickey, is 'bankrupt like every other estate in the West of Ireland. You know they've stopped paying rents again this past month. The Land Leaguers will have nothing to take of what's left'(21). The passing of property from the Russian landowners to an emergent commercial bourgeoisie, the subject of the *Cherry Orchard*, Kilroy translates into the *Seagull* as the Irish land wars that saw the eventual expropriation of the Anglo-Irish in favour of their tenants.

What made the situation so different was the colonial dimension in Ireland, as Kilroy himself stressed: 'The Anglo-Irish represented a foreign, English power in Ireland. Chekhov's gentry at least shared a common Russian nationality with those around and beneath them'.[8]

Though people of the class of the Desmonds would no doubt have seen themselves as wholly Irish not foreigners, the difference of their political interests, accentuated by the difference in religion, made for a gap between them and their fellow Irishmen. This is made manifest in Kilroy's version by the figure of James, the local schoolteacher, counterpart to Chekhov's Medvedenko. When Mary/Masha, disappointed in her love for Constantine, eventually marries James, it is seen as a cross-community misalliance: 'he's a Roman Catholic and he has all that awful family of his down in that awful cottage ... His family look on me as a kind of loot rifled from the Big House'(27). Implied here is that horror of marrying down and marrying out that is such a leitmotif of Anglo-Irish fiction from Maria Edgeworth's *Castle Rackrent* (1800) to Somerville and Ross's *The Big House of Inver* (1925). And the imagined corollary is the predatory perspective of the cottagers on their Anglo-Irish neighbours. This is an Irish rather than a Russian imaginary.

One of Kilroy's most creative inventions in his *Seagull* is the conversion of Treplev's symbolist play-within-a-play into Constantine's Celtic Revival monodrama. Isobel Desmond here becomes the representative of conventional London Victorian theatre against which Yeats, Gregory and Martyn were protesting when they launched the Irish Literary Theatre in 1897. (The geographical landmarks in Kilroy's play place it in East Galway, not far from Coole Park.) Lily appears 'dressed in a long green robe and wearing a kind of crown in the style of contemporary nationalist representations of Ireland' and her speech becomes a wonderful sub-Yeatsian pastiche:

> I am Macha, Queen of Uladh, I am Morrigu, the crow-bird who flies over the battle-field. I am Eire and Fodla and Banba, the daughters of Dagda. I am every woman of the Tuatha de Danann, the people of Light and Air (13).

The monologue, just before it is interrupted by Isobel – 'Do I detect the smell of sulphur?' – is building towards a climactic conflict between Balor, giant 'King of the Fomorions' and his 'bright-faced' opponent, the god Lugh. More than one critic has viewed this imagined battle as a premonitory vision, attributed to both Chekhov and Kilroy, of the Great War to come in the twentieth century.[9] But in context, surely, it has a nationalist anti-colonial colouring. The speaker looks forward to the time when 'the spirit of Darkness is defeated and the spirit of Light shines over the land of Banba' (14). Kilroy no doubt mocks this sort of nationalist rhetoric and the excesses of early Celticism, just as Chekhov in the original made fun of Treplev's Decadent symbolism. However, in the Irish adaptation the historical momentum drives on towards the outcomes we all know. Constantine, the Yeatsian poetaster may go under and commit suicide, but not Yeats, the great impresario of the Celtic Revival. The land wars of the 1880s are stirrings that will feed into the long gestation leading to 1916 and beyond. Where Chekhov's *Seagull* is immersed in the melancholy stagnation of 1890s Russia, Kilroy's version lives within the dynamics of a known historical continuum.

Frank McGuinness salutes Kilroy as initiating a new era in Irish theatre by 'making Chekhov his own'.[10] He was to be closely followed by many others, McGuinness himself with versions of *Three Sisters* and *Uncle Vanya*, Michael West with his *Seagull*, though not in a self-consciously Irish style. Friel's has of course been the most sustained engagement, not only with his *Three Sisters* and *Uncle Vanya* but with what he published as his *Three Plays After*: *The Bear*, *The Yalta Game* (his adaptation of the short story 'The Lady with the Dog'), and *Afterplay*, his own fantasia using characters from two Chekhov plays.[11] Tom Murphy was quite late in the field with his *Cherry Orchard* commissioned for the Abbey Centenary programme in 2004. His version of the play is relatively close to the original, with only a few striking Irish divergences.[12] However, he had already written his response to *The Cherry Orchard* in his play *The House* in 2000.

The house in Murphy's play is not an Irish Big House, capital B, capital H, with all the associations of that term. To start with the owners, the de Burcas, are Catholic not Protestant: they attend the same Mass as their small town neighbours. The de Burca house, also, is literally not all that big. This is no imposing Georgian mansion but, Murphy tells us in a stage direction, 'a four/five bedroom affair, early Victorian'.[13] If there ever was an estate or even a farm that went with the house, it is long gone by the time of the action. The sale in the climactic Scene Nine specifies just over three acres on the property, and it is bought for the sum of £2,400, a very different matter from the thousand-acre estate of the cherry orchard for which Lopakhin gives 90,000 roubles over the mortgage. In this play Murphy is back on his preferred territory, the provincial Irish town of the 1950s, and much of the action is taken

8 *The Seagull*, **Royal Court Theatre, April 1981, directed by Max Stafford Clark: Anton Lesser as (Constantine) and Harriet Walter (Lily).**

up with the emigrant workers who come back each year for their statutory two-week holidays to spend all their savings in one colossal spree. Making due allowances, though, for the differences in scale, place and period, the imaginative starting-point for *The House* is the *Cherry Orchard* situation, specifically the relationship between Lopakhin and Ranyevskaya.

In the first scene of *The Cherry Orchard*, as Lopakhin waits for the return of the owners, he remembers his first encounter with Ranyevskaya, quoted here in Tom Murphy's version.

The eyes, you know: the kindness in them. Always ... I'll never forget it for her: I was fifteen, and my father – oh he'd 'progressed' to having the little shop over in the village then. And we'd come here, to the yard over there, for something or other, and he hit me. Drunk, of course, what else. Smack, here in the face with his fist, and the blood started to pour. And Lyubov Andreyevna, so young then, *so* – slender – took me in. I mean into here, the house, to this room, the washbasin that was over there. 'Do not cry, little peasant, it will get better before you are married ... '[14]

Like Ranyevskaya for Lopakhin, Mrs de Burca represented for Christy a childhood glimpse of an alternative to drunken brutalism. Christy's mother used to work for the de Burcas as a cleaning woman, and he would come along with her; when she died, while he was still just a child, he ran away from his father and showed up at the house: 'I'd like to be this family please',[15] he is remembered as saying. Mrs de Burca would in fact have taken him in and had him educated, but his obstinate father would have none of it. In a childhood where he knew nothing but being beaten until he was old enough to beat his father back, Mrs de Burca stands for maternal tenderness: in the play's stage prefixes she is referred to only as 'Mother'. That motherliness for Christy is associated with the shelter of the house, its superior graciousness of living, its grounds and gardens. And that is the reason why he is so desperate to preserve it.

This is the major twist that Murphy gives to the *Cherry Orchard* situation. Ranyevskaya dreads the idea of having to sell the cherry orchard but will do nothing practical to save it. Lopakhin, the friend of the family and go-ahead businessman, has the solution: clear the land of cherry orchard and house and let the property for the building of holiday homes. In Murphy's *The House*, it is Mrs de Burca who is determined to sell – she is old and ill and, since the death of her husband, she cannot manage such a large place. It is Christy who passionately wants her to stay, for everything to stay the same. He gives up much of his holiday time to cutting the grass, repairing the walls. The key exchange between the two of them comes in Scene Four when he tries to persuade her not to sell the house:

Mother. It's too big. Now. It isn't working out. And – Christy! – the past is the past.
Christy. Aw, I don't know so much about that![16]

Where Lopakhin with his plans for urban summer holiday makers represents the future, Christy needs to retain the past as his only vision of an alternative to his own life, the violent product of a violent upbringing, someone who has worked as a pimp in London to make the money he uses to buy the house. For Christy, like Lopakhin (and again like him reluctantly), becomes the purchaser of the estate when it comes to auction. Lopakhin's great speech when he makes the announcement in Act III of *The Cherry Orchard* is a brilliant study in mixed feelings, awed amazement at being the owner of 'the most beautiful estate in the world', with class triumph in the prospect of destroying it, seeing 'the trees come "tumbelling" down to the tune of Yermolay Lopakhin's axe'.[17] For Christy there is nothing but joy at having saved the house with all it means to him.

He has saved it, but at a terrible cost, no less than murder. Christy's feeling for Mrs de Burca as Mother seems to have created something like an incest taboo in his relations with her three daughters. All three are in love with him, or at least want him as a lover, but his feelings towards them are blocked. There may be something of a suggestion for this in *The Cherry Orchard* where the long planned marriage between Lopakhin and Varya, honorary daughter of the house, fails to materialize. Mrs de Burca similarly would like Christy to marry her oldest daughter Marie, and again nothing comes of it. But the degree of Christy's infantilist fixation becomes apparent in his relationship with the other two sisters. He withdraws from an unsatisfactory affair he has had with the married Louise. And when the neurotic Susanne who, it turns out, also works in the sex trade in London, offers herself to him, he ends up killing her. It is a very dark psychopathology that Murphy explores here. Christy's need to preserve some pure pre-sexual icon of the mother, enshrined in the house, makes it impossible for him to have a normally loving sexual relationship; sexuality remains always for him proximate to violence.

In *The House* we have come a long way from Chekhov. But the object of this essay has been to illustrate how Irish playwrights have been able to take off from Chekhov in their own dramatic visions. There are indeed analogies between late nineteenth-century Ireland and the period of Russian history when Chekhov wrote. The similarities between Irish Big House and Chekhovian country estate, seen from early on, are indeed there. But it took a Thomas Kilroy to seize on them and make his own theatrical capital out of them. In Kilroy's *The Seagull* this involved a re-conception of the play, a reframing of it in terms of the issues of late colonial Ireland with its politics of land and religion. We understand and appreciate his play better when we see how and why it differs from Chekhov, the ways in which the Desmonds' West of Ireland country house is unlike Sorin and Arkadina's Russian estate. Tom Murphy's adaptation of *The Cherry Orchard* is a good actable version but not much more than that. His real response to Chekhov is shown in *The House*, where the passing of property from one class to another, the Lopakhin/Ranyevskaya relationship, comes in for an Irish re-imagining. The late blooming Irish love affair with Chekhov is at its most fruitful where the Russian playwright has enabled playwrights like Kilroy and Murphy to realize their own characteristically Irish theatrical vision.

---

[1] I have found just one possible exception. Pischkik's much-mentioned, non-appearing daughter Dashenka, we are told, hopefully 'will win 200,000 roubles ... she's got a ticket in the sweep', Anton Chekhov, *The Cherry Orchard*, trans. Hubert Butler (London: H.F.W. Deane, 1934): 19. This is probably a reference to the Irish Hospitals Sweepstake, set up in 1930. I am very grateful to Julia Crampton for supplying me with one of the very scarce copies of her father's translation of the play.

[2] Chekhov, *Cherry Orchard*, 15, 19.

[3] Ibid., 28.

[4] See William J. Feeney, *Drama in Hardwicke Street: a History of the Irish Theatre Company* (London and Toronto: Associated University Presses, 1984): 159, 240.

[5] Seamus Kelly, 'Chekhov's Classic as in Russia', *Irish Times* 9 October 1968.

[6] Thomas Kilroy, '*The Seagull*: an Adaptation', *The Cambridge Companion to Chekhov*, eds Vera Gottlieb and Paul Allain (Cambridge: Cambridge University Press, 2000): 80.

[7] Anton Chekhov, *The Seagull*, a new version by Thomas Kilroy (London: Eyre Methuen, 1981): 3-6. All further quotations from Kilroy's version are taken from this edition, with references given parenthetically in the text.

[8] Kilroy, '*The Seagull*: an Adaptation', 81-82.

[9] See Frank McGuinness, 'A Voice from the Trees: Thomas Kilroy's Version of Chekhov's *Seagull*', *Irish University Review*, 21.1 (1991): 3-14, and Joseph Long, 'Diction and Ideology: Chekhov's Irish Voice', *Double Vision: Studies in Literary Translation*, ed. Jane Taylor (Durham: Durham Modern Languages Series, 2002): 163-75.

[10] McGuinness, 'A Voice from the Trees', 14.

[11] Brian Friel, *Three Plays After* (Oldcastle: Gallery, 2002).

12 Notable among these is a rich vein in obscenities that he lends to the semi-senile Firs and some nineteenth-century nationalist declamatory pieces that he puts in the mouth of the Passer-by/Vagrant in Act II. Where Chekhov had quotations from poems by Nadson and Nekrasov, Murphy adds in snatches from a nationalist allegorical poem 'Andromeda' by James Jeffrey Roche, and from Thomas Davis's 'A Ballad of Freedom': see Anton Chekhov, *The Cherry Orchard*, adapted by Tom Murphy (London: Methuen, 2004): 41.

13 Tom Murphy, *Plays: 5* (London: Methuen Drama, 2006): 228.

14 Murphy, *The Cherry Orchard*, 5-6.

15 Murphy, *Plays: 5*, 185.

16 Murphy, *Plays: 5*, 217-18.

17 Murphy, *Cherry Orchard*, 60.

4 | 'All of Ireland is Our Orchard': Maria Knebel's Production of *The Cherry Orchard* at the Abbey in 1968

Ros Dixon

On 21 August 1968 the Soviet Union (together with its Warsaw Pact Allies) delivered its ultimate response to the liberalizing economic and political reforms then being introduced in Czechoslovakia, by invading. This action produced varied forms of angry protests across Western Europe, including in Ireland. By a majority vote of its Executive Council a ban was imposed on all Russian entries to the Cork Film Festival scheduled for the autumn of that year.[1] And the organizers of the Dublin Theatre Festival faced a crisis: they had invited not only the Mime Theatre of Prague to perform at the Olympia but also (following protracted negotiations) Soviet director, Maria Knebel, to direct an Irish cast in *The Cherry Orchard* at the Abbey. At an emergency meeting on 27 August 1968, despite threats that the theatre would be boycotted, the organizers resisted calls for Knebel's invitation to be withdrawn.[2] Her visit marked the first official contact between Irish theatre professionals and a Russian director, and her production would be remembered long afterwards by many as a spectacular theatre event.[3]

The Cherry Orchard had originally been staged by Konstantin Stanislavsky at the Moscow Art Theatre in 1904, with Stanislavsky himself as Gayev and Olga Knipper, Chekhov's wife, as Lyubov Ranyevskaya. He had revived this production for a tour in the 1920s, and again at the MAT in 1928. Knebel, who had begun her career at the Moscow Art, and trained under Stanislavsky, had played Charlotta in the MAT revival, and continued to do so for many years. She directed the play at the Soviet Army Theatre in Moscow in 1965.

That production, the one in Dublin, and indeed her rehearsal techniques, were all therefore indebted to Stanislavsky's approach. In the journal *Teatr* and in *Sovetskaia kul'tura* she published accounts of her time in Dublin which illuminate the differences in theatre practice between Russia and Ireland, give details of her rehearsals, and explore those themes of the drama that proved particularly pertinent to her Irish cast.[4] The differences in theatre practice were apparent from the moment she arrived. Meeting her at the airport some four weeks before the play was due to open, the director of the Festival, Brendan Smith, expressed surprise that she had decided to come so early, and revealed that Siobhán McKenna (who had been cast as Ranyevskaya) and Cyril Cusack (who was to play Gayev) were both out of the country on separate foreign tours. Accustomed to the lengthy rehearsal periods typical of many Soviet theatres, and particularly at the MAT, Knebel was alarmed at the prospect of having to produce so subtle and complex a play in the space of just one month.[5] She was later surprised to discover that she was expected to rehearse on the set of *The Playboy of the Western World*, which was in the middle of its run. The repertoire system in Russian theatres meant that productions were often turned over on a daily basis and therefore sets were dismantled every night to leave a bare stage for daytime rehearsals. Knebel's early concerns were greatly exacerbated on the first day of rehearsal when (in contrast to a Russian cast who would have been thoroughly warmed up, focused and ready), her Irish actors wandered into the rehearsal a good twenty minutes late, chatting and drinking coffee, and in the case of one actor whiskey, from styrofoam cups.[6] Much to her horror, a cup of whiskey had been thoughtfully provided for Knebel too. However, the note of panic that entered her voice when she remarked on how little preparation time remained had an immediate effect. The actors thereafter were not only punctual but prepared to work ten-hour days. Later Knebel had nothing but praise for the enthusiasm, energy and industry of her cast, who gave so much in rehearsal that they treated mere run-throughs as though they were full-scale performances.[7]

In the considerable press coverage that surrounded Knebel's production, reference was often made to the bond that supposedly existed between the Moscow Art Theatre and the Abbey because the two theatres had been established within years of each other, both had adopted a naturalistic style, and both enjoyed world renown. In terms of their professional practice, actor training, choice of repertoire, performance histories, and political imperatives, there are more differences than similarities between the two. Any bond between them is largely superficial. However, Knebel did claim that the natural and unaffected style of her Irish cast had much in common with their Russian counterparts:

> Everything about these Irish actors – their manners, speech, and actions – was enhanced by a lack of inhibition, and by their sincerity, and artistic temperament. I found everything strange, and at the same time unusually familiar. I found to my pleasant surprise that in spite of the language barrier the emotional atmosphere was the same as if I were working with Russian actors. There is a remarkable similarity between them and the Irish in their vital emotions, and their avid committed response to the requirements of their art.[8]

9 *The Cherry Orchard*, **Abbey Theatre, 1968, directed by Maria Knebel: Siobhán McKenna as Madame Ranyevskaia Cyril Cusack as Gayev, and Bernadette McKenna as Ania. [The original spelling of the characters' names has been retained.]**

Early in rehearsals Knebel gathered all her cast and engaged in her standard practice of a very detailed and careful analysis of each character, discussing the roles with individual actors and with the troupe as whole. For one actor in the Abbey company, Joe Dowling, this was a wholly new experience; he had never come across a director who was so concerned for such meticulous detail. This is perhaps not so surprising. As Dowling later reflected in *Theatre Ireland*, with some notable and brilliant exceptions most Irish directors at the time of this production 'tended to be super-stage-managers who maintained discipline and worked out a choreography of moves for the players', but left 'the interpretative aspects to the actors'.[9] Knebel's triumph, he maintained, was in her skill in drawing out the innate talents of the Abbey company. For their part the actors welcomed the way in which Knebel, drawing on her experience of Stanislavsky's approach, explored the characters' inner psychology and motivations, though some of his specific practices were quite unfamiliar at first. Knebel recalled that when she asked McKenna to improvise dialogue for an exercise called 'The Return Home' the actor initially laughed, but having complied became completely carried away, kissing the walls and the cupboard of her beloved nursery.[10] In another rehearsal they found almost by accident a key to the hidden pain that the feckless Ranyevskaya feels at her penury: Knebel asked McKenna to wear a ring to rehearsals and the actor revealed that she had none. She had sold all her jewellery (just as her character might have done) at a time of financial need.[11]

As is very well documented, Stanislavsky's interpretation of *The Cherry Orchard* had expressed his deeply felt belief that the chopping down of the orchard and the destruction of the genteel life that it symbolizes was a tragic loss. In a letter to his wife in 1903, Chekhov had expressed concern that Lopakhin, whom he saw as the central character, should not be played simply as a loudmouthed boor.[12] The playwright had insisted instead that beneath the businessman's coarse exterior there lay a delicacy of spirit, and from the very beginning he had envisaged the role being played by Stanislavsky, a real millionaire from a family of merchants, themselves sprung from peasant stock. But though Stanislavsky had readily agreed with Chekhov's analysis of the character, he showed great reluctance to play him. Initially he rehearsed two parts, Gayev and Lopakhin, but wrote twice to Chekhov, complaining that he could not find the right tone for the peasant-turned-merchant, and in the end he played Gayev.[13] The playwright and the director had disagreed too about the role of Ranyevskaya. Chekhov had been adamant that Knipper should play either Charlotta or Varya. Stanislavsky, again ignoring his wishes, insisted on casting her as Ranyevskaya. Sharon Carnicke has argued that casting two of the company's strongest performers in the roles of the brother and sister, had immediately and inevitably focused attention upon them; it had strengthened Stanislavsky's overriding emphasis on the sufferings of the displaced gentry and shifted the centre of gravity of the play.[14] Knebel by contrast took a broader approach. Her sympathy extended to all the characters and she avoided dividing them into opposite camps according to their social standing. Writing of Knebel's 1965 Moscow production, Tat'iana Shakh-Azizova maintained that 'the characters aroused interest not because of their social status, or class as merchants or aristocrats, but by their human characteristics: they were quite simply fascinating people'.[15] Siobhan McKenna and Cyril Cusack were not part of the regular Abbey ensemble and had long-established reputations as stars of the Irish theatre. Their performances as Ranyevskaya and Gayev were naturally the focus of much critical attention. But as Gus Smith remarked, a great strength of Knebel's work was that the other members of the cast did not become merely 'the poor relations of the production'.[16] On the contrary, according to Dowling, the director demonstrated 'a delicacy of touch in her approach to the characters, both major and minor, which resulted in a truthful and warm sense of the whole'.[17] Nevertheless her careful line of sympathy for the displaced family did not ignore the absurdity of their lifestyles and their failure to adjust to new realities.[18] In rehearsal, Lopakhin was appreciated as a man of sense, whose plan to build dachas was admirably practical. At the same time, Ranyevskaya and Gayev's rejection of his scheme delighted the Dublin cast. As one actor gleefully claimed: 'They're Irish. Totally impractical. Just like us.'[19]

Knebel had performed with Stanislavsky and she recalled the impression he had made as Gayev: tall, handsome, and elegantly aristocratic, and in her Moscow production in 1965 the actor Antony Khodursky had adopted a similar style. But in Dublin, she found, in the diminutive, affectionate, and absent-mindedly smiling Cusack, a completely different but no less convincing Gayev.[20] In fact the role was to become one of Cusack's more memorable triumphs. An adept billiard player, from his first entrance, swinging the gold-topped cane that doubled as his cue, to his final heart-rending exit, (in Dowling's description) Cusack presented a man who operated on two levels of reality, one a state of perfect indolence where the only concern was potting the red, and the other a more intrusive one where the petty details broke in and the reality created a deep sadness.[21] In the final scene, as everyone busied themselves for departure, he gently patted all the furniture as an indulgent grandfather might his adorable grandchildren.[22] This action was all the more poignant because the dresser and chairs that had seemed so familiar and welcoming at Ranyevskaya's arrival were now shrouded in dust-cloths for her departure. As Knebel recalled, after all the other actors had left Cusack sat alone on a last remaining forgotten trunk until someone hurriedly returned to collect it, at which point he rose and delivered a final wistful gesture as though apologizing for delaying everyone.[23] Cusack's gentle other-worldliness was complemented by McKenna's radiance and dynamism as Ranyevskaya. Dressed in crimson, from her first entrance sweeping on to the stage with her entourage she established a commanding presence, but it soon became clear that her rich voice and carefully cultivated urbane style could not mask the pathos of a woman for whom life had provided much pain and many failures.

Stanislavsky, much to Chekhov's dismay, had expanded on his directions for settings. In collaboration with his designer Viktor Simov, Stanislavsky had added in each act a wealth of naturalistic detail, and had written what was in effect a complete score of off-stage sound effects. His production had been criticized for such excessive detail by contemporary commentators. Vsevolod Meyerhold, in particular, had maintained that the orchard and the old life it represents were expressed in Chekhov's play in an openly symbolic form.[24] This idea had been central to the setting designed by Yury Pimenov for Knebel's Moscow production, and which now was recreated on the Abbey stage. There was no attempt at a physical representation of the orchard; the set consisted instead of semi-opaque floating drapes hung around the stage area. Though white, these airy curtains were intended to evoke not the actual presence of blossoming cherry trees but a memory of them. In Knebel's production they and the life they represent had already passed; the audience were not shown the process of time passing but instead presented with a *fait accompli*.[25] Stanislavsky's approach exerted (and often continues to exert) a considerable influence on expectations of how Chekhov should be presented. As Arnold Aronson has argued, unlike 'Shakespearean', or 'Pinteresque', the word 'Chekhovian' does not identify the dramatist's writing technique but evokes instead an instantly recognizable visual style – rooms choc-a-bloc with period furniture, and outdoor scenes that seek to recreate leafy bowers and magic lakes.[26] McKenna, when she heard that there would be no orchard on the Abbey stage, was initially alarmed at this subversion of traditional expectations.[27] Knebel, however, explained that the loss of the orchard was in her view not so much actual as metaphorical:

> It seems to me that in his last play Chekhov understood very well what it means to lose something infinitely beloved. Each of us has lost and will lose our own 'cherry orchard'. Each of us is trying to hold on to it. The moment when you lose 'the cherry orchard', you might think you lose everything. But ahead lies a life, a thousand times richer than any loss.[28]

In the rehearsal process Knebel also explored those themes that resonated most with her Irish actors: the role of the home and hearth in Irish social interaction and the importance of possessing one's own home, and the sorrow felt at its loss. But for the cast such ideas of ownership were less important than the broader notion of a homeland – a place that the young must abandon but which remains the site of childhood memories, and to which the exile feels compelled to return.[29] As McKenna explained to her Russian director, emigration of the young in search of work was a fact of Irish life that had enormous emotional significance: '[It was as] if Chekhov had seen the faces of the mothers who stand on the quayside watching the ships that bear away their children – perhaps, who knows, forever – to distant, foreign countries'.[30] Although these ideas were central to Knebel's Irish production, they were not imposed on Chekhov's play, they evolved instead from an exploration of it. Knebel was not concerned to create on stage a specifically Irish world. On the contrary, she attempted to present an authentic image of Russia. This led to a minor contretemps with the Abbey props department. At one point in the rehearsal process an antique samovar which they had acquired with some considerable difficulty and expense was presented to Knebel. It aroused a great deal of enthusiasm: 'A Russian play, a Russian director, and even a samovar – fantastic!'[31] A samovar, to Western eyes, is probably the commonest signifier of everything that is Russian – they are bought as souvenirs, and images are reproduced on tourist brochures. To Russians they are much less exotic: they are tea-kettles. To the stage management's great disappointment, Knebel politely but quite categorically rejected the samovar; it was a 'completely unnecessary piece of local colour', and the script itself called for a coffee pot.[32] This incident clearly amused her, but is also quite revealing in what it says about our preconceived notions of the other.

Knebel was fêted in the Irish press, her production was given an extended run, played to packed houses and generated some ecstatic reviews.[33] Desmond Rushe described it as a 'supreme joy', praised the 'superlatively fine' acting, and said that he could not recall 'ever having experienced a theatrical performance of such concentrated, sustained, and elevating beauty'.[34] Gus Smith, who was disappointed by other productions in the second week of the festival, described it as a 'sparkling jewel in a far from glittering casket' and wondered why no one had yet suggested that Knebel receive the Freedom of the City of Dublin.[35] Seamus Kelly of *The Irish Times* was less enthusiastic. Although he praised the high standards of the performance of the ensemble in general and of McKenna and Cusack in particular, he suggested that Knebel's production was a 'fine bit of theatrical archaeological digging' and 'a faithful and beautiful period reproduction of the play as it was originally played by Olga Knippur' (*sic*).[36]

Knebel's productions in Moscow in 1965 and in Dublin in 1968 were staged in a period when some other Russian directors were being heavily censured for their daring, often iconoclastic, stagings of Chekhov's work. Knebel's productions were not radical re-interpretations. And they were politically conservative; her suggestion that the play was about the necessity for human beings to endure in the face of loss and look to a brighter future had much in common with the optimism of the official Soviet party line.[37] Knebel's interpretation was indebted too to Stanislavsky's, but it was by no means, as Kelly implies, a carbon copy of his work. As we have seen, she took a more even-handed approach than Stanislavsky in her treatment of the characters and used a setting devoid of all extraneous naturalistic detail. In this she was indebted not to the traditions of the MAT but to the Russian avant-garde: to Meyerhold, but also arguably to Aleksandr Tairov's minimalist treatment of the *Seagull* at the Kamernyi theatre in 1944. Kelly simply failed to see that Knebel's decision to stage *The Cherry Orchard* with no house, no blossoming branches, and little of the paraphernalia of the everyday, was a significant departure from tradition for a director schooled at the MAT.[38]

Kelly also considered Knebel's desire to present an authentically Russian world unsatisfactory because, he maintained:

The truth of Chekhov's thesis would have been more strongly emphasized if it were interpreted in terms of the decaying Irish Great House, with Gombeen-men taking over, and good old Somerville and Ross slaves left behind to die instead of Firs.[39]

The idea that Chekhov's work would be better understood if its social world were viewed through Irish eyes, and its action transposed to an Irish Big House was not new. Thomas McDonagh, who had introduced Chekhov to the Irish stage by directing in 1915 a production of the one-act *Swan Song*, in 1918 wrote a play of his own, *Weeds*.[40] The manuscript has been lost, but to judge from critical commentaries it was in essence a reworking of *The Cherry Orchard*, with the action transplanted to Ireland. Some time before Knebel arrived in Dublin, an Irish version of *The Cherry Orchard* entitled *The Light of Other Days* by Peter Watts had been rejected by the Abbey but was later broadcast on RTE. In more recent times several Irish playwrights have all produced versions and translations of Chekhov plays that explore what they see as the experiences common to Russia and Ireland at the end of the nineteenth century. The experience of creating new versions has also prompted some to create original works, in which the specific details of Chekhov's world may be lost but in which the play's fabric is woven in part from Chekhov's emotional threads.

In 2004 Tom Murphy's *Cherry Orchard*, based on a literal translation by Chris Heaney and Patrick Miles, and advertised as a new version, was staged as part of the Abbey's centenary celebrations. But Murphy's engagement with Chekhov predates this new version of *The Cherry Orchard* by some four years and is clearly seen in his original work *The House*. It concerns how Christy, having emigrated and having made money by dubious means (probably as a pimp), returns with enough to buy up,when it comes up for auction, the old house of the de Burca family whom from childhood he has idolized as Lopakhin has Ranyevskaya. Unlike Lopakhin's, however, his purchase is not a business venture. He has no desire to destroy the house and build something new. On the contrary, he is driven by a desire to preserve the past, himself buying, if needs be, the house which, while not in truth his home, he has always regarded as such. Murphy's play involves sexual infidelity, and violence leading eventually to murder, but in some aspects of its plot, in references to the chopping of trees, and in the creation of this Lopakhin-like figure, it does rework *The Cherry Orchard*. Murphy sets the play in his hometown of Tuam in County

Galway and returns to the theme of exile that he had explored in his earliest works. In his introduction to the first edition of *The House*, Fintan O'Toole has argued that exile in Murphy is not a matter of location. It is a condition so fundamental that it has seeped into the bones of those who stay as much as those who go. It shapes family, friendship, personality, even dreams. It becomes the human condition itself.[41] As Maria Knebel discovered in 1968, and as Murphy explored in 2000, it is perhaps this understanding of the emotional and social impact of emigration – the pain of exile, and the trauma of return – that brings Chekhov's world sharply into focus for an Irish audience.

---

[1] 'Theatre Council to discuss play "problems"', *Irish Independent* 24 August 1968: 13, and 'Resigns over Russian films ban', *Irish Independent* 3 September 1968: 1.

[2] Ibid.

[3] The author has previously published a short account of this production in: Ros Dixon, 'West Meets East: Russian Productions at the Dublin Theatre Festival, 1957-2006', *Interactions: Dublin Theatre Festival 1957-2007*, eds Nicholas Grene and Patrick Lonergan (Dublin: Carysfort, 2008): 75-91 (77-78).

[4] Mariia Knebel', '"Vishnevyi sad" v Irlandii', *Teatr* (May 1969): 158-66. Knebel also wrote about her experiences in Ireland in the following: Mariia Knebel', 'Dublin: Ebbi-teatr', *Sovetskaia kul'tura*, 7 January 1969: 3. The latter article was later translated and published in English as Maria Knebel, 'Dublin – The Abbey Theatre', *The Irish Times* 28 January 1969: 12. Knebel's accounts of her time in Ireland are very largely positive. She was not impressed, however, by what she clearly perceived as the unprofessional practices of some of her actors, and remarked upon them in ways that could (at a stretch) be interpreted as scornful. The present author suspects the Russian director was entirely justified, but following the publication of her views in English Martin D. Bates objected to Knebel's fault-finding in 'A Russian Eye on Ireland', *The Irish Times* 28 March 1981: 13.

[5] Knebel', *Teatr*, 159.

[6] Ibid., 163.

[7] Ibid.

[8] Knebel', *Sovetskaia*, 3.

[9] Joe Dowling, 'Signposts', *Theatre Ireland*, 4 (September – December 1983): 33.

[10] Knebel', *Teatr*, 162.

[11] Ibid.

12 Letter from Chekhov to Knipper, 30 October 1903, *Chekhov i teatr: pis'ma, fel'etony, sovremenniki o Chekhove – dramaturge*, ed. E. Surkov (Moscow: Iskusstvo, 1961): 156.

13 Jean Benedetti, *Stanislavski* (London: Methuen, 1988): 128.

14 Sharon Carnicke, 'Stanislavsky's production of *The Cherry Orchard* in the US', *Chekhov Then and Now*, ed. Douglas Clayton (New York: Peter Lang, 1977): 23.

15 Tatiana K. Shakh-Azizova, 'Chekhov on the Russian Stage', *The Cambridge Companion to Chekhov*, eds Vera Gottlieb and Paul Allain (Cambridge: CUP, 2000): 168.

16 Gus Smith, 'Salute to Madame Knebel', *The Sunday Independent* 13 October 1968: 26.

17 Dowling, 32.

18 Ibid.

19 Knebel', *Teatr*, 164.

20 Ibid., 162-163.

21 Dowling, 33.

22 Ibid.

23 Knebel', *Teatr*, 163.

24 V. E. Meierkhol'd, *Stat'i, pis'ma, rechi, besedy: 1891-1917* (Moscow: Iskusstvo, 1968): 84-86. In English: 'The Naturalistic Theatre and The Theatre of Mood', *Meyerhold on Theatre*, ed. and trans. Edward Braun (London: Eyre Methuen, 1969): 28-33.

25 Tatiana K. Shakh-Azizova, 'Dolgaia zhizn' traditsii', *Chekhovskie chteniia v Ialte: Chekhov i teatr*, ed. V. I. Kuleshov (Moscow: Kniga, 1976): 29.

26 Arnold Aronson, 'The Scenography of Chekhov', *The Cambridge Companion to Chekhov*, 135.

27 Knebel', *Teatr*, 162.

28 Maria Knebel', *Vsia zhizn*, 2nd ed. (Moscow: Iskusstvo, 1993): 570.

29 Knebel', *Teatr*, 164.

30 Knebel', *Sovetskaia*, 3.

31 Knebel', *Teatr*, 164.

32 Ibid.

33 'Henry Kelly Talks to Madame Maria Knebel', *Irish Times* 3 October 1968: 6; Seamus Kelly, 'Producer Speaks of Abbey Skill', *Irish Times* 10 October 1968: 10; Ita Mallon, 'Art that blossoms in "The Cherry Orchard"', *Irish Independent* 27 September 1968: 11.

34 Desmond Rushe, '"The Cherry Orchard" a supreme joy', *Irish Independent* 9 October 1968: 3.

35 Smith, 26.

36 Seamus Kelly, 'Chekhov's Classic as in Russia', *Irish Times* 9 October 1968: 10.

37 James N. Loehlin, *Chekhov: The Cherry Orchard* (Cambridge: CUP, 2006): 149-150.

38 Shakh-Azizova, 'Dolgaia', 30.

[39] Kelly, 'Chekhov's Classic', 10. Kelly's commentary caused a small stir. In a letter to the *Irish Times* an audience member objected to his idea that the play would have been better for Irish audiences had it been presented as an analogue for the decline of the Anglo Irish gentry. Rosemary Lane, 'The Cherry Orchard', *Irish Times* October 12 1968: 16.

[40] Measadoir, 'Weeds', *New Ireland* 7 (18 January 1919): 181. For commentaries on McDonagh's productions of Chekhov and on the reception of the Russian playwright's work in Ireland at the beginning of the twentieth century, see William J. Feeney, *Drama in Hardwicke Street: A History of the Irish Theatre Company* (London and Toronto: Associated University Press, 1984).

[41] Fintan O'Toole, Introduction, *The House*, by Thomas Murphy (London: Methuen, 2000): viii.

5 | Tom Murphy's *The Cherry Orchard* in the Context of Irish Rewritings of Chekhov

Zsuzsa Csikai

Anton Chekhov was worried about the translation of his plays, as he feared that a translation would not be able to convey the full meaning of the selling of the estate in *The Cherry Orchard*.[1] He might have feared that his works in translation would suffer the fate that Cervantes' Don Quixote hints at when pondering the nature of translation: 'It seems to me that translation from one language to another ... is like looking at Flemish tapestries from the back side, because even though you can see the figures, they are covered by threads that hide them, and you can't see the smooth texture of the front side'.[2]

Tom Murphy, one of the several Irish playwrights who have translated, re-translated or reworked Chekhov's works, speculates on the distinction between literal translation and version in terms of Don Quixote's metaphor:

> The objective of a literal translation – to render in another language the exact contextual meaning of the original – differs from the purpose of a version. A version, as I see it, is more subjective and more interpretatively open; it is speculative in its considerations of the 'spirit' of the original and seeks to translate that 'spirit' into a language and movement that have their own dynamic; the ordering in the version attempts to re-create what was alive, musical and vibrant in the original. A version, of itself, wants to avoid looking like the back of the tapestry.[3]

To avoid creating translations (or versions) that look like the back of the tapestry is an ambition of primary importance commonly shared by translators of literary texts, but the methods used are immensely varied. Importantly, when a translator decides, consciously or otherwise, to apply one particular method,[4] his or her choice is just as much governed by the given cultural and political milieu as by individual personal artistic and aesthetic preferences. This paper examines the ways, and the motivations behind them, in which Irish playwrights, in particular Tom Murphy, have attempted to recreate the front of the tapestry when reworking Chekhov's plays.

The two distinctive activities Murphy mentions in connection with literary translations, namely to produce a literal translation of the exact contextual meaning and to translate the 'spirit' of the original into a text that re-creates the original's vitality and musicality in a more subjective and interpretative way, would sound very much like two steps in the regular translation process for those who have ever been engaged in making translations from one language into another. Translators do not come up with their actual version immediately after reading the original, but make a mental 'literal' translation first and then turn it into a functional equivalent, usually striving to preserve the 'spirit' while transposing the source text into the different dynamic of a different language. Murphy, having no knowledge of Russian, relies on someone else doing the first step for him and carries out the second, undoubtedly more creative, step himself, using his own subjective translation strategy.[5] And what his overall strategy amounts to is a break with the Irish tendency to effectively domesticate, Hibernicize the original. His *The Cherry Orchard* (2004), the most recent Irish Chekhov version, does not deny the Russianness of the play, on the contrary, the Russianness is emphasized by preserving the play's otherness.

Although the metaphor of recreating the front as opposed to the back of the tapestry implies that it is an issue of quality, in this exploration of Murphy's and other Irish dramatists' translations of Chekhov's works the central concern will not be whether one particular method has produced a 'better' or more 'faithful' translation than the other. Instead of such a normative approach (which attempts to evaluate the 'faithfulness' or 'equivalence' of a translation), translations will be seen as embodiments of a cultural practice which has its own contexts and its own politics, and which bears the impact of the historical and social milieu the translator is working in. Examining the Irish-English Chekhov versions of the last three decades from such a perspective reveals that, although a small group of works, these translations and adaptations do form a 'body of literature'[6] with recognizably changing patterns of translating/reworking techniques reflecting the effect of changing social and political circumstances.

Different times produce different translations and adaptations, and a shift in approach to translation can occur even within a few decades. While Brian Friel and Thomas Kilroy produced acculturated, Hibernicized Chekhov plays in the 1980s and late 1990s, playwrights who turned to reworking Chekhov later, or belong to a younger generation, created versions that are not so intent on thoroughly Irishing the originals; instead, these playwrights have made some efforts to show the foreign, the other, in their translations, and instead of domestication they favour foreignization. And indeed, whether this or that translation strategy is favoured in the process of translation (and the dilemma usually concerns whether to opt for domestication or foreignization) is not a result of arbitrary choices. Behind each word the translator chooses, adds or leaves out, and the way she or he places them, there is, as Román Álvarez and Carmen-África Vidal claim, 'a voluntary act that reveals his history and the socio-political milieu that surrounds him; in other words, his own culture'.[7]

It seems reasonable to suggest that the changing pattern of recreating Chekhov for the Irish stage signals a shift in the way the authors perceive not only the aim of translation in general but also their own role in shaping the landscape of Irish theatre. The first, domesticating, phase of Chekhov rewritings, i.e. Kilroy's adaptation of *The Seagull* (1981), and the production of Friel's first translations of Chekhov's major plays, *Three Sisters* (1981), and later *Uncle Vanya* (1998), shows a similar general approach to rewriting. To a lesser or greater extent, these plays can be seen as associated with the aspirations that characterized the Field Day project, which, 'especially in its early years, had been part of the more general attempt by artists and intellectuals to circumvent politics through culture'.[8] The governing idea was to further 'the decolonization process of the imagination' through art, which in Friel's opinion was 'very important if a new Irish personality is to emerge'.[9] In an attempt to displace the established Anglicized Chekhov translations by providing recognizably Irish versions, Kilroy and Friel both contributed to this endeavour.[10]

What these versions of Chekhov wanted to avoid looking like is translations felt to be too Anglicized for Irish tastes. Interestingly, the heavy acculturation chosen by Kilroy and Friel in their versions of the Russian plays was seen as justified not merely because at the time it was a means for these dramatists to search for ways of asserting cultural independence for Irish theatre. Their Hibernicized versions were also seen as much needed attempts to ensure a revitalization of Chekhov for English-language audiences, as the established English Chekhov translations and productions had long been perceived as problematic by Chekhov scholars and translation studies scholars alike. The early translations, like Constance Garnett's, first presented Chekhov to the British, and consequently to the Irish, in the disguise of an honorary English gentleman. As Vera Gottlieb points out, ignoring the plays' political, historical and cultural specificity, the Anglicized translations created an apolitical, sentimental 'sorrowing evocation of valuable way of life gone forever'.[11] This was an image of Chekhov that later provoked dissatisfaction and motivated attempts at its correction. Among the more recent reinterpretations of Chekhov, the late twentieth-century Irish-English versions are seen as some of the most innovative. They succeed in rediscovering the Russian dramatist's comic genius and his use of irony, and, even more importantly, in restoring a sharper political edge to the plays.

It is a paradox of translation, however, that while the Irish dramatists rediscover Chekhov and attempt to restore to his work what was lost in earlier Standard English translations, they accomplish it by way of altering the original text just as much. Kilroy's adaptation of *The Seagull* was originally commissioned by Max Stafford-Clark for the London Royal Court Theatre[12] with the aim to bring the play closer to its contemporary English audience by relocating it, paradoxical as it might seem, into Ireland. Friel's versions are also in part reactions against the established, genteel, Anglicized Chekhov but his translations move Chekhov out of Bloomsburyland only to resettle him in Ireland.

However, the potential new dimensions that an Irish version (in opposing earlier English ones) may bring to Chekhov create the sense, as Michael West aptly points out, that 'Irishness has come to signify authenticity on the stage,' and that 'the Irishness makes the Russian more real: this is Chekhov in English, but not an English Chekhov'.[13] Going back to Don Quixote's metaphor, Friel and Kilroy in their recreation of the Chekhovian tapestry introduce new lines, contours, colours, and figures, all of them in an Irish hue, which was perceived by most viewers as a successful restoration of the original front.

Tom Murphy's new version of *The Cherry Orchard* stands out against the backdrop of the established Irish tradition of Hibernicizing Chekhov. His version of the Russian play shows the emergence of a strikingly different pattern of translational/- adaptational choices. Although undoubtedly an Irish English version, it is one that represents a move away from the late twentieth-century Irish trend to thoroughly acculturate and domesticate the original.[14] In contrast, it allows space to the Russianness, the otherness of Chekhov's play. In terms of underlying motives, it seems to lack the subtle but inherent political dimension that made the earlier Chekhov translations and adaptations part of the intellectual and aesthetic decolonization process. The change of motivation is signalled by the fact that Murphy's Chekhov text features a significantly smaller measure of alteration through domestication; instead the Irish author creates a version rather close to the original Russian play text and manages in various ways to preserve some of its foreignness.

Although Murphy was commissioned by the Abbey to do the play, and the choice of this particular play 'was exclusively their decision',[15] it was a fortunate one, as *The Cherry Orchard* fits seamlessly into the playwright's intense exploration of the meaning of home, a preoccupation central in his original plays. Concerned with a search for home, *The House* (2000) has conspicuous echoes of Chekhov's *The Cherry Orchard* in terms of plot, characters and subject matter, with the Irish play's focus on the decline of the land-owning classes and its portrayal of lives arrested in the past. It would come as no surprise, therefore, if, in line with the Irish dramatic tradition, Murphy domesticated *The Cherry Orchard*, transposing it into his Irish reality, or if he integrated the Russian play, similarly to Friel, into his own oeuvre through a series of alterations and adjustments. Contrary to these expectations, Murphy's *The Cherry Orchard* cannot be classed as an attempt at conscious and provocative domestication. Despite writing inevitably in a language that has Irish rhythms and cadences, Murphy makes no emphatic attempt at acculturating the Russian text; in fact, not only does he follow the original very closely, but through various foreignizing techniques his translation ensures that the play is not deprived of its roots in the Russian culture.[16]

What prompts the move away from acculturation towards a tendency to retain the foreign element in the source? To a great extent, it seems it is the changes in the social and cultural conditions of Ireland that facilitate the emergence of this new approach to the rewriting process. By the late 1990s and early 2000s, the issues Friel's and Kilroy's resistant translations/adaptations set out to address have lost their relevance for more recent rewriters of Chekhov (as well as for Friel himself in his later career), not to mention the representatives of a younger generation. The search for ways to achieve Irish cultural assertion, a central issue even in the last decades of the twentieth century, appears less urgent, or even out of place, in the context of the manifold successes and new problems of Celtic Tiger Ireland. The advent of a different cultural milieu in a post-nationalist, more and more multicultural Ireland entails a greater openness to foreign voices in Irish culture and a general opening up towards the international, global context. The economic development is coupled with a new confidence, which is manifest as a cultural confidence as well. McGuinness's words with regard to his translations and versions imply this. He claims that creating versions with foreign voices, for him 'is the mark of a new confidence in Irish theatre, that we are not frightened to do that. We no longer need to assert that we have a right to do these plays, we take it for granted, of course we do it'.[17] This attitude is reflected in Murphy's Chekhov play too.

Deeply rooted expectations, however, are hard to change and are easily taken for granted. The tradition of domesticating Chekhov into an Irish context has become so established in public perception that if an Irish playwright deals with Chekhov, the expectation seems to be that it is a version in which the original is significantly altered so that it reflects Irish historical, social or cultural issues. It is generally expected that the Russian reality of Chekhov's works be used as an analogy for the Irish one. Michael West, who translated *The Seagull* (first produced in 1999), claims that his is a very close translation without any conscious attempt at Hibernicization, which might account for why it was met with rather hostile criticism.[18] It is also noteworthy that Murphy's Chekhov is described and promoted by the publisher on the back cover of its book version as 'a fine adaptation with its Irish vernacular [which] allows us to re-imagine the events of the play in the last days of Anglo-Irish colonialism, giving *The Cherry Orchard* a vivid new life within our own history and social consciousness'.[19] This reading of Murphy's version seems to be symptomatic of the extent to which Irish readers and audiences are conditioned by the earlier adaptations to automatically see (and expect) Russia as a counterpart for Ireland, and to place all Chekhov adaptations within this context.

If we go beyond this conditioning, we see that Murphy's rewriting techniques indicate a new approach to the translation of Chekhov in Ireland in that his *The Cherry Orchard*, far from being a consistently Hibernicized adaptation, is a rather close rendering of the original, featuring foreignizing techniques that make the play's text oscillate between the familiar and the foreign. Although it is rendered into English as it is spoken in Ireland (which is, however, not a decision as politically loaded as it was in the time of Friel's and Kilroy's pioneering Chekhov versions), thus ensuring naturalness, the play also preserves enough of the original text's features to disrupt at times the sense of absolute familiarity which a fluent, transparent translated language would aim to create. With the retention of, and even emphasis on, the foreign elements, the playwright challenges the target language culture by exposing its audience to the difference inherent in Chekhov's text rooted in a foreign culture.

One typical feature of a translation that intends to signal the foreignness of the original text instead of totally integrating it into the receiving culture is that it follows the original closely. Although Murphy in his introduction claims that he has 'not followed the literal translation line by line or speech by speech', he is rather close to doing so. His version does not exhibit any radical departure from the original; there are no significant changes in the play's structure and hardly any instances of editing out or adding to the original text. The ones that do occur are well within the sphere of normal translation practice, which aims at reproducing the sense and the impact of the original for a target audience, i.e., making 'the target text function in the target culture the way the source text functioned in the source culture'. [20]

If we take Murphy's rendering of Petya's famous 'All of Russia is our orchard' speech, we can see that it may very well sound as if it was adjusted to reflect the Irish predicament. The speech ends with the following lines in Murphy's version:

> We haven't come very far. We have nothing yet. No *conscious* attitude to the past. Theories, melancholy and vodka. And to live in the present, the past has to be consciously acknowledged, and atoned for by suffering and work.[21]

An Irish audience, conditioned to search for Irish relevance in Chekhov's works, will undoubtedly interpret these lines as a reference to the past political stagnation in Northern Ireland, or as an allusion to Ireland's obsession with her past and the acknowledged need to come to terms with its legacy. Compare, however, a possible so-called 'literal' translation of Petya's speech:

> We are at least two hundred years behind our times, we don't have anything yet, no clear attitude to the past, we can only philosophize, complain about despondency or drink vodka. But it is so obvious that in order to start living in the present we have to start to atone for our past, to get over it, but it is only through suffering, only through working ceaselessly and especially hard that we can atone for it.[22]

Beyond doubt, the speech in Murphy's conspicuously close rendering does allow a re-imagining of the events 'in terms of the Anglo-Irish colonial past', but only as much as a 'literal' translation would.

The lack of significant additions or omissions also indicates an intention to preserve as much of the original as possible. The very few lines Murphy added to the original text merely function as a means to enhance characterization. Lyubov says in Murphy that her sin is 'squandering my inheritance' (34), which is a reference to a central theme. Lopakhin's added line: 'But you know the place is going to be sold, you know that, don't you?' (17), is a means of underlying Lopakhin's desperate attempt to make his voice heard and save the family from destruction, which indicates that he is not to be considered the villain of the play. The additions, therefore, unlike in Friel's *Three Sisters* and *Uncle Vanya*, do not introduce specifically Irish concerns, political, social or cultural;[23] they merely make the figures of the tapestry come out with a sharper contour.

The general tendency to follow the original closely and make cultural difference visible is manifest in Murphy's decision to retain all the Russian culture-specific elements, like the Russian terms of endearment and patronymics that Chekhov's texts abound in. Murphy's play is peppered with expressions like 'Petya' or 'Anyechka', 'mamochka', people address each other as Lyubov Andreyevna (16), Peter Sergeich, (10), Boris Borisovich (20), Leonid Andreich (27) or Avdotya Fyodorovna (31), which will definitely convey a sense of foreignness for Irish audiences, and this in turn works towards hindering an automatic identification of the Russian reality with the Irish one.

In several cases, Murphy not only preserves but also intensifies the Russian effect by adding a few of his own creation: he expands, for instance, the single word '*rodnaia*'[24] when he renders it as 'my pet, my love, my darling little sister, my ...'(28); or when he translates the line '*milaia moia, prekrasnaia komnata*'[25] (literally, my darling, beautiful room) into 'sweet, darling, beautiful, *angel* of a room' (9, emphasis in original). Murphy emphasizes the foreign effect when he has Pishchik address Lopakhin as 'my dearest heart' (70) instead of the emotionally less charged phrase in the original, '*gromadneishevo uma chelovek*',[26] which means 'man of the greatest intellect'. Also, Gayev, the landowner, parts with the peasants with the words: 'Thank you, my brothers, my little brothers' (62), which is the direct translation of the Russian phrase, '*spasibo, brattsy, spasibo vam*'.[27] In Murphy, Firs, the old servant, is addressed by Ranyevskaya as 'Firs, dear little old friend' (15), and the servants in the kitchen as 'our old dears in the kitchen' (31).

Carrying these features, foreign to English (including Irish-English) ears and customs, over into the translation instead of omitting them or toning them down contributes to the image of the Russians as more emotional than English speakers, thus emphasizing cultural difference and exposing the target audience to the original's otherness.

Although most of the idiomatic phrases are rendered by their corresponding English phrases creating a contemporary feel: 'Time to call it a day' (13), 'head over heels, I am' (16), for instance, Murphy allows at least one such phrase to stick out, sounding unidiomatic due to its being a mirror translation from Russian. He renders the Russian saying '*do svad'by zazhivet*'[28] as 'it will get better before you are married' (6). In Russian this is said when comforting a crying, injured child, and would thus be closer to 'be a brave boy' in contemporary English. Although the mirror translation's meaning is perfectly clear in the given context, its foreignness and unidiomatic nature can still be sensed.

There is one type of change in the texture of the original that Murphy is consistent in carrying out. Chekhov's full grammatical speeches tend to be broken into shorter, fragmented, elliptical sentences, thus making the original, often highly expository speeches give way to questions, gaps, which creates suggestiveness. The very first utterance in Murphy's play is: 'Well, it's in' (5), the referent of which becomes clear only in the subsequent lines: 'What time it is?' 'Nearly two'. 'So how late does that make the train?' (5).

In the original the first line states: 'The train has arrived.' Instead of such expository sentences in Chekhov, perceived as an outdated mode of introducing new information for the audience, we have questions and elliptical sentences. Chekhov's lines: 'Lyubov Andreyevna has lived for five years abroad, I don't know what she has become like ... She is a good person' becomes: 'What will she be like after her five years abroad? She won't have changed ... The eyes, you know: the kindness in them. Always ...' (5).

Elliptical sentences dominate the dialogues in Murphy. Characters regularly converse in half sentences while the rest of the meaning is indicated in italics in the stage directions, thus remaining unseen and unheard for the audience, only to be guessed. For instance, the complete Russian sentence, *'Esli by ia mogla zabyt' moe proshloe!'*[29] (literally, If only I could forget my past), is rendered as 'If only I too could forget (... *the past)*' (20)[30]; or the sentence *'dachi i dachniki – eto tak poshlo prostite'*[31] (literally, cottages and cottagers! Oh, please, this is so vulgar!) turns into 'But cottages, 'bungalows' (*The vulgarity of the idea)*' (34). 'Mama' (*meaning 'Mama bought it')*, [emphasis in original] (16), or 'it's changing' (*the world is)*' (61) represent the same strategy. What is achieved is an updating of the language, making Chekhov sound just as contemporary and realist for the twenty-first century as he did for his own audience. [32]

Emphasizing the above foreign features in various ways while resisting complete domestication in his translation of *The Cherry Orchard*, Murphy does not only manage to make his version avoid looking like the back of the tapestry where the threads hide the original figures, but he equally avoids weaving in new threads that would change the shades and colours of the figures. His translational choices allow the Russianness and otherness of the original to filter through, making the audience experience the cultural climate of the original. If the Hibernicized versions enabled their audiences to rediscover Chekhov after a long tradition of Anglicization, the more recent foreignizing approaches to the Russian works allow yet another revision. With less emphasis on Hibernicization, Murphy's version has the potential to enable Irish audiences to rediscover the Russian playwright once again, this time more on his own terms and with a greater awareness of his foreignness. The new approach to translation of classics of which Murphy's version is an example demonstrates an opening up to a larger scale of other voices in Irish theatre, which instead of defining itself in opposition to the English influence now conceives of itself as part of a global, multicultural world.

---

[1] As Emma Polotskaya, quoting Chekhov's letters, reminds us, Chekhov was worried that due to the cultural differences, 'the French would never understand Ermolaj and the selling of the estate'; quoted in Emma Polotskaya, 'Nedotiopa i vrazdrob' (O trudnostiah perevoda piesy)' ['On the difficulties of translating a play']. *http://rus.1september.ru/articlef.php?ID=200300409.*

[2] Quoted in Howard Mancing, *Cervantes' Don Quixote: A Reference Guide* (Westport: Greenwood Press, 2006): xi.

[3] Tom Murphy, *The Cherry Orchard* (London: Methuen, 2004): 2.

[4] Murphy for instance says, in a letter to the author, that as for the language of his version he 'did not have a system of techniques or governing approach to what I did, it was a matter of instinct and judgement'.

[5] For the purposes of this analysis, 'translation' is used in a wider sense generally accepted in the field of translation studies to allow for a much wider definition of the nature of translation, making room for the exploration of irregular translations and methods. Murphy himself refers to his *The Cherry Orchard* as a 'version', which is an undefined category. One might well argue, however, that a version like his, as well as adaptations in general, often operate with techniques of translation.

[6] Rachel May observes that 'translations are not merely stand-ins for their originals, but they themselves form a body of literature, subject to its own historical and political constraints, observing its own rules of syntax and communication'; Rachel May, *The Translator in the Text. On Reading Russian Literature in English* (Evanston, IL: Northwestern University Press, 1994): 144.

[7] Román Álvarez and M. Carmen-África Vidal, 'Translating: A Political Act', *Translation, Power, Subversion,* eds Román Álvarez and M. Carmen-África Vidal (Clevedon: Multilingual, 1996): 5.

[8] Marilynn J., Richtarik, *Acting between the Lines. The Field Day Theatre Company and Irish Cultural Politics 1980-1984* (Oxford: Clarendon, 1994): 7.

[9] Quoted in Richtarik, 121.

[10] One of Friel's concerns at the time, that 'we must make English identifiably our own language'[10], is not only a central issue in *Translations* (1980), but it is also manifest in the translation philosophy discernible in his *Three Sisters* (and later in *Uncle Vanya*). Friel's translation techniques reflect the underlying agenda of resisting and challenging the Anglicization of Irish culture. Privileging Hiberno-English over Standard English when translating a world classic is one way of resisting a residual English cultural

influence. This kind of resistant translation acts as a reassertion of the status of Hiberno-English as a legitimate language for the mediation of European classics for English-language audiences. That Friel works against the traditional role of Standard English as a mediator of culture for the Irish is most clearly apparent in his method of using not a 'literal', or close, translation as a basis for his version of *Three Sisters*, but five already existing Standard English translations.

[11] Vera Gottlieb, ' "The dwindling scale": the politics of British Chekhov', *Chekhov on the British Stage*, ed. Patrick Miles (Cambridge: CUP,1993): 151.

[12] Introduction to Thomas Kilroy. *The Seagull*. (Loughcrew: Gallery, 1993): 12.

[13] Michael West, 'Authentic Fictions', *Irish Theatre Magazine* 4.16 (Autumn 2003): 15 -22.

[14] Frank McGuinness's *Three Sisters* (1990) and *Uncle Vanya* (1995) also display a lack of intense Hibernicization, and Friel's own approach to re-translating Chekhov changed noticeably too, in his later Chekhov plays, *The Yalta Game* (2001), *The Bear* (2002), and *Afterplay* (2002), as he seems concerned with exploring private matters rather than the ways theatre may be able to change the political landscape.

[15] Murphy's correspondence with the author.

[16] Certain ideas appearing in this analysis of Murphy's *The Cherry Orchard* have been discussed in Zsuzsa Csikai 'Recreating the Front of the Tapestry: Tom Murphy's Version of *The Cherry Orchard*', *'Alive in Time': The Enduring Drama of Tom Murphy*, ed. Christopher Murray (Dublin: Carysfort Press, 2010).

[17] 'Frank McGuinness in Conversation with Joseph Long', *Theatre Talk: Voices of Irish Theatre Practitioners*, eds Lilian Chambers, Ger Fitzgibbon, and Eamonn Jordan (Dublin: Carysfort, 2001): 298-307.

[18] Oral communication with Michael West.

[19] Tom Murphy, *The Cherry Orchard* (London: Methuen, 2004).

[20] André Lefevere and Susan Bassnett, 'Introduction: Proust's Grandmother and the Thousand and One Nights: The 'Cultural Turn' in Translation Studies', *Translation, History and Culture*, eds Susan Bassnett and André Lefevere (London, New York: Pinter, 1990): 8.

[21] Murphy, *The Cherry Orchard* (London: Methuen, 2004): 43.

[22] Translation by Zsuzsa Csikai. The original text is as follows: *Мы отстали по крайней мере лет на двести, у нас нет еще ровно ничего, нет определенного отношения к прошлому, мы только философствуем, жалуемся на тоску или пьем водку. Ведь так ясно, чтобы начать жить в настоящем, надо сначала искупить наше прошлое, покончить с ним, а искупить его можно только страданием, только необычайным,*

непрерывным трудом; A. P. Chekhov, *Dramaticheskie proizvedeniia* (Leningrad: Iskusstvo, 1985): 301-02.

23 In the case of Friel's *Three Sisters*, for instance, the play's Irishing is due not only to the use of Hiberno-English. The sense of its being a double for the Irish reality is conjured up by the numerous added speeches with specifically Irish resonances. Friel's audience of 'the land of saints and scholars' hear Andrey complain their provincial town 'has not produced one person of any distinction – not one saint, not one scholar, not one artist' (111). In Friel's *Uncle Vanya*, Vanya's added lines might well be seen to make an ironic comment on the futility of empty political rhetoric in the (Northern) Irish context: 'For fifty long years we have been expressing opinions and reading pamphlets and debating and arguing. [We thought that] the very essence of life could be found in a pamphlet or in a cause or in a political belief. Chaff. ... Trumpery. Guff. Smoke. The essence of life isn't there' (19).

24 A. P. Chekhov, *Dramaticheskie proizvedeniia*, (Leningrad: Iskusstvo, 1985): 290.

25 Ibid.: 277.

26 Ibid.: 320.

27 Ibid.: 315.

28 Ibid.: 275.

29 Ibid.: 286.

30 Murphy uses brackets to indicate what is left unsaid.

31 A. P. Chekhov, *Dramaticheskie proizvedeniia.*, (Leningrad: Iskusstvo, 1985): 295.

32 Another re-translator of *The Cherry Orchard*, Trevor Griffiths, convincingly explains the need for similar alterations he carried out in his 1977 version, saying 'The writing is often highly expositional: characters tell each other things they all know already, in order that the audience will gain a firm biographical picture of character, relationships, history. This method of introducing information now seems dated. There is a history of realism that spans some eighty years beyond Chekhov: a realism of the stage, but also a realism of film. The craft of realism, of shaping realist texts, has advanced in some ways beyond what Chekhov was able to achieve –particularly in levels of obliqueness.' (Quoted in David Allen, ' 'The Cherry Orchard': a new English version by Trevor Griffiths', *Chekhov on the British Stage*, ed. Patrick Miles (Cambridge: CUP, 1993): 161.

6 | Playwrights Speak Out – Round-table Discussion on Translation and Adaptation with Thomas Kilroy and Michael West

Adrian Frazier: I wonder if I could ask Tom first about these three terms that Cynthia has used – collision, hybridization, and acculturation.[1] Collision, she told us, maintains an awareness of difference in the translated text of the original and forces a sense of alienation. Hybridization mimics the colloquialisms of the receiving culture but allows an amount of domestic inscription. Acculturation is an adaptation, a sort of free adaptation that finds parallels in the target culture. Tom, you have not only done *The Seagull*; you have also done a great deal of major translations including Ibsen and Pirandello.[2] It would be possible to admit that *The Seagull* in 1982 could have been two of these things. It was an instance of acculturation in which the premise of the translation was 'do a parallel that uses Irish culture in the late nineteenth century'. Yet, because it was staged originally in England, it was received as an instance of collision: 'This is not what we expected of Chekhov, you have done something different and forced us into an awareness of alienation and an awareness of difference'. It just was not a case of collision between Russian culture and English, but between English culture and Irish culture by way of the Russian original.

Thomas Kilroy: I think it's very helpful to have a scale of the engagement with the original. All writers are influenced by the writing of other writers, and it is just the matter of the degree. And this is particularly acute in theatre. I have described before somewhere that the history of theatre is a history of adaptation, of constant recycling. This is also true of the sister art of cinema. It is certainly true, whether it has to do with the representation of otherness, the imaginative quality, or the nature of the medium. In theatre you have a whole variety of engagements, and it is very useful to have that scale in place.

In my own case, it is literally true that in each of the adaptations which I have made I was asked to do it by a management. In the case of *Ghosts* I was approached by Phyllis Ryan and the late great Siobhan MacKenna. Siobhan wanted to play the Mrs Alving part; she was interested in the psycho-sexual relationship between the woman and the priest. Phyllis was more generally interested in using Ibsen as a vehicle to portray provincial Ireland before the Catholic Church lost its power. So there were very specific demands coming from these people. And I think that we need to remind ourselves of the fact that this whole question of adaptation is heavily related to the practical business of making theatre.

In Max Stafford-Clark's case, his father was a very famous Scottish Freudian analyst, and he became the adviser on John Huston's film *Freud*. And when Max was a student in Trinity (this is a roundabout way of telling you of his interest in *The Seagull*), Huston was living here in Co. Galway and living the life of an eighteenth-century squire. He invited Max down, and Max came and became entranced by this whole business of the Irish country estate house. Max actually had the very specific agenda of transferring *The Seagull* into an Anglo-Irish country house in the west of Ireland. So that I was presented with a job of journeywork in both of these cases, almost. I have also been invited to do many other versions and I said no. And the reason I said no is that I was not able to find a personal entry into the play. In each of the cases of the ones which I have done, I found that personal entry.

In the case of *The Seagull*, again we are back to practical theatre. Max had this idea that we would cast it half English and half Irish, so that Anna Massey, Alan Rickman, and Harriet Walter became the Anglo-Irish, and you had actors like T.P. McKenna and Veronica Duffy playing the native Irish, or whatever you want to call them. And it worked. It worked in the sense that the Anglo-Irish parts, so to speak, are written in a certain kind of idiom. And the more native Irish are written in a kind of idiomatic West of Ireland thing.

I first of all started thinking in terms of setting the play in the 1890s. And I couldn't get around this. It didn't work. And I pushed it back then. One of the reasons Max picked me to do this was that he had read my novel *The Big Chapel* (1971), which is set in the 1870s. I pushed it back a couple of decades, and immediately all the cultural references, all the references to English theatre, English literature and so on, started to leap out at me. I just had to catch them and put them down. It was amazing. In other words, it was just a mechanical shift in time and then the thing kind of worked out.

10 Thomas Kilroy, *The Seagull*, Royal Court Theatre, April 1981, directed by Max Stafford Clark: T.P. McKenna (Dr Hickey), Anna Massey (Isobel Desmond), Maggie McCarthy (Pauline), Alan Devlin (Cousin Gregory), Stuart Burge (Peter). Photo: John Haynes. Courtesy of John Haynes and Lebrecht Music & Arts Photo Library.

I was fascinated by the discussion earlier about the house, the Big House. And of course the Big House, the house in Chekhov is a place that is notorious for its traffic. The amount of people moving in and out of these houses is startling. You think of the house in terms of family or of relations. But in Chekhov, there are people there, and you don't know what they are doing there. And they are in and out, and they take their place there, and they go off, and they are back again – this constant traffic. It is highly theatrical, and it is wonderfully theatrical. One of my sources for translating *The Seagull* was reading nineteenth-century Irish novels and in particular George Moore. When you read something like *A Drama in Muslin* (1886), you realize a number of things, one of which is that in the West of Ireland the distinction between the landlord and the peasant is a spurious one, the distinction between the Protestants and the Catholics is a spurious one. The West of Ireland houses had an equivalent traffic. You had the parish priest for dinner with the Protestant landlord one day. You had the aspiring Catholic petit-bourgeois in the town dining with the landlord. You had this break-down of class. You have something similar going on in Chekhov; the lines are confused. It makes very fascinating material to work with.

There is also the question of the change which Nicky [Nicholas Grene] quite rightly saw in my version of *The Seagull*, and that is the emphasis that I place on the lack of money in my particular version.[3] This is not in the original. The reason for that is that all of the West of Ireland houses, ones that I explored and researched, were literally on their last legs and very poor. It was a kind of a gentility which was very threadbare. But in some way that is also Chekhovian. Chekhov was obsessed all his life with money and where the money was coming from or was not coming from. The letters are filled with details of cash.

Adrian Frazier: Can I move now to Michael? Michael, I did not manage to see your version of *The Seagull* (1999), and I really would like to hear the story of what it was like. The Corn Exchange Theatre since then, on your strength, has become a very famous company, but in 1999 it wasn't.

Michael West: To begin with I have to confess a certain sense of humility and deep amusement at sharing the table with Tom. I am pretty confident that nobody has seen my version of *The Seagull*. It was performed in a very small theatre in Dublin for three weeks a long, long time ago. So it was personally very interesting to me, but it hardly merits discussion in the same terms as Tom's. Tom's is archetypal as the start of Irish approaches to dealing with Chekhov.

Our production set out to be a very faithful translation; we did not try and set it in Ireland as such. What we tried to do was set it in the theatre; that's how we approached it. And I think this is a legacy of the freedom that is now open to everyone writing in Ireland. Translation is in the eye and the ear of the beholder. People just did not notice the English versions, up to a certain point; then they became weird, and why would you stage one of those? They don't fit in our mouths. I was very interested to hear Nicky tell about Seamus Kelly.[4] It took fifty years for those things to be driven through. It is kind of shocking. Audiences know instantly what's missing and what's wrong. But it's not always their job to fix the thing.

In terms of Irish Chekhov, Tom's version was performed in England for English audiences, so its Irishness had a different value. Our approach to it was to write in Irish-English but not in Ireland. In terms of the scale of approach to translation and adaptation, I would propose different terms to collision, hybridization, and acculturation. My own ones would be evasion, paraphrase, and water-carrying, because you are constantly faced with the impossibility of what you are doing, whether or not you speak the original language. I have done plenty of translations,[5] and sometimes I am fortunate or unfortunate enough to have some understanding of the original language. In case of the Russian I did not, so I had to work from a literal translation. That was the approach.

We set out to do it as a very faithful translation, and the reason I was asked to do it was because it was cheaper to get me to do it than to pay someone else for the rights of one of the extant versions. That's really what it came down to. It's always a shame to remember the words of critics. But this one did stick in my head: 'this is a production which robs the word travesty of any meaning.' The translation is indeed in the eye of the beholder, because we were astonished. We thought ours was an absolutely faithful rendition of the original play. We were not fiddling with it in any way. The characters' names were Russian. We had a slightly heightened theatrical style that we were bringing to it, but at the same time it was quite extraordinary that we got this kind of reaction. Then again we had audiences that we disappointed in that we did not take Chekhov and give him a good kicking. That's what they wanted, on the one hand. On the other hand any deviation from the Gate way of doing it – with long dresses – was regarded as insanity.

I suppose these issues of evasion, paraphrase, and water carrying are always open for debate because the performance arts are uniquely prone to adaptation and transportation – they are interpretive arts in their essence. They don't exist until you see them.

Adrian Frazier: I'll ask Cynthia if she wants to say anything at this time

Cynthia Marsh: I am fascinated. This is my anthropological research.

Michael West: I like very much the point about *The Seagull*. *The Seagull* is almost a textbook case of mistranslation: the title does not work at all. I found this out when I was in France talking about the brilliant translation I have done of *Le Goéland*. There was great tittering, because *goéland* is the big ugly brute that kills pensioners. And in France they say 'non, non, c'est la mouette'. I guess we could start at the beginning and call it *The Tern* or something like that.

Cynthia Marsh: Too late.

Adrian Frazier: We are back to the papers by Nicky [Nicholas Grene] and Bob [Robert Tracy] about Chekhov in the period between 1915 and 1925. Some of the comments that greeted these early performances were 'nothing is happening', 'this is incredibly boring', 'we can't bear it'. Yet in the context of the plays of the sixties and seventies, the experience of watching the plays of Chekhov in the last twenty years is quite different. In Chekhov there is generally a gun involved, the gun goes off, there are men and women, there are different classes. Chekhov's plays come off by comparison really rigidly plotted with the great building of tension. They are quite exciting plays. In the early years of the twentieth century, they were compared presumably to melodrama or patriotic action plays, and in that sense they were flat and philosophical. But compared to Beckett or Pinter, they offer almost a return to the world of romance and lyricism. I wonder if it's not always the case with translation that the target is a reaction against the theatrical norm in the culture in which it is being produced. The strangeness, in other words, that you are seeking is really just some surprise on stage. So for instance, let's say you do a strange Chekhov in a different acting style in different dresses. And people experience it as 'this is shocking'. This is actually a theatrical experience, being shocked by something in a new form.

Thomas Kilroy: The making of theatre is one of the sources of all of this, just simply the excitement of the challenge of doing something from outside your own culture. But there is also the personal trait of the writer who is making this version. I have taken a lot of stick for this because it looks parasitic, and it looks abusive of the original, but in my case it's a kind of experience with this writer: experiencing this writer in a very private kind of way as somebody. In other words I am imaginatively stimulated by this writer. I used to have a wonderful agent in London called Peggy Ramsay. Peggy was one of the great figures in English theatre in her day. She said to me when I was starting this job: 'Darling, it will be like a privileged conversation with the dead author'. That describes it beautifully. You are having a very privileged access to something, something enormous, beyond your scope and ken. But you have been allowed into this as a privilege. And for that reason you take off imaginatively; you are no longer the agent providing a vehicle for this great classic author – you are gone on another trip.

A certain point comes then when you feel that you have gone so far that you are no longer tied to the original. You may change the title for that reason, but you have to acknowledge that you came out of this. The version of Wedekind's *Spring Awakening* which I am doing in February at the Abbey has a title *Christ Deliver Us*[6] for the simple reason that I moved very, very far away from *Spring Awakening*. It's the work that inspired me to write this other play, a play which now happens to be about school kids in 1950s Ireland and about the particular monsters – it's the play behind the clerical scandals. I never experienced sexual abuse in school or at all, but I experienced a great deal of physical abuse. And the play is about that awful deadly world that kids were growing up in, in Ireland in the 1950s. The play is inspired by the Wedekind, and that will always have to be acknowledged, but it's become something else.

Cynthia Marsh: One of the wonderful things about foreign theatre is that it is constantly retranslated; it is constantly renewed. That is one of the great positive benefits of it. In their own cultures the texts are locked in the language in which they are written, so there's a certain limitation on what you can do with the language. Translation is a great liberating force.

Pat Burke: Can I ask Tom and Michael: have you seen any of your works in translation? What was that like?

Thomas Kilroy: Yes I have. I have also experienced something else. I have one play *The Death and Resurrection of Mr Roche*, a very early play which has influenced other plays, partly because it is the kind of classic formula of the enclosed group and an intruder who comes into the group. But there have been imitations of this play. So I have been at the other end of the stick. Very shortly after it was done in Hampstead and London, I saw a full television play which clearly borrowed its whole plot. My producer at the time, Michael Coston, said: 'We'll sue them'. But I said: 'No, I am very flattered', which I was, and amazed actually.

I have seen a few strange ones, including a Japanese university production of one of the plays. Very recently I got a new agent in Paris. I had my plays published and translated by academics before and I gave her these plays, but she said: 'O no, no, these are unactable.' So there is a kind of a translation industry which is not theatrical and won't work in the theatre, and you have to kind of get professional theatre translators to do it.

Michael West: I have been lucky enough to see some of my work. I saw a production of a play of mine in Dutch, and as a result I spoke Dutch incredibly well for about an hour and ten minutes. Unfortunately when the play ended my capacity to understand Dutch just disappeared. It was nearly gone. But it was uncanny. It was a really extraordinary thing. Your parallel translator in your head is going: 'Oh, I am following this, absolutely'.

Academic translations serve a very important purpose: they are for people like us to steal and use for our adaptations. But apart from that, the relationship between the literal translation, as it is often misleadingly called, and the original is a very important one. I had a very interesting translation experience of working on a production of Chekhov's *Ivanov* by the Katona József Theatre. It was an astonishing production which featured in the Dublin festival two years ago. They needed an English version of the sur-titles, so I worked with a Hungarian dramaturge on that. And it was like doing a crossword puzzle. I really enjoyed it. The palette was thirty-five characters, and I had to write in couplets, which means that I had seventy characters, including punctuation and spaces, per line. So I had to do a condensed form of the play. It was such an extraordinary version to work on. I was only half-way through the process when I realized, looking at the video, that the timing was important: 'I don't know what we are doing here, I need help, I don't speak Hungarian.' My job was to write water; the translation had to be transparent. You don't want any Hibernian, you don't want any intrusive elements. You want an audience in Ireland to pretend they have not even seen it.

Adrian Frazier: It was a beautiful show.

Michael West: It was a beautiful, beautiful show. In terms of questions of the canonicity of texts, we now can see Chekhov performed in Hungarian or indeed in Russian. *The Three Sisters* production was over recently and that's a very new experience.[7] I don't know when the first Russian production of Chekhov came to Ireland, but that's a whole other thing, and that's a very interesting issue of translation. There are sur-titles, but for an audience to sit and watch something for three hours in another language changes things. You have the illusion of understanding things, and it's a very interesting experience.

Nicholas Grene: Michael, I did not see your *Seagull*. I did see Tom's, but the reason why I did not see yours was because when I went to the box office they turned me and some thirty other possible people down on the grounds that they were booked out entirely. So this is my let-out. Could you tell us a little bit more about the style? You talked about the heightened style of the theatrical production.

Michael West: The Corn Exchange is a company that I worked with a lot. Annie Ryan, the director, keeps trying to get rid of the style and she might have finally done it, but she brought it to Ireland from America: full frontal delivery, percussion, whiteface, the use of stock characters, and emotional range reduced to official emotional states: happiness, sadness, fear, and anger.[8] It sounds like a workshop. It is naturalism under a Bunsen burner. The style heightens the moment and intensifies the actual flow of narrative. There must always be one moment that you are watching rather than a whole bunch of things. It's a tool for focusing. One of the problems with our production of *The Seagull* is we have not quite gone far enough. We had a comparatively long rehearsal period to explore the idea.

We set it in the notional seventies, and the idea was to use the kind of pancake makeup that I remember first seeing in productions of *The Mikado* in school where teachers put this weird gunk on their faces and drew lines on their foreheads (as if they did not have any)

11 *The Seagull*, **in a version by Michael West, Corn Exchange Company, directed by Annie Ryan, June 1999. Photograph: Paul McCarthy. Courtesy of Corn Exchange Theatre.**

and put on jumpers and sang. It was not that far off from the time when boys dressed up as girls, and it was perfectly normal too. It was that world. So the convention was that pancake makeup. And you imagine it would be so in an empty space. We just did the play without any comment other than its look. It was certainly not nineteenth century or early twentieth century. It was clearly a rehearsal room.

My job was to absolutely stick with that. But the question is: how do you turn down the volume on your style? I am not sure that you can. Sometimes you want a bit of flavour. You just have to have your ear pitched for difference. And there are always choices. It is an act of homage, irritation, engagement, and complete befuddlement working with another writer. It's a great experience, but there is always a range of options. Nothing is quite right. You have to decide which one is quite wrong enough for the moment.

Conor Graham: I would like to refer to the paper by Cynthia Marsh. She mentioned that there's a degree of collision, hybridization, or acculturation in each translation. You mentioned literal translations. You could not put them on in the theatre because people wouldn't be able to engage with them. I am just quite interested in the remainder, in what's left out. Would it be dangerous to be put on a literal translation of Chekhov?

Michael West: Because it would be so good or so bad? We can use terms like collision, hybridization or acculturation, or my own ones of evasion, paraphrase or water-carrying. But my point is that they happen all at the same time. There is no way of knowing. One person's literal translation is another person's travesty, and the question is infinitely complex in terms of character names, units of currency, objects on the table, and the idioms. To use an obvious example, in *The Seagull* Arkadina says: 'When it comes to my appearance I am as fussy as an Englishman'. How do you translate that in English? Obviously you need to decide what you are going to do with that. Are you going just to step over it like a little dead body or a drunk in the street, or do you give it a good shake and make it come alive and punch you in the face, or do you just try and avoid it somehow?

Conor Graham: If you did not have someone with agendas, with your knowledge of the original script, would it be viable to stage a direct translation?

Thomas Kilroy: In my case, each of those plays that I became involved with I knew very well and would have seen different productions down the years, so that I was coming to a revered text. But then it's a question of the effect of that text on your own imagination. I did a version of *Six Characters in Search of an Author* for the Abbey some years ago, and I stayed very close to this text. I did make a kind of a frame for this play which I felt was implied in the Pirandello, but it's when you start to move away from it, that's when something strange is happening. There are ghostly versions of classical plays behind a great number of modern plays, and you can see them, you can sense that shadow there. Very often it is unacknowledged by the writer; maybe the writer does not even see. But there is this haunting presence. The amount of echoes of classical Greek plays in modern theatre is just extraordinary. And some of them, as I say, are not even acknowledged. And it's a case of really being part of the fraternity or the sorority of theatre that you have this immense body of work which is there for your illumination for you to try to do something of your own out of it.

I was startled by the use of the word 'remainder' in reference to translation. Like most contemporary playwrights, I don't have too many languages. In fact I would not have any Russian, Norwegian, or Italian, a bit of Italian maybe, but not enough to read Pirandello. So in each case I worked with a literal translation (and usually this literal translation is commissioned by the theatre you are working for). So the Abbey commissioned somebody to do a Pirandello translation, a verbatim translation. In the Royal Court we had the Moscow English language version of *The Seagull*, which was not only unactable but virtually unreadable. Yet it was accurate to the extent that as we worked through the play in rehearsal, we used it as a kind of a baseline. This was some authenticity that we referred to, and that we had deferred to. It was particularly useful when we hit things which were Kilroy's inventions, and I had to defend myself against questions such as 'why was I doing this', which was very interesting.

Adrian Frazier: Defended in that in some ways there had to be some form of an echo of something in the original that was necessary?

Thomas Kilroy: If it was using the words of *The Seagull* and was describing itself as a version of a Chekhov play, then it had to stand up and provide some degree of truthfulness in relation to that play. And in a strange kind of way I was pleased with the end-product.

Conor Graham: I suppose it goes back to what Cynthia was saying about the acculturation of the plays; maybe some people know Russia through Chekhov, so they might not know the play. They just know what they have seen of the play.

Cynthia Marsh: Absolutely, the play is their perception of Russia.

Michael West: The interpretive arts, they are all just deeply unstable. If the national theatres pay Tom Stoppard to do a version of *The Seagull*, the reviewers, the building, and everybody who goes to see the play will want to see plenty of Tom Stoppard. And they will attribute the good bits to Stoppard more likely than to Chekhov. I did a translation of Molière. At first read, the director came steaming to me. It was Fergus Lynn, in fact, who ended up producing it. And he was absolutely white with rage. I said: 'What's wrong?'. I thought somebody had an accident, if ever it could be me? Fergus found it quite hard to speak, and he said: 'It's too short'. I was not entirely sure what he meant. He said: 'You have cut it! You have cut it!' 'Beg your pardon, I have translated it. I haven't cut it at all'. 'No, no, I know the play, and we can't have an interval, and we need to have an interval'. He was convinced I had savaged it ... and, of course, I may have done. But it certainly wasn't shorter than the original.

Irina Ruppo Malone: Tom, you mentioned that translating a play is like having an intimate kind of conversation with the playwright. Could you comment on the differences between these conversations with Ibsen and with Chekhov?

Michael West: Whom would you rather have a drink with?

Thomas Kilroy: Neither, I think. I don't know. I immediately start thinking of Chekhov's hostility to Ibsen. Here were these two great writers who had such wonderful perception of the ordinary and made something extraordinary of it. You'd imagine a kind of a togetherness there, but in fact Chekhov was scathing about Ibsen. He made one or two remarks that could be seen as half praise, but he found him problematic, formulaic, and controlling. Chekhov said that the mysteries were left out, which I think is very harsh on Ibsen.

Cynthia Marsh: One way of reading *The Seagull* is as a parody of *The Wild Duck*, a vicious parody.

Thomas Kilroy: One thing we did not mention about Chekhov is that he is a very funny writer. The early days of writing farce contributed a great deal to the four main plays. There are scenes in *The Seagull* that are absolutely hilarious and should be played for farce to get the effect right.

Cynthia Marsh: There is a production currently in Bristol of *Uncle Vanya*, which has been reviewed (I have not seen it yet) as absolutely the best comic production of Chekhov.[9]

Beth Phillips: I saw a production of *The Cherry Orchard* by the Maly Theatre company, and it was bordering on slapstick. It was amazing.

Cynthia Marsh: You mean Lev Dodin, at the Maly Theatre of St Petersburg. Dodin is dedicated to re-vitalizing perceptions of Chekhov.

Miglena Ivanova: I was struck by the comment that Chekhov found Ibsen controlling. Yet Chekhov denied every single request for any of his works to be translated, because he did not think he wanted anything changed.

Cynthia Marsh: That's actually much more an issue of copyright, than maybe a desire or emotion. You had to be extremely careful.

Nicholas Grene: I only know of one remark about the French version of *The Cherry Orchard* that nobody could understand. One of the extraordinary things is that Chekhov is the most portable Russian dramatist, but he did not believe that. He believed that his texts were so local, so specific that they would not travel outside Russia. I think there is one comment where quite unaccountably Chekhov says: 'Ibsen, he is my favourite writer'.[10] And I think he was extremely volatile in his opinions. They changed all the time with his mood. There is this reaction against Ibsen and the controlling, but Chekhov could flip also and see what an extraordinary playwright Ibsen was. Could we push you to talk more about *Ghosts*, and following up on what has been said about how you found working with Ibsen in this privileged conversation you were talking about?

Thomas Kilroy: I am not entirely happy with my version of *Ghosts*. I think that it tries too hard to make the Irish skeleton hold the whole thing up, and, in particular, the transference into a Catholic culture. I think that's awkward. Siobhan used to talk about how it would give the opportunity to portray a relationship between a priest and a woman at this particular point in Irish history. This may be effective, but in some way it loses the complexity of the

Ibsen. For me the wonderful quality in Ibsen's work is this character complexity and the kind of subtlety of motivation which makes him a wonderful writer for actors. With Chekhov it's a much more random world that you are in. There is this trying to hold on to this randomness where unusual things can happen and an unusual kind of flux, a kind of fluidity. There is a sternness and a rigour to Ibsen which precludes this.

Adrian Patterson: I have two questions: one about the reputation of the writer and the freeing nature of this reputation, and the other in relation to the difference between writing a translation for acting only and producing a translation for publication. I was very glad to hear that you felt the freedom to bring something to your version of *The Seagull*, in spite of the awful weight of reputation that Chekhov or Ibsen have. Does writing for the theatre differ from writing for publication in this respect? Can the knowledge that your version is going to be printed affect the way you write and the freedom with which you change texts?

Michael West: I am not sure that reputation is important. Tom talked about the personal relationship with the writer, and sometimes it just does not work. I started to translate some things, and I had nothing to say. I couldn't understand the temperature of the characters. I couldn't read the way they were facing. I started writing for the theatre by doing translation; that is my apprenticeship, and I'd still go back to it. It cleanses the palate and refines vocabulary. It's like going on holiday. You are suddenly working with someone who is much better than you and who solved all the horrible problems. You are able to relax and think about things, and sometimes it is very difficult.

I used to think the older the text, the more free I could be, and then I found out it was not the case. One of the most interesting things I had to do was a fifteenth century Bohemian text that I was asked to translate for a French director.[11] That production was a seminal version; but this was the breakthrough. His approach is very interesting: the productions are extraordinary meditations on life and death. For me he is the opposite of the French auteur director. He believes in the text and in nothing else – just take away the set. I found that play so old that I had to hold on like I was on a rock face 600 feet above ground. It was so alien, if I let go again I was gone.

I worked with a German dramaturge with a contemporary German text, a whole bunch of dictionaries, and a lot of time. For that reason it was extremely liberating, and literally my stupidity is a great aid. It does not always work. I really learnt something about craft and work, because I had to go so slowly. All theories go out of the window.

Thomas Kilroy: You mentioned the word cannibalism, Cynthia, at one point. Translating is a strange, parasitic, cannibalistic activity, so you have to develop a high degree of tact and judgment, because there is a line that you cannot cross. Maybe you can't see the line. You have to be careful at all times in that regard.

Cynthia Marsh: But respect is central to the understanding of cannibalism. People ate other people because they liked them; they actually ate them to get their essences, their personalities. [12]

Adrian Frazier: In an entirely cannibalistic act, this conversation will be printed and put into a book now. Thanks to Tom, and Michael, and Cynthia. It's been wonderful talking to you.

---

[1] Cynthia Marsh, 'Making Foreign Theatre or Making Theatre Foreign: Russian Theatre in English', 117-33.

[2] Thomas Kilroy's version of Ibsen's *Ghosts* was produced at the Abbey Theatre in 1989 and his adaptation of *Six Characters in Search of an Author* was produced at the Abbey Theatre in 1996.

[3] Nicholas Grene, 'Chekhov and the Irish Big House', 150.

[4] Ibid., 149.

[5] Michael West's translations and adaptations include *Death and the Ploughman*, after Johannes Van Saaz, (2001), *Don Juan* (1990), *Lolita* (2002), *Tartuffe* (1992), *The Marriage of Figaro* (1900), *The Seagull* (1990), and *The Tender Trap* (1992).

[6] *Christ Deliver Us!* was premièred at the Abbey Theatre on 9 February 2010.

[7] *Three Sisters*, by Cheek By Jowl, was performed in Dublin on 29 September – 4 October 2009 as part of the Ulster Bank Theatre Festival.

[8] See http://www.cornexchange.ie, especially the note on the version of Commedia dell'Arte as a style practised by the company.

[9] *Uncle Vanya* (a Bristol Old Vic co-production with Shakespeare at the Tobacco Factory, directed by Andrew Hilton) premièred in Bristol in November 2009 and was subsequently performed in Galway on 13-17 July 2010 as part of the Galway Arts Festival.

[10] Chekhov to A.L. Vishnevksy, 7 November 1903, *Letters of Anton Chekhov to His Family and Friends with Biographical Sketch*, trans. Constance Garnett (London: Macmillan, 1920).

[11] '*Der Ackermann und der Tod*' (1401) by Johannes Van Saaz, adapted for the stage as *Death and the Ploughman* (2001), produced by Project Arts Centre and Comédie de Reims in association with the Corn Exchange Theatre, directed by Christian Schiaretti.

[12] On this point see Marsh, 'Making Foreign Theatre or Making Theatre Foreign'. Marsh refers to Else Ribeiro Pires Viera, 'Liberating Calibans: *Antropofagia* and Haroldo de Campos' Poetics of Transcreation', *Post-Colonial Translation*, eds Susan Bassnett and Harish Trivedi (London: Routledge 1999): 95-113, where an argument is put forward (98) for cannibalism as a form of respect.

Appendix

List of Previous Works by Ros Dixon

'From Iconoclast to Traditionalist: A Study of Anatolii Efros's
Productions of Chekhov, Gogol and Turgenev', PhD Dissertation
(University of Nottingham, 2002).

Peer-Reviewed Articles

'"Slaughtering Sacred Seagulls": Anatolii Efros's Production of the
Seagull at the Lenkom, 1967', *Irish Slavonic Studies* 21 (2000):
49–73.
'"Don't Throw Me Out": Anatolii Efros'1967 Production of *Three Sisters*',
Essays in Poetics 31 (Autumn 2006): 85-113.
'"The avant-garde, you know, can easily become the rearguard. All it
takes is a change of direction". Anatolii Efros's production of *A
Month in The Country*: A Dialogue with Stanislavsky', *Turgenev and
Russian Culture*, eds Joe Andrew, Derek Offord and Robert Reid
(Amsterdam and New York: Rodopi, 2008): 193-204.
'West Meets East: Russian Productions at the Dublin Theatre Festival,
1957-2006', *Interactions: Dublin Theatre Festival 1957-2006*, eds
Nicholas Grene and Patrick Lonergan (Dublin: Carysfort Press,
2008):75-91.

Encyclopedia Entries and Essays

'Russian Set Design', *The Columbia Encyclopedia of Modern Drama*,
eds Gabrielle H. Cody and Evert Sprinchorn, 2 vols (New York:
Columbia University Press, 2007), vol. 2: 1172-73.
'Socialist Realism, Soviet Union', *The Columbia Encyclopedia of
Modern Drama*, eds Gabrielle H. Cody and Evert Sprinchorn, 2 vols
(New York: Columbia University Press, 2007), vol. 2: 1256-57.
'Mesiats v derevne [A Month in the Country]' *The Literary
Encyclopedia*, 14 July 2007, http://www.litencyc.com/.

'Revizor' *The Literary Encyclopedia*, 15 September 2008, http://www.litencyc.com/.
'Chekhov Bogged Down? Tom Kilroy's version of *The Seagull*', *Renegotiating and Resisting Nationalism in Twentieth-Century Irish Drama*, ed. Scott Boltwood (Gerrards Cross: Colin Smythe, 2009):97-110.

Book Reviews

Review of Moscow Performances: The New Russian Theatre, 1991–1996 by John Freedman, Irish Slavonic Studies 20 (1999): 96-99.
Review of *A History of Russian Theatre*, eds Robert Leach and Victor Borovski, *Irish Slavonic Studies* 22 (2001): 96-99.
Review of *A Triptych from the Russian Theatre: An Artistic Biography of the Komissarzhevskys* by Victor Borovsky, Irish Slavonic Studies
Review of Lev Dodin and The Maly Drama Theatre by Maria Shevtsova, Modern Languages Review 101.3 (2006): 920-921.
Review of *The Joy of Rehearsal* by Anatoly Efros, trans. James Thomas, *Slavonica* 15 (April 2009): 75-75.

Theatre Reviews

'Dr. Faustus', *Irish Theatre Magazine* 5: 22 (Spring 2005): 60-62.
'Frongach', *Irish Theatre Magazine* 5: 23 (Summer 2005): 74-76.
'Anna Karenina', *Irish Theatre Magazine* 7: 30 (Summer 2007): 83-86.
'The Official Version', *Irish Theatre Magazine* 6:29 (Winter 2006): 111-113

Programme Notes

Gorky's *Vacationers*, Programme Note, Omsk State Drama, Dublin Theatre Festival Sept.-Oct. 2006.
Chekhov's *Ivanov*, Programme Note, Josef Kantor Company, Dublin Theatre Festival Sept.-Oct. 2007.

Radio Interview

15 minute Interview on Today FM on the occasion of the death of American playwright Arthur Miller. 11 February 2005.

Conference Papers and Invited Lectures

'Letter to Brezhnev, Andropov and Gorbachev', Conference of the Irish Association of Russian and East European Studies, Queen's University, Belfast, May 1998.
'Anatolii Efros's *Seagull*', Conference of the Irish Association of Russian and East European Studies, Queen's University, Belfast, May 2000.

'"Don't Vaudevillize *Marriage*, Overcoat it!" A study of Efros's 1975 seminal production of Gogol's *Marriage*', Conference of the British Association of Slavonic and Eastern European Studies, Cambridge, April 2003.

'Chekhov Bogged Down or Not? Tom Kilroy's version of *The Seagull*', Conference of the Academy of Irish Cultural Heritages, University of Ulster, Derry. April 2004.

'Chekhov in Ireland', Conference of the British Association for Slavonic and Eastern European Studies, Cambridge, April 2004.

'"Ne goni menia!"': Anatolii Efros's *Three Sisters*', Conference of the Neo-Formalist Circle, Oxford, September 2004.

'Anatolii Efros at the Lenkom 1964-1967', Conference of the International Federation of Theatre Researchers, University of Maryland, June 2005.

'Oh, Chekhov Thou Art Translated!', Conference of International Association for the Study of Irish Literature, Charles University, Prague, July 2005.

'"The avant-garde, you know, can easily become the rearguard. All it takes is a change of direction." Anatolii Efros's production of *A Month in The Country*: A Dialogue with Stanislavsky'. Conference of the Neo-Formalist Circle, Oxford, September 2006.

'"All of Ireland is Our Orchard": Two Abbey Productions of *The Cherry Orchard*, 1968 and 2004', Conference of SOFEIR, Sorbonne, Paris, March 2007.

'Tom Murphy's *The Cherry Orchard*', Conference of the British Association for Slavonic and Eastern European Studies, Cambridge, April 2007.

'Russian Productions at the Dublin Theatre Festival', Conference of the Irish Theatrical Diaspora, Project Arts Centre, Dublin, 4-5 October 2007.

'Brian Friel's *Three Sisters*', Lecture, Synge Summer School 2008, Avondale, Wicklow, 29 June -5 July 2008.

'From Riot to Riotous Laughter: *The Playboy of the Western World* at the Abbey in 1907 and 2007', IASIL 2008 Porto, Portugal, 28 July-1 August 2008.

'"All of Ireland is Our Orchard": Maria Knebel's The Cherry Orchard at the Abbey 1968', Ibsen and Chekhov on the Irish Stage, National University of Ireland, Galway, 6-7 November 2009.

Bibliography

Translations and Adaptations of Ibsen's Plays Cited

Ibsen, Henrik, *The Collected Works*, ed. William Archer, 11 vols (New York: Charles Scribner's Sons, 1908-1910).

---, *The Complete Major Prose Plays*, trans. Rolf Fjelde (London: Faber, 1978).

---, *An Enemy of the People*, trans. Christopher Hampton (London: Faber, 1997).

---, *Ghosts and Other Plays,* trans. Peter Watts (Hamondsworth: Penguin Books, 1979).

---, *John Gabriel Borkman,* translated and introduced by Inga-Stina Ewbank and Peter Hall (London: Athlone Press, 1975).

---, *The Lady from the Sea,* a new version by Frank McGuinness from a literal translation by Charlotte Barslund (London: Faber, 2008).

---, *Namhaid Don Phobal* [*Enemy of the* People], trans. Gearóid Ó Lochlainn (Dublin: Oifig an tSolathair, 1947).

---, *The Oxford Ibsen*, ed. James McFarlane, 8 vols (New York: Oxford, 1960-1977).

---, *Peer Gynt*, a version by Frank McGuinness (London: Faber, 1990).

---, *Plays*, trans. Michael Meyer (London: Methuen, 1980).

---, *When We Dead Awaken; Rosmersholm: Two Plays*, trans. David Rudkin (Bath: Absolute Classics, 1990).

Translations and Adaptations of Chekhov's Plays Cited

Chekhov, Anton, *The Cherry Orchard*, trans. Hubert Butler (London: H.F.W. Deane, 1934).

---, *The Complete Plays*, trans. Laurence Senelick (New York; London: Norton, 2006).

---, *The Seagull*, a new version by Thomas Kilroy (London: Eyre Methuen, 1981).

Friel, Brian, *Three Sisters* (Dublin: Gallery Press, 1981).

Kilroy, Thomas, *The Seagull* (London: Eyre Methuen, 1981).

Murphy, Tom, *The Cherry Orchard*, (London: Methuen, 2004).

Books and Articles

Allen, David, '*The Cherry Orchard*: a new English version by Trevor Griffiths', *Chekhov on the British Stage*, ed. Patrick Miles (Cambridge: CUP, 1993):156-68.

Álvarez, Román and M. Carmen-África Vidal, 'Translating: A Political Act', *Translation, Power, Subversion*, eds Román Álvarez and M. Carmen-África Vidal (Clevedon: Multilingual, 1996):1-9.

Andermann, Gunilla M., *Europe on Stage: Translation and Theatre* (London: Oberon Books, 2005).

Archer, William, *William Archer on Ibsen: The Major Essays, 1889-1919*, ed. Thomas Postlewait (London: Greenwood Press, 1984).

Aronson, Arnold, 'The Scenography of Chekhov', *The Cambridge Companion to Chekhov*, eds Vera Gottlieb and Paul Allain (Cambridge: Cambridge University Press, 2000): 134-48.

Bates, Martin D., 'A Russian Eye on Ireland', *Irish Times* 28 March 1981: 13.

Benedetti, Jean, *Stanislavski* (London: Methuen, 1988).

Bennett, Arnold, *Books and Persons* (New York, 1917).

Bloom, Harold, *The Western Canon: The Books and School of the Ages* (London: Macmillan, 1994)

Blythe, Ernest, *The Abbey Theatre* [pamphlet] (Dublin: The National Theatre Society Ltd, n.d.).

Boyd, Ernest A. *The Contemporary Drama of Ireland* (Dublin: Talbot Press; London: Fisher Unwin, 1918).

---, 'The Work of the Irish Theatre', *Irish Monthly* 47 (February 1919): 71-76.

Brandt, George W., ed., *Modern Theories of Drama: A Selection of Writings on Drama and Theatre 1850-1990* (Oxford: Clarendon Press, 1998).

Brække, Jonas, 'Peer Gynt inntar pyramidene' [Peer Gynt Takes the Pyramids], *Dagsavisen* 25 October 2006: 50-51.

Brook, Peter, *The Empty Space* (Harmondsworth: Penguin, 1968).

Brustein, Robert, *Critical Moments: Reflections on Theater and Society 1973-1979* (New York: Random House, 1980).

Bull, Francis, 'Henrik Ibsen og Norge' [Henrik Ibsen and Norway], *Edda* 56 (1956): 245-53.

Carnicke, Sharon, 'Stanislavsky's production of *The Cherry Orchard* in the US', *Chekhov Then and Now*, ed. Douglas Clayton (New York: Peter Lang, 1977): 19-30.

Carr, Marina, 'Dealing with the Dead', *Irish University Review* 28.1(Spring-Summer, 1998): 190-96.

Casanova, Pascale, *The World Republic of Letters* [1999], trans. M. B.. DeBevoise (Boston: Harvard University Press, 2004).

Chambers, Lilian, Ger Fitzgibbon, and Eamonn Jordan, eds, *Theatre Talk: Voices of Irish Theatre Practitioners* (Dublin: Carysfort Press, 2001).

Chekhov, Anton Pavlovich, *Dramaticheskie proizvedeniia* (Leningrad: Iskusstvo, 1985).

Csikai, Zsuzsa, 'Recreating the Front of the Tapestry: Tom Murphy's Version of *The Cherry Orchard*', *'Alive in Time': The Enduring Drama of Tom Murphy*, ed. Christopher Murray (Dublin: Carysfort Press, 2010).

Colum, Padraic, 'Ibsen and National Drama', *Sinn Fein* 2 June 1906: 3.

Corkery, Daniel, *Synge and Anglo-Irish Literature* [1931] (Cork: Mercier Press, 1966).

De Figueiredo, Ivo, *Henrik Ibsen: Mennesket* [Henrik Ibsen: the Man] (Oslo: Aschehoug, 2006).

DeGiacomo, Albert J., *T.C. Murray, Dramatist: Voice of Rural Ireland* (Syracuse: SUP, 2003).

Devane, R.S. *Indecent Literature: Some Legal Remedies* (Dublin: Brown and Nolan, n.d [1925]).

Dixon, Ros, 'West Meets East: Russian Productions at the Dublin Theatre Festival, 1957-2006', *Interactions: Dublin Theatre Festival 1957-2007*, eds Nicholas Grene and Patrick Lonergan (Dublin: Carysfort Press, 2008): 75-91.

Dowling, Joe, 'Signposts', *Theatre Ireland* 4 (September – December 1983): 32-33.

Doyle, Paul A., *Paul Vincent Carroll* (Lewisburg: Bucknell UP, 1971).

'Dramatic Ideals and the Irish Literary Theatre', *Freeman's Journal*, 6 May 1899: 5.

Durbach, Errol, 'Ibsen and the Dramaturgy of Uncertainty', *Ibsen Studies* 6.2 (2006): 124-38.

---, 'Sacrifice and Absurdity in The Wild Duck', *Mosaic: A Journal for the Interdisciplinary Study of Literature* 7.4 (1974): 99-107.

Edwards, Ruth Dudley, *Patrick Pearse: the Triumph of Failure* [1977] (Dublin: Poolbeg, 1990).

Eglinton, John, W. B. Yeats, AE, and W. Larminie, *Literary Ideals in Ireland* (London: Fisher Unwin, 1899).

Ervine, St John, 'Review of *The Cherry Orchard*', *Observer* 18 July 1920.

Fallon, Gabriel, 'The Abbey Theatre Acting Tradition', *The Story of the Abbey Theatre*, ed. Sean McCann (London: New English Library, 1967).

Fay, Frank J., *Towards a National Theatre: The Dramatic Criticism of Frank J. Fay*, ed. Robert Hogan (Dublin: Dolmen Press, 1970).

Feeney, William J., *Drama in Hardwicke Street* (London and Toronto: Associated University Presses, 1984).

Frazier, Adrian, *George Moore, 1852-1933* (New Haven and London: Yale UP, 2000).

Friel, Brian, *Performances* (Oldcastle: Gallery Press, 2003).

---, *Selected Plays* (London and Boston: Faber 1984).

--- , *Three Plays After* (Oldcastle: Gallery Press, 2002).

Fulsås, Narve, 'Litteraturen, universitetet og det moderne gjennombrotet', *Kunnskapens betingelser: Festskrift til Edgeir Benum* [Conditions of Knowledge: A Festschrift for Edgeir Benum], eds John Peter Collett, Jan Eivind Myhre, and Jon Skeie (Oslo: Vidarforlaget, 2009): 168-92.

Gibbons, Luke: '"Famished Ghosts": Bloom, Bible Wars, and "U.P. up" in Joyce's Dublin', *Dublin James Joyce Journal* 2 (2009): 1-23.

Gottlieb, Vera'"The dwindling scale": the Politics of British Chekhov', *Chekhov on the British Stage*, ed. Patrick Miles (C UP,1993): 147-55.

Gosse, Edmund, 'Ibsen, the Norwegian Satirist', *Fortnightly Review* 19 (1873): 74-88.

Gregory, Lady Augusta, *Our Irish Theatre: A Chapter of Autobiography*, ed. Roger McHugh (Gerrards Cross: Colin Smythe, 1972).

Gwynn, Denis, *Edward Martyn and the Irish Revival* [1930] (New York: Lemma, 1974).

Halvorsen, J.B., 'Ibsens verdensry' [Ibsen's World Reputation], *Henrik Ibsen: Festskrift*, ed. Gerhard Gran (Bergen: John Grieg, 1898): 284-304.

Haugan, Jørgen, 'Krisen i norsk Ibsen-forskning' [The Crisis in Norwegian Ibsen Research], *Edda* 1 (1983): 45-47.

Hemmer, Bjørn, 'Ibsen and the Realistic Problem Drama', *The Cambridge Companion to Ibsen*, ed. James McFarlane (Cambridge: CUP, 1994).

Hogan, Robert, *After the Irish Renaissance: A Critical History of the Irish Drama Since The Plough and the Stars* (London: Macmillan, 1968).

---, and James Kilroy, *The Modern Irish Drama: A Documentary History*, vol. 3: *The Abbey Theatre: The Years of Synge 1905-1909* (Dublin: Dolmen Press; Highlands, NJ: Humanities Press, 1978).

---, Richard Burnham and Daniel P. Poteet, *The Modern Irish Drama: A Documentary History*, vol. 4: *The Rise of the Realists 1910-1915* (Dublin: Dolmen, 1979).

Holroyd, Michael, *Bernard Shaw: The One-Volume Definitive Edition* (London: Vintage, 1998).

Hyldig, Keld, *Realisme, symbol og psykologi: Norsk Ibsen-tradition belyst gennem udvalgteforestillinger på Nationaltheatret 1899-1940* [Realism, Symbols and Psychology: the Norwegian Ibsen Tradition Illustrated through Selected Performances at the National Theatre], PhD Dissertation (University of Bergen), 2000.

---, 'Ibsen-tradisjonen i norsk teater' [The Ibsen Tradition in Norwegain Theatre], *Norsk Shakespeare- og teatertidsskrift* 3-4 (2006): 6-11.

Humphreys, Madeleine, *The Life and Times of Edward Martyn: An Aristocratic Bohemian* (Dublin: Irish Academic Press, 2007).

'Ibsen-året 2006' [The Ibsen Year], *Aftenposten* 11 January 2006: 3.

'Ibsen at the Abbey Theatre', *Irish Times* 1 December 1926: 11.
'Ibsen Play in Limerick: A Very Successful Production', *Irish Times* 20 January 1930: 4.
'Ibsen Centenary: "John Gabriel Borkman" at the Abbey', *Irish Times* 4 April 1928: 4.
Innes, Christopher, '"Nothing but talk, talk, talk, – Shaw talk": Discussion Plays and the Making of Modern Drama', *The Cambridge Companion to George Bernard Shaw*, ed. Christopher Innes (Cambridge: CUP, 1998): 162-79.
Isherwood, Charles, 'At the Top of the Ladder, Confronting His Demons', Review of *The Master Builder*, *New York Times* 24 October 2008.
James, Henry, 'John Gabriel Borkman', *Harper's Weekly* 6 February 1897: 78.
Johannessen, Gisle L., 'Norges Ibsen eller Ibsens Norge?' [Norway's Ibsen or Ibsen's Norway], *Bergens Tidende* 4 December 2005: 3.
Johnston, David, '*En otras palabras*: Frank McGuinness and Spanish Drama', *The Dreaming Body: Contemporary Irish Theatre*, eds Melissa Sihra and Paul Murphy (Gerrards Cross UK: Colin Smythe, 2009).
Johnston, Denis, *The Dramatic Works of Denis Johnston*, 2 vols (Gerrards Cross: ColinSmythe, 1977-1979).
Keller, T. G., 'The Genius of Ibsen', *Dublin Magazine* 3 (April–June 1928): 44–47.
Kelly, Henry, 'Henry Kelly Talks to Madame Maria Knebel', *Irish Times* 3 October 1968: 6.
Kelly, Seamus, 'Chekhov's Classic as in Russia', *Irish Times* 9 October 1968: 10.
Kelly, Seamus, 'Producer Speaks of Abbey Skill', *Irish Times* 10 October 1968: 10.
Kilroy, Thomas,'*The Seagull*: an Adaptation', *The Cambridge Companion to Chekhov*, eds Vera Gottlieb and Paul Allain (Cambridge: Cambridge University Press, 2000): 80-90.
Knebel, Maria, '"Vishnevyi sad" v Irlandii' [*The Cherry Orchard* in Ireland], *Teatr* (May 1969):158-66.
---, 'Dublin: Ebbi-teatr' [Dublin: the Abbey Theatre], *Sovetskaia kul'tura* 1 January 1969: 3.
---, 'Dublin – The Abbey Theatre', *Irish Times* 28 January 1969: 12.
---, *Vsia zhizn* [My Whole Life], 2nd ed. (Moscow: Iskusstvo, 1993).
Lane, Rosemary, 'The Cherry Orchard', *Irish Times* 12 October 1968: 16.
Laurence, Dan H. and Nicholas Grene, eds, *Shaw, Lady Gregory and the Abbey: A Correspondence and a Record* (Gerrards Cross: Colin Smythe, 1993).
Lefevere, André and Susan Bassnett, 'Introduction: Proust's Grandmother and the Thousand and One Nights: The 'Cultural Turn'

in Translation Studies', *Translation History and Culture*. eds Susan
Bassnett and André Lefevere (London, New York: Pinter, 1990):1-13.

Loehlin, James N., *Chekhov The Cherry Orchard* (Cambridge: CUP, 2006).

Lojek, Helen Heusner, 'Letters from Frank: A Playwright Reflects on His Work', *Irish University Review* 40:1 (Spring-Summer 2010): 26-34.

Long, Joseph, 'Diction and Ideology: Chekhov's Irish Voice', *Double Vision: Studies in Literary Translation*, ed. Jane Taylor (Durham: Durham Modern Languages Series, 2002):163-75.

Lunde, Ådne, 'Verdenspeer' [The World's Peer], *Bergens Tidende*, 14 January 2006.

MacDonagh, Thomas, *Pagans: A Modern Play in Two Conversations* (Dublin: Talbot, 1920).

MacLiammóir, Mícheál, *All for Hecuba: an Irish Theatrical Autobiography* (London: Methuen, 1947).

---, 'Problem Plays', *The Irish Theatre*, ed. Lennox Robinson (London: Macmillan, 1939): 199-227.

Mallon, Ita, 'Art that Blossoms in "The Cherry Orchard"', *Irish Independent* 27 September 1968: 11.

Malone, A.E., 'A Doll's House': Gwen Ffrangcon-Davies as Nora', *Irish Times* 26 July, 1938: 8.

Malone, Irina Ruppo, 'Ibsen and the Irish Free State: The Gate Theatre Productions of Peer Gynt', *Irish University Review* 39:1 (Spring-Summer 2009), 42-64.

---, *Ibsen and the Irish Revival* (Basingstoke: Palgrave Macmillan, 2010).

Mancing, Howard, *Cervantes' Don Quixote: A Reference Guide* (Westport: Greenwood Press, 2006).

Marker, Frederick J. and Lise-Lone Marker, *Ibsen's Lively Art* (Cambridge: CUP, 1989).

Marsh, Cynthia, 'The Implications of Quotation in Performance: Masha's Lines from Pushkin in Chekhov's *Three Sisters*', *Slavonic and East European Review* 44.3 (2006): 446-59.

---, 'Whose Text is it Anyway? On Translating and Directing Gorky's *Egor Bulychev*', *Drama Translation and Theatre Practice*, eds Sabine Coelsch-Foisner and Holger Klein (Frankfurt: Peter Lang, 2004): 137-49.

Martyn, Edward, 'The Cherry Orchard of Tchekoff', *New Ireland* 8 (21 June 1919): 108-09.

---, 'A Plea for the Revival of the Irish Literary Theatre,' *Irish Review* 4 (April 1914): 79-84.

Massingham, H. W. (H.W. M.), 'The Sigh of Failure', *Nation* 16 May 1914: 265.

May, Rachel, *The Translator in the Text. On Reading Russian Literature in English* (Evanston: Northwestern University Press, 1994).

McDonald, Jan, 'Shaw and the Court Theatre', *The Cambridge Companion to George Bernard Shaw*, ed. Christopher Innes (Cambridge: CUP, 1998): 261-82.

McGuinness, Frank, 'A Voice from the Trees: Thomas Kilroy's Version of Chekhov's *Seagull*', *Irish University Review*, 21.1 (1991): 3-14.

---, 'I'm not entirely respectable. I couldn't be', Interview with Charlotte Higgins, *The Guardian* 18 October 2008.

Measadóir, 'New Forms in Drama', *New Ireland* 8 (21 June 1919): 109-10.

---, 'Weeds', *New Ireland* 7 (18 January 1919): 181.

Meierkhol'd, V. E., *Stat'i, pis'ma, rechi, besedy: 1891-1917* [Articles, Essays, Speeches, and Conversations: 1891-1917] (Moscow: Iskusstvo, 1968).

---, 'The Naturalistic Theatre and The Theatre of Mood', *Meyerhold on Theatre*, ed. and trans. Edward Braun (London: Eyre Methuen, 1969): 28-33.

Meyer, Michael, *Ibsen* (Garden City: Doubleday, 1971).

---, 'The Weight of Tradition', *New York Times* 14 December 1988: C21.

Moi, Toril, *Henrik Ibsen and the Birth of Modernism* (New York: OUP, 2006).

Morash, Christopher, *A History of Irish Theatre 1601-2000* (Cambridge: CUP, 2002).

Murphy, Tom , *Plays: 5* (London: Methuen Drama, 2006).

Murray, Christopher, ed. *Brian Friel: Essays, Diaries, Interviews: 1964-1999* (London: New York, 1999).

---, 'Padraic Colum's *The Land* and Cultural Nationalism', *Hungarian Journal of English and American Studies*, 2.2 (1996): 5-15.

---, *Twentieth-Century Irish Drama: Mirror up to Nation* (Manchester: Manchester University Press, 1997).

Murray, T.C. (Thomas Cornelius), *The Selected Plays of T. C. Murray*, ed. Cave, Richard Allen (Gerrards Cross: Colin Smythe; Washington: Catholic University of America Press, 1998).

Níc Shiubhlaighh, Máire, *The Splendid Years* (Dublin: James Duffy, 1955).

O'Casey, Sean, *Autobiographies*, 2 vols (London: Macmillan, 1963).

---, *Collected Plays*, vol. 1 (London: Macmillan, 1949).

---, 'Sean O'Casey's *The Cooing of Doves*: A One-Act Play Rediscovered', introduced and edited by Christopher Murray, *Princeton University Library Chronicle*, XVIII No. 1 & 2 (autumn 2006-winter 2007): 327-56.

---, *Under a Colored Cap* (London: Macmillan, 1964).

O'Driscoll, Denis, ed., *Stepping Stones: Interviews with Seamus Heaney* (London: Farrar Straus, 2008).

O'Farrell, Ciara, *Louis D'Alton and the Abbey Theatre* (Dublin: Four Courts, 2004).

O'Hara, Sarah, 'Productive Lives', *The Irish Press* 17 March 1982.

Ó hAodha, Mícheál, *Plays and Places* (Dublin: Progress House, 1961).

O'Mahony, John, 'A Happy Marriage' (Interview with Frank
    McGuinness), *The Guardian* 24 April 2008.
O'Neill, Michael J., *Lennox Robinson* (Boston: Twayne, 1964).
O'Toole, Fintan, 'Judged by Its Peers', Review of *Peer Gynt, Theatre
    Ireland* (December 1988/March 1989):17.
Parks, Edd Winfield and Aileen Wells Parks, *Thomas MacDonagh: the
    Man, the Patriot, the Writer* (Athens: University of Georgia Press,
    1967).
Peter, John, 'The Pitfalls of the Creative Translator', *Sunday Times* 7
    June 1987.
Polotskaya, Emma 'Nedotiopa i vrazdrob' (O trudnostiah perevoda
    piesy)' [On the difficulties of translating a play].
    http://rus.1september.ru/articlef.php?ID=200300409
Pickering, Michael, *Stereotyping: the Politics of Representation*
    (Basingstoke: Palgrave, 2001).
Plunkett Dillon, Geraldine, *All in the Blood*, ed. Honor O Brolchain
    (Dublin: A. & Farmar, 2006).
Rem, Tore, *Født til frihet: En biografi om Jens Bjørneboe* [Born to
    Freedom: a Biography of Jens Bjørneboe] (Oslo: Cappelen Damm,
    2010).
---, *Henrik Ibsen/Henry Gibson: Den provinsielle verdensdikter*
    [Henrik Ibsen/Henry Gibson: the Provincial Poet of the World]
    (Oslo: Cappelen 2006).
---, 'Ute av kontroll: Ibsen-året i skyggen av pyramidene' [Out of
    Control: the Ibsen Year in the Shadow of the Pyramids] , *Samtiden* 1
    (2007): 128-39.
'Resigns over Russian films ban', *Irish Independent* 3 September 1968:
    1.
Ribeiro, Else Pires Viera, 'Liberating Calibans: *Antropofagia* and
    Haroldo de Campos' Poetics of Transcreation', *Post-Colonial
    Translation*, eds Susan Bassnett and Harish Trivedi (London:
    Routledge, 1999): 95-113.
Richtarik, Marilynn J., *Acting between the Lines. The Field Day
    Theatre Company and Irish Cultural Politics 1980-1984* (Oxford:
    Clarendon, 1994).
Robinson, Lennox, *Curtain Up: An Autobiography* (London: Michael
    Joseph, 1942).
---, 'Ibsen's Influence on Irish Drama', *Irish Times* 31 March 1928: 6.
---, *I Sometimes Think* (Dublin: Talbot Press, n.d. [1956]).
---, *The Lost Leader: A Play in Three Acts* (Dublin: Thomas Kiersey,
    1918).
---, *Selected Plays: Lennox Robinson*, ed. Christopher Murray
    (Gerrards Cross: Colin Smythe, 1981).
---, *The White Blackbird* (Dublin: Talbot Press, 1926).
Rushe, Desmond, '"The Cherry Orchard" a Supreme Joy', *Irish
    Independent* 9 October 1968: 3.

Schäffner, Christina and Beverley Adab, 'The Idea of the Hybrid Text in Translation Revisited', *Across Languages and Cultures* 2.2 (2001): 277-302.

Selnes, Gisle, 'Peer og imperiet' [Peer and Empire], *Klassekampen* 7 November 2006: 14-15.

Setterquist, Jan. *Ibsen and the Beginnings of Anglo-Irish Drama I. John Millington Synge* (Dublin: Hodges, Figgis and Co.; Upsala: A.-B. Lundequistska Bokhandeln, 1951).

Shakh-Azizova, Tatiana K., 'Chekhov on the Russian Stage', *The Cambridge Companion to Chekhov*, eds Vera Gottlieb and Paul Allain (Cambridge: Cambridge University Press, 2000): 162-75.

---, 'Dolgaia zhizn' traditsii' [The Long Life of a Tradition], *Chekhovskie chteniia v Ialte: Chekhov i teatr* [Chekhov Readings in Yalta: Chekhov and Theatre], ed. V. I. Kuleshov (Moscow: Kniga, 1976): 22-35.

Shaw, George Bernard, *Collected Letters 1898-1910*, ed. Dan H. Laurence (London: Max Reinhardt, 1972).

---, *Complete Plays with Prefaces*, vol. 1 (New York: Dodd, Mead, 1963).

---, *The Matter with Ireland*, eds David H. Greene and Dan H. Laurence (London: Hart-Davis, 1962).

---, *Our Theatres in the Nineties*, 3 vols (London: Constable, 1932).

---, *Shaw on Theatre*, ed. E.J. West (New York: Hill and Wang, 1959)

---, *The Quintessence of Ibsenism: Now Completed to the Death of Ibsen* (New York: Hill and Wang, 1957).

Smith, Gus, 'Salute to Madame Knebel', *The Sunday Independent* 13 October 1968: 26.

Surkov, E., ed., *Chekhov i teatr: pis'ma, fel'etony, sovremenniki o Chekhove – dramaturge* [Chekhov and the Theatre: Letters, Pamphlets, and Comments by Contemporaries on Chekhov as a Dramatist], (Moscow: Iskusstvo, 1961).

Strindberg, August, *Plays: One*, trans. Michael Meyer (London, Secker & Warburg,1975).

Synge, J.M., *The Collected Letters of John Millington Synge*, ed. Ann Saddlemyer, vol. 1 1871-1907 (New York: OUP, 1983).

Szondi, Peter, *Theory of the Modern Drama* (Cambridge: Polity Press, 1987).

Taylor, John Russell, *The Rise and Fall of the Well-Made Play* (London: Methuen, 1967).

Templeton, Joan, *Munch's Ibsen: A Painter's Visions of a Playwright* (Seattle: University of Washington Press; Copenhagen: Museum Tusculanum Press, 2008).

'Theatre Council to Discuss Play "Problems"', *Irish Independent* 24 August 1968: 13.

Titley, Alan, *Tagann Godot: Coiméide Thraigeídeach Dhá Ghníomh* (Dublin: An Clóchomhar Tta, 1991).

Turco, Alfred, Jr., *Shaw's Moral Vision: The Self and Salvation* (Ithaca: Cornell UP, 1976).

Tysdahl, Bjørn J., *Joyce and Ibsen – A Study In Literary Influence* (Oslo: Norwegian Universities Press; New York: Humanities Press, 1968).

Venuti, Lawrence, *The Scandals of Translation: Towards an Ethics of Difference* [1998] (London and New York: Routledge, 2003).

Verma, Jatinder, 'The Challenge of Binglish: Analysing Multi-Cultural Productions', *Analysing Performance,* ed. Patrick Campbell (Manchester: Manchester University Press, 1996): 193-202.

Vormann, Hartmut, *The Art of Lennox Robinson: Theoretical Premises and Theatrical Practice* (Trier: Wissenschaftlicher Verlag, 2001).

Wellek, René, 'From Tolstoy to Ibsen', *The Norton Anthology of World Masterpieces* [1956], eds Maynard Mack 4th ed. (London: Norton, 1979): 728.

West, Michael, 'Authentic Fictions', *Irish Theatre Magazine* 4.6 (Autumn 2003): 15-22.

Whitman, Robert F., *Shaw and the Play of Ideas* (Ithaca and London: Cornell UP, 1977).

Williams, Raymond, *Drama from Ibsen to Brecht*, revised edition (London: Penguin, 1968).

Yeats, William Butler, *Autobiographies* (London: Macmillan, 1961).

– – , *Poems,* ed. Richard J. Finneran (New York: Macmillan, 1983).

– – , *The Writing of the Player Queen: Manuscripts of W.B. Yeats*, ed. Curtis Baker Bradford (DeKalb: Northern Illinois University Press, 1977).

Zucker, Carole, 'Interview with Stephen Rea', *Canadian Journal of Irish Studies* 26.1 (Spring 2000).

Contributors

Patrick Burke retired in 2008, after a career of almost forty years at St Patrick's College, Drumcondra, now a college of Dublin City University. His was among the first institutions to include Ibsen on academic courses. He was Director of MA in Theatre Studies at St Patrick's from 1998 to 2007. Dr Burke has lectured and published extensively on drama and theatre, especially the work of Friel, Murphy, Murray, McGuinness, and Carr. He is well-known also as a play director and adjudicator, most celebrated for *The Winter's Tale*, *Macbeth*, *Faith Healer* and *Conversations on a Homecoming*.

Zsuzsa Csikai is an Assistant Lecturer in the Department of English Literatures and Cultures, University of Pécs, Hungary. She has completed her PhD dissertation on Irish English translations and adaptations of Chekhov's plays. Her academic interests include Irish drama, Irish culture, and translation studies.

Ros Dixon (1967-2010) was Lecturer in Drama and Theatre Studies and Director of the BA Connect with Theatre and Performance at the National University of Ireland, Galway. She was a specialist in Soviet theatre history and wrote several articles, essays, book chapters, and conference papers on the work of Anatolii Efros, and on modern productions of the works of Chekhov, Gogol, and Turgenev. She was awarded grants by the Irish Research Council for the Humanities and Social Sciences and by the Millennium Research Fund for her research on productions of Russian plays in Ireland and Irish plays in Russia, a study concerning issues of translation, adaptation, and cross-cultural exchange.

Adrian Frazier is Director of the MA in Writing and MA in Drama and Theatre Studies, National University of Ireland, Galway. He is the author of *Behind the Scenes: Yeats, Horniman, and the Struggle for the Abbey Theatre* (1990), *George Moore 1852-1933* (2000); editor of 'Irish Theatre', the *Irish Review* (Autumn 2002), and *Hollywood Irish: John Ford, Abbey Actors and the Irish Revival in Hollywood* (2011).

Nicholas Grene is Professor of English Literature at Trinity College Dublin. He has written widely on drama and on Irish literature: his books include *The Politics of Irish Drama* (Cambridge University Press,1999), *Shakespeare's Serial History Plays* (Cambridge University Press, 2002) and *Yeats's Poetic Codes* (Oxford University Press, 2008). *Synge and Edwardian Ireland*, the collection of essays he has edited with Brian Cliff, will be published by Oxford University Press later in 2011.

Thomas Kilroy is a playwright, novelist, and academic. He served as play editor at the Abbey in 1977 and was appointed to the Board of Field Day Theatre Company in 1988. Kilroy was Professor of English at UCG and has published a number of academic essays and studies. In 1989, he resigned his professorship, to concentrate fully on writing. His plays include *Double Cross, Talbot's Box, Tea and Sex and Shakespeare, The Death and Resurrection of Mr. Roche, The Madame MacAdam Travelling Theatre, The O'Neill, The Secret Fall of Constance Wilde, The Shape of Metal*, and adaptations of Henrik Ibsen's *Ghosts*, Luigi Pirandello's *Six Characters in Search of an Author*, and Anton Chekhov's *The Seagull*. His many awards include the Guardian Fiction Prize, the Heinemann Award for Literature, the AIB Literary Prize and an Irish PEN Award. Thomas Kilroy is a Fellow of the Royal Society of Literature and a member of the Irish Academy of Letters and Aosdána. He was honoured with a special Lifetime Achievement Award at the ESB/Irish Times Theatre Awards in 2004.

Helen Lojek is Professor Emeritus of English at Boise State University (Idaho), where she also served as Associate Dean of the College of Arts and Sciences and Director of New Faculty Services. At present she is director of the university's Foundational Studies Program. She is the author of *Contexts for Frank McGuinness's Drama* (2004) and numerous articles about contemporary Irish drama. Her *Spaces of Irish Drama: Stage and Place in Contemporary Plays* is forthcoming from Palgrave Macmillan in Autumn 2011.

Irina Ruppo Malone is a graduate of the Hebrew University of Jerusalem, Trinity College Dublin, and the National University of Ireland, Galway, where she teaches courses on Irish and European drama, James Joyce, and contemporary Irish fiction. She is the author of *Ibsen and the Irish Revival* (Palgrave Macmillan, 2010).

Cynthia Marsh is Professor Emeritus of Russian Drama and Literature in the Department of Russian and Slavonic Studies, University of Nottingham, UK. Her research and publications have mostly been focused on the plays of Chekhov and Gorky, and on issues of translation and cultural transference. Her fourth book: *Staging Russian Theatre in Britain, 1945-2005* is near completion. She has extensive experience of directing plays in translation.

Chris Morash is Professor of English at National University of Ireland, Maynooth. His publications include *A History of the Irish Theatre, 1601-2000* (2002) and *A History of the Media in Ireland* (2010), which covers the period from 1551 to the present. He is a Member of the Royal Irish Academy.

Christopher Murray is Emeritus Professor in the School of English, Drama and Film Studies at University College Dublin, where he taught Ibsen and Shaw for many years both in the context of modern drama and the Irish dramatic movement. In 1978, to mark Ibsen's 150th birthday, he organized a small conference at UCD where John Northam gave the keynote and Jim Sheridan with his brother Peter led a lively session on the contemporary Irish community theatre project. Among Christopher's publications are *Twentieth-Century Irish Drama: Mirror Up to Nation* and *Sean O'Casey: Writer at Work, A Biography*. In 2010 Carysfort Press published *'Alive in Time': The Enduring Drama of Tom Murphy, New Essays*, which Christopher has edited. He is currently writing a book on Brian Friel for Methuen Drama.

Máiréad Ní Chróinín is co-director of Moonfish Theatre, which she founded with her sister Ionia in 2006 in Galway. She studied Politics in the University of Glasgow, and in Charles University in

Prague. She also worked for the European Commission in Brussels before returning to Galway in 2006. Directing credits for Moonfish include *Namhaid don Phobal* (*An Enemy of the People*) – an Irish-language staging of Henrik Ibsen's classic; *After the End* by Dennis Kelly for the Galway Theatre Festival 08; and *Bonny & Read*, which the company toured to the Edinburgh Fringe Festival '07. She has also worked with Moonfish company members to devise two family shows, *Noah's Ark* and *Aucassin & Nicolette*, which were presented at festivals in Galway, Dublin, Athenry and Waterford. Most recently, Moonfish presented a devised family show for the Galway Theatre Festival '09, based on the children's classic *The Secret Garden*. In 2008, she received a Travel and Training Award from the Arts Council to study with Teatr Gardzienicie in Poland. Inspired by this experience, she helped organize a two-week live-in workshop for Moonfish company members in Kinvara, Co. Galway, to explore various devising processes. In September - October 2009 Máiréad participated in 'The Next Stage' theatre training programme organized by Theatre Forum, in conjunction with the Dublin Theatre Festival and the Abbey Theatre. Máiréad is also a member of the Green Party, and stood as a candidate in the Local Elections 2009, in the Galway City Centre constituency.

Lynne Parker is Artistic Director and co-founder of Rough Magic. Productions for Rough Magic include *Phaedra* by Ellen Cranitch and Hilary Fannin, *The Importance of Being Earnest* at the Gaiety Theatre, Dublin, *Sodome, my love* with Olwen Fouere, *Spokesong* and *Pentecost* by Stewart Parker, *Don Carlos* (Best Production, Irish Times Irish Theatre Awards 2007), *The Taming of the Shrew* (Dublin and National Tour; Best Production, 2006 Irish Times Irish Theatre Awards), *Improbable Frequency* (Dublin, Edinburgh, Poland, National Tour, New York; Best Production and Best Director, 2004 Irish Times/ESB Irish Theatre Awards), *Take me Away*, *Shiver*, *Copenhagen* (Best Production, 2002 Irish Times/ESB Irish Theatre Awards), *The Sugar Wife*, *Midden*, *Three Days of Rain*, *Northern Star*, *The Way of the World*, *Halloween Night*, *Hidden Charges*, *The Dogs*, *Down Onto Blue*, *Danti-Dan*, *New Morning*, *I Can't get Started*, *Love and a Bottle*, *Digging for Fire*, *Lady Windermere's Fan*, *Aunt Dan and Lemon*, *Serious Money*, *Nightshade*, *The Country Wife*, *Decadence* and *Top Girls*.
  Productions at the Abbey and Peacock Theatres include *The Trojan Women*, *Tartuffe*, *Down the Line*, *The Sanctuary Lamp*,

The Drawer Boy (Galway Arts Festival co-production), *The Shape of Metal and Heavenly Bodies* (Best Director, 2004 Irish Times/ESB Irish Theatre Awards). Other work outside Rough Magic inclues productions for Druid, Tinderbox, 7:84 Scotland, and Opera Theatre Company. Lynne was an associate artist of Charabanc for whom she adapted and directed *The House of Bernarda Alba*. Other directing credits include *The Clearing* (Bush Theatre), *The Playboy of the Western World*, *The Silver Tassie* and *Our Father* (Almeida Theatre), *Brothers of the Brush* (Arts Theatre), *The Shadow of a Gunman* (Gate, Dublin**)**, *Playhouse Creatures* (The Peter Hall Company at the Old Vic), *The Importance of Being Earnest* (West Yorkshire Playhouse), *Love me?!* (Corn Exchange's Car Show), *The Comedy of Errors* (RSC), *Olga* and *Shimmer* (Traverse Theatre, Edinburgh), *The Drunkard* and *Benefactors* (b*spoke) *Only the Lonely* (Birmingham Rep), *A Streetcar Named Desire* (Opera Ireland) and most recently, *The Girl Who Forgot to Sing Badly* (The Ark/Theatre Lovett). She was the recipient of the 2008 Irish Times Irish Special Tribute Theatre Award and in 2010 was awarded an Honorary Doctorate by Trinity College Dublin.

Arthur Riordan is a playwright and actor, and a founder-member of Rough Magic Theatre Company. As an actor he has worked extensively with Rough Magic, and with most of Ireland's leading companies, including Druid, The Abbey, Bedrock, Fishamble, and most recently, Pan Pan, as well as making numerous TV and film appearances. For Rough Magic Arthur wrote the book and lyrics for the widely acclaimed musical, *Improbable Frequency*, which was first staged in the Dublin Theatre Festival in 2004, and subsequently went to the Edinburgh Fringe and the Kontakt Festival, Thorun, in 2006, toured Ireland in 2007, and was staged in 59E59 Theater, New York, 2008/2009. Extracts from his verse translation of *Peer Gynt* were presented by Rough Magic as part of the Ulster Bank Dublin Theatre Festival In Development program, 2008; the translation was performed in the Dublin Ulster Bank Theatre Festival in 2011. Other Rough Magic productions of Arthur's work include *Hidden Charges*, and *The Emergency Session*, a one-man show, and *Boomtown*. For The Performance Corporation, Arthur has adapted Flann O'Brien's unfinished novel, *Slattery's Sago Saga*, for the stage. He has also co-written two plays with Des Bishop: *Shooting Gallery*, a farce, and *Rap Éire*, a rap musical.

Tore Rem is Professor of English Literature in the Department of Literature, Area Studies and European Languages, University of Oslo. He is Head of the Board of the Centre for Ibsen Studies in Oslo, and has published extensively on British and Scandinavian nineteenth-century literature. He has recently written a two-volume biography of the Norwegian writer Jens Bjørneboe, and is working on a study of Ibsen's early European reception.

Kurt Taroff is a Lecturer in Drama at the Queen's University of Belfast. His primary work concerns the subjective dramatic form of monodrama, of which *Peer Gynt* may be seen as an excellent example. Kurt is also the convenor of the Translation, Adaptation, and Dramaturgy working group of the International Federation for Theatre Research. He has published in the *Journal of Adaptation in Film and Performance, Forum Modernes Theater, Modern Mask,* and the *Journal of the Pirandello Society of America.*

Robert Tracy is Professor Emeritus of English and of Celtic Studies at the University of California, Berkeley. He has been Visiting Professor of American Literature at the University of Leeds, of Russian Literature at Wellesley, and of Irish Literature at Trinity College Dublin. His publications include recent articles on Dickens, Trollope, Seamus Heaney and Brian Friel; Trollope's Later Novels (1978); editions of works by Synge, Trollope, Le Fanu, and Flann O'Brien; *Stone* (1981), a translation of Osip Mandelstam's *Kamen'*; and *The Unappeasable Host: Studies in Irish Identities* (1998). In 1997 the Russian Academy of Science published (in Russian) his 'Cexov i Irlandskii teatr' (Chekhov and the Irish Theatre) in volume 1 of a two volume compilation, *Cexov i mirovaya literatura* (Chekhov and World Literature). Never published in English, this essay covers performances and the 'influence' and reception of Chekhov in Ireland from the beginnings through Shaw and O'Casey to Friel and Kilroy.

Michael West is a playwright and translator. His work for The Corn Exchange includes *Man of Valour*, which plays in Edinburgh and Dublin Fringe Festival in 2011; *Freefall*, which won the Irish Theatre Award and the Irish Writers' Guild Award for best new play; *Everyday*; *Dublin By Lamplight*; *Foley*, and a version of *The Seagull*. His adaptation of Nabokov's *Lolita* was presented at the Abbey in a co-production between The Corn Exchange and the

National Irish Theatre. He has translated or adapted many classical and contemporary texts, among them *The Marriage of Figaro*, *Don Juan*, Jean-Pierre Siméon's *Stabat Mater Furiosa*, and Calderón's *The Separation of Body and Soul*. Other work includes his acclaimed translation of *Death and the Ploughman*, a fifteenth century Bohemian text; an adaptation of *The Canterville Ghost* for the English National Ballet; and two plays for children, *Jack Fell Down* and *Forest Man*.

Index

Carysfort Press was formed in the summer of 1998. It receives annual funding from the Arts Council.

The directors believe that drama is playing an ever-increasing role in today's society and that enjoyment of the theatre, both professional and amateur, currently plays a central part in Irish culture.

The Press aims to produce high quality publications which, though written and/or edited by academics, will be made accessible to a general readership. The organisation would also like to provide a forum for critical thinking in the Arts in Ireland, again keeping the needs and interests of the general public in view.

The company publishes contemporary Irish writing for and about the theatre.

Editorial and publishing inquiries to:
Carysfort Press Ltd.,
58 Woodfield,
Scholarstown Road,
Rathfarnham,
Dublin 16,
Republic of Ireland.

T (353 1) 493 7383
F (353 1) 406 9815
E: info@carysfortpress.com
www.carysfortpress.com

HOW TO ORDER

TRADE ORDERS DIRECTLY TO:
Irish Book Distribution
Unit 12, North Park, North Road,
Finglas, Dublin 11.

T: (353 1) 8239580
F: (353 1) 8239599
E: mary@argosybooks.ie
www.argosybooks.ie

INDIVIDUAL ORDERS DIRECTLY TO:
eprint Ltd.
35 Coolmine Industrial Estate,
Blanchardstown, Dublin 15.
T: (353 1) 827 8860
F: (353 1) 827 8804 Order online @
E: books@eprint.ie
www.eprint.ie

FOR SALES IN NORTH AMERICA AND CANADA:
Dufour Editions Inc.,
124 Byers Road,
PO Box 7,
Chester Springs,
PA 19425,
USA

T: 1-610-458-5005
F: 1-610-458-7103

Tom Swift Selected Plays

With an introduction by Peter Crawley.

The inaugural production of Performance Corporation in 2002 matched Voltaire's withering assault against the doctrine of optimism with a playful aesthetic and endlessly inventive stagecraft.

Each play in this collection was originally staged by the Performance Corporation and though Swift has explored different avenues ever since, such playfulness is a constant. The writing is precise, but leaves room for the discoveries of rehearsals, the flesh of the theatre. All plays are blueprints for performance, but several of these scripts – many of which are site-specific and all of them slyly topical – are documents for something unrepeatable.

ISBN: 978-1-904505-56-3   €20

Synge and His Influences: Centenary Essays from the Synge Summer School

Edited by Patrick Lonergan

The year 2009 was the centenary of the death of John Millington Synge, one of the world's great dramatists. To mark the occasion, this book gathers essays by leading scholars of Irish drama, aiming to explore the writers and movements that shaped Synge, and to consider his enduring legacies. Essays discuss Synge's work in its Irish, European and world contexts – showing his engagement not just with the Irish literary revival but with European politics and culture too. The book also explores Synge's influence on later writers: Irish dramatists such as Brian Friel, Tom Murphy and Marina Carr, as well as international writers like Mustapha Matura and Erisa Kironde. It also considers Synge's place in Ireland today, revealing how *The Playboy of the Western World* has helped to shape Ireland's responses to globalisation and multiculturalism, in celebrated productions by the Abbey Theatre, Druid Theatre, and Pan Pan Theatre Company.

Contributors include Ann Saddlemyer, Ben Levitas, Mary Burke, Paige Reynolds, Eilís Ní Dhuibhne, Mark Phelan, Shaun Richards, Ondřej Pilný, Richard Pine, Alexandra Poulain, Emilie Pine, Melissa Sihra, Sara Keating, Bisi Adigun, Adrian Frazier and Anthony Roche.

ISBN: 978-1-904505-50-1   €20.00

Constellations - The Life and Music of John Buckley

Benjamin Dwyer

Benjamin Dwyer provides a long overdue assessment of one of Ireland's most prolific composers of the last decades. He looks at John Buckley's music in the context of his biography and Irish cultural life. This is no hagiography but a critical assessment of Buckley's work, his roots and aesthetics. While looking closely at several of Buckley's compositions, the book is written in a comprehensible style that makes it easily accessible to anybody interested in Irish musical and cultural history.   *Wolfgang Marx*

As well as providing a very readable and comprehensive study of the life and music of John Buckley, Constellations also offers an up-to-date and informative catalogue of compositions, a complete discography, translations of set texts and the full libretto of his chamber opera, making this book an essential guide for both students and professional scholars alike.

ISBN: 978-1-904505-52-5   €20.00

'Because We Are Poor': Irish Theatre in the 1990s
Victor Merriman

"Victor Merriman's work on Irish theatre is in the vanguard of a whole new paradigm in Irish theatre scholarship, one that is not content to contemplate monuments of past or present achievement, but for which the theatre is a lens that makes visible the hidden malaises in Irish society. That he has been able to do so by focusing on a period when so much else in Irish culture conspired to hide those problems is only testimony to the considerable power of his critical scrutiny." Chris Morash, NUI Maynooth.

ISBN: 978-1-904505-51-8   €20.00

'Buffoonery and Easy Sentiment':
Popular Irish Plays in the Decade Prior to the Opening of The Abbey Theatre

Christopher Fitz-Simon

In this fascinating reappraisal of the non-literary drama of the late 19th - early 20th century, Christopher Fitz-Simon discloses a unique world of plays, players and producers in metropolitan theatres in Ireland and other countries where Ireland was viewed as a source of extraordinary topics at once contemporary and comfortably remote: revolution, eviction, famine, agrarian agitation, political assassination.

The form was the fashionable one of melodrama, yet Irish melodrama was of a particular kind replete with hidden messages, and the language was far more allusive, colourful and entertaining than that of its English equivalent.

ISBN: 978-1-9045505-49-5   €20.00

The Fourth Seamus Heaney Lectures, 'Mirror up to Nature':

Ed. Patrick Burke

What, in particular, is the contemporary usefulness for the building of societies of one of our oldest and culturally valued ideals, that of drama? The Fourth Seamus Heaney Lectures, 'Mirror up to Nature': Drama and Theatre in the Modern World, given at St Patrick's College, Drumcondra, between October 2006 and April 2007, addressed these and related questions. Patrick Mason spoke on the essence of theatre, Thomas Kilroy on Ireland's contribution to the art of theatre, Cecily O'Neill and Jonothan Neelands on the rich potential of drama in the classroom. Brenna Katz Clarke examined the relationship between drama and film, and John Buckley spoke on opera and its history and gave an illuminating account of his own *Words Upon The Window-Pane*.

ISBN 978-1-9045505-48-8   €12

The Theatre of Tom Mac Intyre: 'Strays from the ether'

Eds. Bernadette Sweeney and Marie Kelly

This long overdue anthology captures the soul of Mac Intyre's dramatic canon – its ethereal qualities, its extraordinary diversity, its emphasis on the poetic and on performance – in an extensive range of visual, journalistic and scholarly contributions from writers, theatre practitioners.

ISBN 978-1-904505-46-4   €25

Irish Appropriation Of Greek Tragedy

Brian Arkins

This book presents an analysis of more than 30 plays written by Irish dramatists and poets that are based on the tragedies of Sophocles, Euripides and Aeschylus. These plays proceed from the time of Yeats and Synge through MacNeice and the Longfords on to many of today's leading writers.

ISBN 978-1-904505-47-1 €20

Alive in Time: The Enduring Drama of Tom Murphy

Ed. Christopher Murray

Almost 50 years after he first hit the headlines as Ireland's most challenging playwright, the 'angry young man' of those times Tom Murphy still commands his place at the pinnacle of Irish theatre. Here 17 new essays by prominent critics and academics, with an introduction by Christopher Murray, survey Murphy's dramatic oeuvre in a concerted attempt to define his greatness and enduring appeal, making this book a significant study of a unique genius.

ISBN 978-1-904505-45-7 €25

Performing Violence in Contemporary Ireland

Ed. Lisa Fitzpatrick

This interdisciplinary collection of fifteen new essays by scholars of theatre, Irish studies, music, design and politics explores aspects of the performance of violence in contemporary Ireland. With chapters on the work of playwrights Martin McDonagh, Martin Lynch, Conor McPherson and Gary Mitchell, on Republican commemorations and the 90th anniversary ceremonies for the Battle of the Somme and the Easter Rising, this book aims to contribute to the ongoing international debate on the performance of violence in contemporary societies.

ISBN 978-1-904505-44-0 (2009) €20

Ireland's Economic Crisis - Time to Act. Essays from over 40 leading Irish thinkers at the MacGill Summer School 2009

Eds. Joe Mulholland and Finbarr Bradley

Ireland's economic crisis requires a radical transformation in policymaking. In this volume, political, industrial, academic, trade union and business leaders and commentators tell the story of the Irish economy and its rise and fall. Contributions at Glenties range from policy, vision and context to practical suggestions on how the country can emerge from its crisis.

ISBN 978-1-904505-43-3 (2009) €20

Deviant Acts: Essays on Queer Performance

Ed. David Cregan

This book contains an exciting collection of essays focusing on a variety of alternative performances happening in contemporary Ireland. While it highlights the particular representations of gay and lesbian identity it also brings to light how diversity has always been a part of Irish culture and is, in fact, shaping what it means to be Irish today.

ISBN 978-1-904505-42-6 (2009) €20

Seán Keating in Context: Responses to Culture and Politics in Post-Civil War Ireland

Compiled, edited and introduced by Éimear O'Connor

Irish artist Seán Keating has been judged by his critics as the personification of old-fashioned traditionalist values. This book presents a different view. The story reveals Keating's early determination to attain government support for the visual arts. It also illustrates his socialist leanings, his disappointment with capitalism, and his attitude to cultural snobbery, to art critics, and to the Academy. Given the national and global circumstances nowadays, Keating's critical and wry observations are prophetic – and highly amusing.

ISBN 978-1-904505-41-9 €25

Dialogue of the Ancients of Ireland: A new translation of Acallam na Senorach

Translated with introduction and notes by Maurice Harmon

One of Ireland's greatest collections of stories and poems, The Dialogue of the Ancients of Ireland is a new translation by Maurice Harmon of the 12th century *Acallam na Senorach*. Retold in a refreshing modern idiom, the *Dialogue* is an extraordinary account of journeys to the four provinces by St. Patrick and the pagan Cailte, one of the surviving Fian. Within the frame story are over 200 other stories reflecting many genres – wonder tales, sea journeys, romances, stories of revenge, tales of monsters and magic. The poems are equally varied – lyrics, nature poems, eulogies, prophecies, laments, genealogical poems. After the *Tain Bo Cuailnge*, the *Acallam* is the largest surviving prose work in Old and Middle Irish.

ISBN: 978-1-904505-39-6 (2009) €20

Literary and Cultural Relations between Ireland and Hungary and Central and Eastern Europe

Ed. Maria Kurdi

This lively, informative and incisive collection of essays sheds fascinating new light on the literary interrelations between Ireland, Hungary, Poland, Romania and the Czech Republic. It charts a hitherto under-explored history of the reception of modern Irish culture in Central and Eastern Europe and also investigates how key authors have been translated, performed and adapted. The revealing explorations undertaken in this volume of a wide array of Irish dramatic and literary texts, ranging from *Gulliver's Travels* to *Translations* and *The Pillowman*, tease out the subtly altered nuances that they acquire in a Central European context.

ISBN: 978-1-904505-40-2 (2009) €20

Plays and Controversies: Abbey Theatre Diaries 2000-2005

Ben Barnes

In diaries covering the period of his artistic directorship of the Abbey, Ben Barnes offers a frank, honest, and probing account of a much commented upon and controversial period in the history of the national theatre. These diaries also provide fascinating personal insights into the day-to- day pressures, joys, and frustrations of running one of Ireland's most iconic institutions.

ISBN: 978-1-904505-38-9 (2008) €35

Interactions: Dublin Theatre Festival 1957-2007. Irish Theatrical Diaspora Series: 3

Eds. Nicholas Grene and Patrick Lonergan with Lilian Chambers

For over 50 years the Dublin Theatre Festival has been one of Ireland's most important cultural events, bringing countless new Irish plays to the world stage, while introducing Irish audiences to the most important international theatre companies and artists. Interactions explores and celebrates the achievements of the renowned Festival since 1957 and includes specially commissioned memoirs from past organizers, offering a unique perspective on the controversies and successes that have marked the event's history. An especially valuable feature of the volume, also, is a complete listing of the shows that have appeared at the Festival from 1957 to 2008.

ISBN: 978-1-904505-36-5 €25

The Informer: A play by Tom Murphy based on the novel by Liam O'Flaherty

The Informer, Tom Murphy's stage adaptation of Liam O'Flaherty's novel, was produced in the 1981 Dublin Theatre Festival, directed by the playwright himself, with Liam Neeson in the leading role. The central subject of the play is the quest of a character at the point of emotional and moral breakdown for some source of meaning or identity. In the case of Gypo Nolan, the informer of the title, this involves a nightmarish progress through a Dublin underworld in which he changes from a Judas figure to a scapegoat surrogate for Jesus, taking upon himself the sins of the world. A cinematic style, with flash-back and intercut scenes, is used rather than a conventional theatrical structure to catch the fevered and phantasmagoric progression of Gypo's mind. The language, characteristically for Murphy, mixes graphically colloquial Dublin slang with the haunted intricacies of the central character groping for the meaning of his own actions. The dynamic rhythm of the action builds towards an inevitable but theatrically satisfying tragic catastrophe. ' [The Informer] is, in many ways closer to being an original Murphy play than it is to O'Flaherty...' Fintan O'Toole.

ISBN: 978-1-904505-37-2 (2008) €10

Shifting Scenes: Irish theatre-going 1955-1985

Eds. Nicholas Grene and Chris Morash

Transcript of conversations with John Devitt, academic and reviewer, about his lifelong passion for the theatre. A fascinating and entertaining insight into Dublin theatre over the course of thirty years provided by Devitt's vivid reminiscences and astute observations.

ISBN: 978-1-904505-33-4 (2008) €10

Irish Literature: Feminist Perspectives

Eds. Patricia Coughlan and Tina O'Toole

The collection discusses texts from the early 18th century to the present. A central theme of the book is the need to renegotiate the relations of feminism with nationalism and to transact the potential contest of these two important narratives, each possessing powerful emancipatory force. Irish Literature: Feminist Perspectives contributes incisively to contemporary debates about Irish culture, gender and ideology.

ISBN: 978-1-904505-35-8 (2008) €25

Silenced Voices: Hungarian Plays from Transylvania

Selected and translated by Csilla Bertha and Donald E. Morse

The five plays are wonderfully theatrical, moving fluidly from absurdism to tragedy, and from satire to the darkly comic. Donald Morse and Csilla Bertha's translations capture these qualities perfectly, giving voice to the 'forgotten playwrights of Central Europe'. They also deeply enrich our understanding of the relationship between art, ethics, and politics in Europe.

ISBN: 978-1-904505-34-1 (2008) €25

A Hazardous Melody of Being:
Seóirse Bodley's Song Cycles on the poems of Micheal O'Siadhail

Ed. Lorraine Byrne Bodley

This apograph is the first publication of Bodley's O'Siadhail song cycles and is the first book to explore the composer's lyrical modernity from a number of perspectives. Lorraine Byrne Bodley's insightful introduction describes in detail the development and essence of Bodley's musical thinking, the European influences he absorbed which linger in these cycles, and the importance of his work as a composer of the Irish art song.

ISBN: 978-1-904505-31-0 (2008) €25

Irish Theatre in England: Irish Theatrical Diaspora Series: 2

Eds. Richard Cave and Ben Levitas

Irish theatre in England has frequently illustrated the complex relations between two distinct cultures. How English reviewers and audiences interpret Irish plays is often decidedly different from how the plays were read in performance in Ireland. How certain Irish performers have chosen to be understood in Dublin is not necessarily how audiences in London have perceived their constructed stage personae. Though a collection by diverse authors, the twelve essays in this volume investigate these issues from a variety of perspectives that together chart the trajectory of Irish performance in England from the mid-nineteenth century till today.

ISBN: 978-1-904505-26-6 (2007) €20

Goethe and Anna Amalia: A Forbidden Love?

Ettore Ghibellino, Trans. Dan Farrelly

In this study Ghibellino sets out to show that the platonic relationship between Goethe and Charlotte von Stein – lady-in-waiting to Anna Amalia, the Dowager Duchess of Weimar – was used as part of a cover-up for Goethe's intense and prolonged love relationship with the Duchess Anna Amalia herself. The book attempts to uncover a hitherto closely-kept state secret. Readers convinced by the evidence supporting Ghibellino's hypothesis will see in it one of the very great love stories in European history – to rank with that of Dante and Beatrice, and Petrarch and Laura.

ISBN: 978-1-904505-24-2 €20

Ireland on Stage: Beckett and After

Eds. Hiroko Mikami, Minako Okamuro, Naoko Yagi

The collection focuses primarily on Irish playwrights and their work, both in text and on the stage during the latter half of the twentieth century. The central figure is Samuel Beckett, but the contributors freely draw on Beckett and his work provides a springboard to discuss contemporary playwrights such as Brian Friel, Frank McGuinness, Marina Carr and Conor McPherson amongst others. Contributors include: Anthony Roche, Hiroko Mikami, Naoko Yagi, Cathy Leeney, Joseph Long, Noreem Doody, Minako Okamuro, Christopher Murray, Futoshi Sakauchi and Declan Kiberd

ISBN: 978-1-904505-23-5 (2007)   €20

'Echoes Down the Corridor': Irish Theatre - Past, Present and Future

Eds. Patrick Lonergan and Riana O'Dwyer

This collection of fourteen new essays explores Irish theatre from exciting new perspectives. How has Irish theatre been received internationally - and, as the country becomes more multicultural, how will international theatre influence the development of drama in Ireland? These and many other important questions.

ISBN: 978-1-904505-25-9 (2007)   €20

Musics of Belonging: The Poetry of Micheal O'Siadhail

Eds. Marc Caball & David F. Ford

An overall account is given of O'Siadhail's life, his work and the reception of his poetry so far. There are close readings of some poems, analyses of his artistry in matching diverse content with both classical and innovative forms, and studies of recurrent themes such as love, death, language, music, and the shifts of modern life.

ISBN: 978-1-904505-22-8 (2007)   €25 (Paperback)
ISBN: 978-1-904505-21-1 (2007)   €50 (Casebound)

Brian Friel's Dramatic Artistry: 'The Work has Value'

Eds. Donald E. Morse, Csilla Bertha and Maria Kurdi

Brian Friel's Dramatic Artistry presents a refreshingly broad range of voices: new work from some of the leading English-speaking authorities on Friel, and fascinating essays from scholars in Germany, Italy, Portugal, and Hungary. This book will deepen our knowledge and enjoyment of Friel's work.

ISBN: 978-1-904505-17-4 (2006)   €30

The Theatre of Martin McDonagh: 'A World of Savage Stories'

Eds. Lilian Chambers and Eamonn Jordan

The book is a vital response to the many challenges set by McDonagh for those involved in the production and reception of his work. Critics and commentators from around the world offer a diverse range of often provocative approaches. What is not surprising is the focus and commitment of the engagement, given the controversial and stimulating nature of the work.

ISBN: 978-1-904505-19-8 (2006) €35

Edna O'Brien: New Critical Perspectives

Eds. Kathryn Laing, Sinead Mooney and Maureen O'Connor

The essays collected here illustrate some of the range, complexity, and interest of Edna O'Brien as a fiction writer and dramatist. They will contribute to a broader appreciation of her work and to an evolution of new critical approaches, as well as igniting more interest in the many unexplored areas of her considerable oeuvre.

ISBN: 978-1-904505-20-4 (2006) €20

Irish Theatre on Tour

Eds. Nicholas Grene and Chris Morash

'Touring has been at the strategic heart of Druid's artistic policy since the early eighties. Everyone has the right to see professional theatre in their own communities. Irish theatre on tour is a crucial part of Irish theatre as a whole'. Garry Hynes

ISBN 978-1-904505-13-6 (2005) €20

Poems 2000-2005 by Hugh Maxton

Poems 2000-2005 is a transitional collection written while the author – also known to be W.J. Mc Cormack, literary historian – was in the process of moving back from London to settle in rural Ireland.

ISBN 978-1-904505-12-9 (2005) €10

Synge: A Celebration

Ed. Colm Tóibín

A collection of essays by some of Ireland's most creative writers on the work of John Millington Synge, featuring Sebastian Barry, Marina Carr, Anthony Cronin, Roddy Doyle, Anne Enright, Hugo Hamilton, Joseph O'Connor, Mary O'Malley, Fintan O'Toole, Colm Toibin, Vincent Woods.

ISBN 978-1-904505-14-3 (2005) €15

East of Eden: New Romanian Plays

Ed. Andrei Marinescu

Four of the most promising Romanian playwrights, young and very young, are in this collection, each one with a specific way of seeing the Romanian reality, each one with a style of communicating an articulated artistic vision of the society we are living in. Ion Caramitru, General Director Romanian National Theatre Bucharest.
ISBN 978-1-904505-15-0 (2005) €10

George Fitzmaurice: 'Wild in His Own Way', Biography of an Irish Playwright

Fiona Brennan

'Fiona Brennan's introduction to his considerable output allows us a much greater appreciation and understanding of Fitzmaurice, the one remaining under-celebrated genius of twentieth-century Irish drama'. Conall Morrison

ISBN 978-1-904505-16-7 (2005) €20

Out of History: Essays on the Writings of Sebastian Barry

Ed. Christina Hunt Mahony

The essays address Barry's engagement with the contemporary cultural debate in Ireland and also with issues that inform postcolonial critical theory. The range and selection of contributors has ensured a high level of critical expression and an insightful assessment of Barry and his works.

ISBN: 978-1-904505-18-1 (2005) €20

Three Congregational Masses

Seoirse Bodley

'From the simpler congregational settings in the Mass of Peace and the Mass of Joy to the richer textures of the Mass of Glory, they are immediately attractive and accessible, and with a distinctively Irish melodic quality.' Barra Boydell

ISBN: 978-1-904505-11-2 (2005) €15

Georg Büchner's Woyzeck,

A new translation by Dan Farrelly

The most up-to-date German scholarship of Thomas Michael Mayer and Burghard Dedner has finally made it possible to establish an authentic sequence of scenes. The wide-spread view that this play is a prime example of loose, open theatre is no longer sustainable. Directors and teachers are challenged to "read it again".

ISBN: 978-1-904505-02-0 (2004) €10

Playboys of the Western World: Production Histories

Ed. Adrian Frazier

'The book is remarkably well-focused: half is a series of production histories of Playboy performances through the twentieth century in the UK, Northern Ireland, the USA, and Ireland. The remainder focuses on one contemporary performance, that of Druid Theatre, as directed by Garry Hynes. The various contemporary social issues that are addressed in relation to Synge's play and this performance of it give the volume an additional interest: it shows how the arts matter.' Kevin Barry

ISBN: 978-1-904505-06-8 (2004) €20

The Power of Laughter: Comedy and Contemporary Irish Theatre

Ed. Eric Weitz

The collection draws on a wide range of perspectives and voices including critics, playwrights, directors and performers. The result is a series of fascinating and provocative debates about the myriad functions of comedy in contemporary Irish theatre. Anna McMullan

As Stan Laurel said, 'it takes only an onion to cry. Peel it and weep. Comedy is harder'. 'These essays listen to the power of laughter. They hear the tough heart of Irish theatre – hard and wicked and funny'. Frank McGuinness

ISBN: 978-1-904505-05-1 (2004) €20

Sacred Play: Soul-Journeys in contemporary Irish Theatre

Anne F. O'Reilly

'Theatre as a space or container for sacred play allows audiences to glimpse mystery and to experience transformation. This book charts how Irish playwrights negotiate the labyrinth of the Irish soul and shows how their plays contribute to a poetics of Irish culture that enables a new imagining. Playwrights discussed are: McGuinness, Murphy, Friel, Le Marquand Hartigan, Burke Brogan, Harding, Meehan, Carr, Parker, Devlin, and Barry.'

ISBN: 978-1-904505-07-5 (2004) €25

The Irish Harp Book

Sheila Larchet Cuthbert

This is a facsimile of the edition originally published by Mercier Press in 1993. There is a new preface by Sheila Larchet Cuthbert, and the biographical material has been updated. It is a collection of studies and exercises for the use of teachers and pupils of the Irish harp.

ISBN: 978-1-904505-08-2 (2004)   €35

The Drunkard

Tom Murphy

'The Drunkard is a wonderfully eloquent play. Murphy's ear is finely attuned to the glories and absurdities of melodramatic exclamation, and even while he is wringing out its ludicrous overstatement, he is also making it sing.' The Irish Times

ISBN: 978-1-90 05-09-9 (2004)   €10

Goethe: Musical Poet, Musical Catalyst

Ed. Lorraine Byrne

'Goethe was interested in, and acutely aware of, the place of music in human experience generally - and of its particular role in modern culture. Moreover, his own literary work - especially the poetry and Faust - inspired some of the major composers of the European tradition to produce some of their finest works.' Martin Swales

ISBN: 978-1-9045-10-5 (2004)   €40

The Theatre of Marina Carr: "Before rules was made"

Eds. Anna McMullan & Cathy Leeney

As the first published collection of articles on the theatre of Marina Carr, this volume explores the world of Carr's theatrical imagination, the place of her plays in contemporary theatre in Ireland and abroad and the significance of her highly individual voice.

ISBN: 978-0-9534257-7-8 (2003)   €20

Critical Moments: Fintan O'Toole on Modern Irish Theatre

Eds. Julia Furay & Redmond O'Hanlon

This new book on the work of Fintan O'Toole, the internationally acclaimed theatre critic and cultural commentator, offers percussive analyses and assessments of the major plays and playwrights in the canon of modern Irish theatre. Fearless and provocative in his judgements, O'Toole is essential reading for anyone interested in criticism or in the current state of Irish theatre.

ISBN: 978-1-904505-03-7 (2003)   €20

Goethe and Schubert: Across the Divide

Eds. Lorraine Byrne & Dan Farrelly

Proceedings of the International Conference, 'Goethe and Schubert in Perspective and Performance', Trinity College Dublin, 2003. This volume includes essays by leading scholars – Barkhoff, Boyle, Byrne, Canisius, Dürr, Fischer, Hill, Kramer, Lamport, Lund, Meikle, Newbould, Norman McKay, White, Whitton, Wright, Youens – on Goethe's musicality and his relationship to Schubert; Schubert's contribution to sacred music and the Lied and his setting of Goethe's Singspiel, Claudine. A companion volume of this Singspiel (with piano reduction and English translation) is also available.

ISBN: 978-1-904505-04-4 (2003)   €25

Goethe's Singspiel, 'Claudine von Villa Bella'

Set by Franz Schubert

Goethe's Singspiel in three acts was set to music by Schubert in 1815. Only Act One of Schuberts's Claudine score is extant. The present volume makes Act One available for performance in English and German. It comprises both a piano reduction by Lorraine Byrne of the original Schubert orchestral score and a bilingual text translated for the modern stage by Dan Farrelly. This is a tale, wittily told, of lovers and vagabonds, romance, reconciliation, and resolution of family conflict.

ISBN: 978-0-9544290-0-3 (2002)   €20

Theatre of Sound, Radio and the Dramatic Imagination

Dermot Rattigan

An innovative study of the challenges that radio drama poses to the creative imagination of the writer, the production team, and the listener.
"A remarkably fine study of radio drama – everywhere informed by the writer's professional experience of such drama in the making…A new theoretical and analytical approach – informative, illuminating and at all times readable." Richard Allen Cave

ISBN: 978- 0-9534-257-5-4 (2002)   €20

Talking about Tom Murphy

Ed. Nicholas Grene

Talking About Tom Murphy is shaped around the six plays in the landmark Abbey Theatre Murphy Season of 2001, assembling some of the best-known commentators on his work: Fintan O'Toole, Chris Morash, Lionel Pilkington, Alexandra Poulain, Shaun Richards, Nicholas Grene and Declan Kiberd.

ISBN: 978-0-9534-257-9-2 (2002)   €15

Hamlet: The Shakespearean Director

Mike Wilcock

"This study of the Shakespearean director as viewed through various interpretations of HAMLET is a welcome addition to our understanding of how essential it is for a director to have a clear vision of a great play. It is an important study from which all of us who love Shakespeare and who understand the importance of continuing contemporary exploration may gain new insights." From the Foreword, by Joe Dowling, Artistic Director, The Guthrie Theater, Minneapolis, MN

ISBN: 978-1-904505-00-6 (2002) €20

The Theatre of Frank Mc Guinness: Stages of Mutability

Ed. Helen Lojek

The first edited collection of essays about internationally renowned Irish playwright Frank McGuinness focuses on both performance and text. Interpreters come to diverse conclusions, creating a vigorous dialogue that enriches understanding and reflects a strong consensus about the value of McGuinness's complex work.

ISBN: 978-1904505-01-3. (2002) €20

Theatre Talk: Voices of Irish Theatre Practitioners

Eds Lilian Chambers, Ger Fitzgibbon and Eamonn Jordan

"This book is the right approach - asking practitioners what they feel." Sebastian Barry, Playwright "... an invaluable and informative collection of interviews with those who make and shape the landscape of Irish Theatre." Ben Barnes, Artistic Director of the Abbey Theatre

ISBN: 978-0-9534-257-6-1 (2001) €20

In Search of the South African Iphigenie

Erika von Wietersheim and Dan Farrelly

Discussions of Goethe's "Iphigenie auf Tauris" (Under the Curse) as relevant to women's issues in modern South Africa: women in family and public life; the force of women's spirituality; experience of personal relationships; attitudes to parents and ancestors; involvement with religion.

ISBN: 978-0-9534257-8-5 (2001) €10

'The Starving' and 'October Song':

Two contemporary Irish plays by Andrew Hinds

The Starving, set during and after the siege of Derry in 1689, is a moving and engrossing drama of the emotional journey of two men.

October Song, a superbly written family drama set in real time in pre-ceasefire Derry.

ISBN: 978-0-9534-257-4-7 (2001) €10

Seen and Heard: Six new plays by Irish women

Ed. Cathy Leeney

A rich and funny, moving and theatrically exciting collection of plays by Mary Elizabeth Burke-Kennedy, Síofra Campbell, Emma Donoghue, Anne Le Marquand Hartigan, Michelle Read and Dolores Walshe.

ISBN: 978-0-9534-257-3-0 (2001) €20

Theatre Stuff: Critical essays on contemporary Irish theatre

Ed. Eamonn Jordan

Best selling essays on the successes and debates of contemporary Irish theatre at home and abroad. Contributors include: Thomas Kilroy, Declan Hughes, Anna McMullan, Declan Kiberd, Deirdre Mulrooney, Fintan O'Toole, Christopher Murray, Caoimhe McAvinchey and Terry Eagleton.

ISBN: 978-0-9534-2571-1-6 (2000) €20

Under the Curse. Goethe's "Iphigenie Auf Tauris", A New Version

Dan Farrelly

The Greek myth of Iphigenie grappling with the curse on the house of Atreus is brought vividly to life. This version is currently being used in Johannesburg to explore problems of ancestry, religion, and Black African women's spirituality.

ISBN: 978-09534-257-8-5 (2000) €10

Urfaust, A New Version of Goethe's early "Faust" in Brechtian Mode

Dan Farrelly

This version is based on Brecht's irreverent and daring re-interpretation of the German classic. "Urfaust is a kind of well-spring for German theatre… The love-story is the most daring and the most profound in German dramatic literature." Brecht

ISBN: 978-0-9534-257-0-9 (1998) €10